HANDBOOK
OF
MEDICAL STAFF
MANAGEMENT

Contributors

Ruth A. Buck, CMSC
Medical Staff Coordinator
Valley Children's Hospital
Fresno, California

Marialice (Mimi) Cruse, BA, CMSC
President-elect
National Association Medical Staff Services
Director, Medical Staff Services
St. John and St. John and West Shore Hospital
Westlake, Ohio

F.C. Dimond, Jr., MD
Director of Quality and Risk Management
Hospital Group
National Medical Enterprises, Inc.
Los Angeles, California

Joyce M. Gardner, BA, ART, CMSC
Medical Staff Coordinator
Hurley Medical Center
Flint, Michigan

Cindy A. Orsund-Gassiot, CMSC
Medical Staff Management Consultant
Grapevine, Texas
Formerly, Manager
Medical Staff Services
Saint Joseph Hospital
Fort Worth, Texas

Sue King, CMSC
Medical Staff Management Consultant
Vista, California

Howard L. Lang, MD
Chairman, American Medical Association
  Hospital Medical Staff Section
Board-Certified Gynecologist in Private
  Practice
Kentfield, California

Sharon Lindsey, BSN, EdM, CMSC
Instructor
Health Care Support Services
Chemeketa Community College
Salem, Oregon

Charles R. Mathews, MD
Assistant Secretary for Health Services
Florida Department of Corrections
Tallahassee, Florida

Janet Thompson Reagan, PhD
Professor and Director
Health Administration Programs
California State University
Northridge, California

Steven V. Schnier, Esq.
Partner
Hanson, Bridgett, Marcus, Vlahos and Rudy
San Francisco, California

Vicki L. Searcy, CMSC
Principle
Lefkowitz-Ziegler, Searcy and Associates
Santa Ana, California

Meg L. Terry, MS
Vice President
HealthLine Systems, Inc.
San Diego, California

Carla D. Thompson, Esq.
Attorney
Guest Lecturer, Chemeketa Community
  College
Salem, Oregon

Richard E. Thompson, MD
President, Thompson, Mohr and Associates, Inc.
Dunedin, Florida

HANDBOOK OF MEDICAL STAFF MANAGEMENT

Edited by

Cindy A. Orsund-Gassiot, CMSC
Medical Staff Management Consultant
Grapevine, Texas

Sharon Lindsey, BSN, EdM, CMSC
Instructor, Health Care Support Services
Chemeka Community College
Salem, Oregon

AN ASPEN PUBLICATION®
Aspen Publishers, Inc.
Gaithersburg, Maryland
1990

Library of Congress Cataloging-in-Publication Data

Handbook of medical staff management / edited by
Cindy A. Orsund-Gassiot, Sharon S. Lindsey.
p. cm.
Includes bibliographical references.
Includes index.
ISBN: 0-8342-0177-1
1. Hospitals—Personnel management—Handbooks, manuals, etc. I.
Orsund-Gassiot, Cindy A. II. Lindsey, Sharon S.
[DNLM: 1. Credentialing. 2. Medical Staff, Hospital—organization &
administration. 3. Quality of Health Care. WX 203 H236]
RA972.H28 1990
362.1'1'0683—dc20
DNLM/DLC
for Library of Congress
90-1024
CIP

Aspen Publishers, Inc., grants permission for photocopying for limited
personal or internal use. This consent does not extend to other kinds of
copying, such as copying for general distribution, for advertising or promo-
tional purposes, for creating new collective works, or for resale. For
information, address Aspen Publishers, Inc., Permissions Department,
200 Orchard Ridge Drive, Suite 200, Gaithersburg, MD 20878.

Editorial Services: Ruth Bloom

Library of Congress Catalog Card Number: 90-1024
ISBN: 0-8342-0177-1

Printed in the United States of America

1 2 3 4 5

To John,
whose support never wanes

C.O.G.

To Mark
and all of my former students

S.L.

Table of Contents

Preface

As the health care delivery system consumes more of the gross national product each year, the structure of the system as we have known it in the post–World War II era is changing. The traditional fee-for-service, physician-controlled format is evolving into many different models. Increased federal regulation has assisted in shaping this evolution, and new professions have begun to take on a greater role. One of these important new professions is medical staff services management.

Defining the new professions is a challenge that has been taken up by the federal government, accrediting bodies, and professional organizations. Whatever the final outcome, the goal is to provide the best health care at the most reasonable cost. By clearly defining its role, each profession can contribute to the efficient provision of care.

The *Handbook of Medical Staff Management* was written with the intent that it become the standard text for the evolving field of medical staff services management. Frustrated by the lack of one comprehensive written work on this important field, the editors set about gathering a group of authoritative contributors who could remedy this deficiency.

In addition to being a definitive text, this book can serve as a valuable resource for medical staff service practitioners and an aid for those preparing to earn their credentials in the field. Physicians who have assumed a leadership position in a medical staff organization but have little or no prior education in health care administration should find this text useful. It also will serve as a reference for the nonprofessional in medical staff services who wishes to learn more about this challenging area of hospital administration.

The editors gratefully acknowledge the efforts of the contributors: Without their work the book would not have been possible. Our thanks also to Aspen Publishers, which had the foresight to recognize the value of the project.

Cindy Orsund-Gassiot
Sharon Lindsey

Part I

The Health Care Stage

All the world's a stage.

Shakespeare, *As You Like It*

Chapter 1

Health Care Delivery Systems

Janet Thompson Reagan, PhD

A BRIEF HISTORY

Health care is one of the largest industries in the United States, both in size of expenditures and persons employed. In 1987 expenditures on health care totaled $500.3 billion, or 11.1 percent of the gross national product (GNP). Expenditures for hospital care totaled $194.7 billion, followed by expenditures for physician services ($102.7 billion).[1] In 1987 hospitals employed 4,440,000 people, and over 7 million were involved in health services delivery.[2] The industry is rapidly changing in response to legal, cultural, technological, and economic developments within its environment. Terms commonly used to describe the environment include "turbulent," "unstable," and "complex."

What began as a cottage industry of individual providers has evolved into a complex array of providers, service delivery mechanisms, payment mechanisms, and regulatory agencies. Torrens described the development of the health care system according to the predominant health problem of the period, the technology available, and the social organization for applying the technology.[3] He divided the history of the industry into four periods: 1850 to 1900, 1900 to World War II, World War II to roughly 1980, and from now into the future. Other authors have used similar approaches in tracing the development of the health care system. For example, Odin W. Anderson discussed the periods from 1875 to 1930, 1930 to 1965, and 1965 to the present (1985).[4] This brief overview of the industry will begin at an earlier point, the pre-1750 era, and then will focus on the periods of development described by Torrens.

Pre-1750

During the pre–Industrial Revolution years (pre-1750), the practice of medicine was relatively primitive.[5] The scientific viewpoint was undeveloped, and medical practice was often based on speculation, trial and error, and even superstition. Medical education was neither standardized nor regulated. Hospitals in their current form did not exist. Institutions for care were essentially pesthouses or almshouses established and run by religious organizations or, in some cases, by local governments. Medical technology and the kind of social organization required for its application were largely nonexistent.

During this period, activities focused on attempts to control epidemics, prevent the entry of new diseases, and ensure a safe water supply. For example, in 1647 the Massachusetts Bay Colony passed a regulation to prevent pollution of the Boston Harbor, and in 1701 the Commonwealth of Massachusetts passed a law requiring isolation of persons with smallpox.[6]

The Industrial Revolution (1750–1850)

During the Industrial Revolution, developments occurred largely in the area of public health. Local and state health agencies were established in response to epidemics and the need to ensure safe water supplies and adequate sanitation. Medical science advanced as a result of an increasing emphasis on logical experimentation and controlled observation. Medical training improved, beginning with the establishment of the first American medical school at the College of Philadelphia in 1765.[7] The American Medical Association was founded in 1847 and had as one of its primary goals the improvement of medical education. Yet, rigorous training was still rare. "In 1800 there were only four functioning medical colleges; in 1825 there were eighteen."[8]

Hospitals were still primarily almshouses serving the indigent. Yet toward the end of this period, hospitals began to emerge as legitimate providers of care, and not only for individuals with communicable diseases who had to be isolated and for the indigent who had no other options for care but also for individuals in the larger community who had the resources to pay.

The Shattuck Report of 1850 can be viewed as the culmination of advances in public health during this period. Although the report did not initially stimulate dramatic changes in the provision of public health services, it set out far-reaching recommendations that not only held true for that time, but continue to hold true. For example, Shattuck included recommendations regarding the control of alcoholism, smoke nuisances, routine physical examinations, and family records of illness, to name only a few.[9]

1851–1900

The period from 1851 to 1900 was characterized by only moderate progress in the medical field. Diagnostic and therapeutic techniques were improved and anesthesia and antisepsis were developed.[10] Medical education and practice, however, were still at a low level. Although many medical schools existed, over 450 at times, many of the new schools were proprietary and curricula and programs varied widely.[11] Schools were not held accountable for the ability or the quality of the physicians produced. At the end of this period, licensure of physicians emerged as medical practice acts began to be enacted by the states in the 1870s.

Nursing emerged as the first allied health profession, and hospital-based training programs for nurses were established. Although Florence Nightingale is credited with the "transformation of nursing into a profession," it was Dorothea Dix who recruited nurses and encouraged nursing training programs in this country during the Civil War.[12] Permanent schools of nursing were established in the post–Civil War years. The health care team now consisted of the physician and the nurse.

Hospitals became legitimate providers of care. As surgery developed, the affluent sought the services of surgeons, who in turn sought to practice in hospitals. "By 1900 there were 4,000 general hospitals in the United States."[13]

1901–1945

The period from 1901 to roughly 1945 included remarkable medical advances, the expansion of state and federal subsidies for health services, the revamping of medical education, and the emergence of the framework for the health care system as it currently exists. During this period, the focus of health care shifted from epidemics to individual episodes of acute disease.[14] Support for medical research was greatly expanded, and advances were made in diagnosis, treatment, and prevention of disease. The period of antibiotics began with the discovery of penicillin in 1941. With the advances in medical science, health care professionals began to combat successfully individual episodes of acute disease.

Medical education was revolutionized as a result of the efforts of the American Medical Association, the advances in medical science, and the publication of the Flexner Report in 1910.[15] Although the number of medical schools declined as a result of the closure of substandard schools (down to 85 in 1920), those that remained built their curricula on a sound scientific base, and a four-year program of preparation became standard. Additionally, "by 1925 forty-nine boards (for medical licensure) required candidates for their examinations to be graduates of a medical college."[16] During this period, many of the medical specialties developed. Only 1 specialty existed in 1920; by 1940 there were 16.[17]

Government involvement at both the state and federal level increased. At the federal level, the Pure Food and Drug Act was passed in 1906. The Sheppard-Towner Act of 1921 made small federal grants available to state and local governments for maternal and child health programs and for the development and strengthening of local health departments.[18] Other federal action included the 1935

Social Security Act. Title V of this act increased federal assistance to maternal and child health programs and greatly expanded assistance to state and local health departments. Another outcome of this legislation was the growth in proprietary nursing homes. Guaranteed monthly incomes through old age survivors insurance and old age assistance programs enabled the elderly to pay for boarding home or nursing home care. Payments were not made to the elderly in almshouses or government facilities. Finally, the 1944 Public Health Service Act brought all the federal public health programs together under one agency.

The Committee on the Costs of Medical Care was created in 1927 through the support of private foundations.[19] A series of 27 field studies were conducted and a total of 28 reports published. The last report, published in 1932, recommended that health services be delivered through organized groups and that the costs of medical care be financed on a group basis. This restructuring of the health care system was proposed as a means of addressing economic inefficiency and reducing preventable pain and needless deaths.

It was during this period that the third-party pay system emerged as an important source of financing for health services. During the Depression, the Blue Cross and Blue Shield plans were developed to ensure that individuals would have access to hospital and physician services. The first commercial insurers also entered the marketplace, and the first prepaid group, the Ross-Loos Plan, was established.

Any attempt to summarize the medical advances during this period would be futile. Progress was made on all fronts. New diagnostic procedures developed; treatments, especially surgical procedures, were improved; and prevention of diseases, especially infectious diseases, became more successful.

1946–1965

The period from 1946 to 1965 included rapid advancement in the medical sciences, expansion of federal effort in the health care field, and the continued growth of third-party payers. "From 1947 to 1963 federal support of medical research increased at an average annual rate of 26 percent."[20] The National Institutes of Health increased in prestige and set the agenda for medical research during this period.

The role of the federal government in health services was greatly expanded. With the passage of the Hill-Burton Act (Hospital Survey and Construction Act) in 1946, the federal government began to subsidize the construction of hospitals. Between 1947 and 1971, Hill-Burton funds helped to build 345,000 hospital beds.[21] Through amendments to the original legislation, funds were later used for hospital renovations and for the construction of ambulatory clinics and nursing homes. Mental health services were supported through the 1946 Mental Health Act and later through the 1963 Mental Retardation Facilities and Community Mental Health Centers Construction Act.[22]

The federal government also subsidized the development of human resources through a variety of programs, including the Vocational Education Act of 1946, the Grants-in-Aid to Schools of Public Health in 1958, and the Health Professions Education Assistance Act of 1963. New occupations emerged in response to the introduction of new technology and advances in medical practice. The practice of medicine became increasingly specialized.

1966–Present

The mid-sixties are considered by many to be a turning point in the health care industry. The predominant health care focus shifted from individual episodes of acute disease to chronic health conditions, partly as a result of our aging population and partly as a result of medicine's success in preventing and treating acute disease.[23]

The federal government began to play an even larger role in health services. Lawrence Brown identified the main function of the federal government from 1966 to the mid-seventies as the provision of financing.[24] With the implementation of Medicare and Medicaid in 1966, the federal government became a major source for financing of health services. Medicare is a federal insurance program for those qualifying for Social Security benefits, and Medicaid is a federal-state assistance program for the indigent.

Although a description of these programs is beyond the scope of this chapter, an indication of their impact on the health care system is essential. Expenditures for both programs soon far exceeded projected levels. Since both were entitlement programs, expenditures were difficult to project and control. Federal expenditures for Medicare alone went from $4.5 billion in 1967 to $15.6 billion in 1976.[25] For Medicaid, the federal response was to allow states to reduce covered services, restrict the eligible population, and modify reimbursement methods to control expenditures. For Medicare, the federal government sought to control expenditures through regulation and reimbursement, for example, through the introduction of professional standards review organizations (PSROs) in 1972 and the prospective payment system (PPS) in 1983.

Brown characterizes federal policy in the 1970s as one of reorganization and regulation.[26] Reorganization was seen as a way of increasing system efficiency and controlling expenditures. The Health Maintenance Organization (HMO) Act of 1973 is an example of action in this area. Additionally, Title XIX of the Social Security Act was amended to encourage the enrollment of persons covered by Medicaid in alternative delivery systems, usually prepaid groups.

The federal government sought to regulate the system through the new health planning legislation passed in 1974 (P.L. 41-93), replacing the planning system authorized in 1966. The Social Security Amendments of 1972 authorized PSROs, whose function was to monitor the appropriateness and quality of care rendered under the Medicaid and Medicare programs. PSROs were replaced by professional review organizations (PROs) in 1982 with the passage of the Tax Equity and Fiscal Responsibility Act (TEFRA). TEFRA also modified the method of reimbursement under Medicare. A prospective payment system based on diagnosis related groups (DRGs) replaced the retrospective cost-based system.

In the 1980s the health care industry continued to evolve. Innovations included the development of new alternative delivery systems, the introduction of new financing mechanisms, and the first attempts by states (Hawaii and Massachusetts) to provide universal health insurance coverage. For a summary of the history, see Table 1-1.

THE HOSPITAL SECTOR

The preceding discussion of the evolution of the health care system traced the development of hospitals as one component of the larger service delivery system. Hospitals have evolved from simple institutions to organizations that provide a wide array of health services, utilize sophisticated technology and numerous health professionals and allied health personnel, and exist under a variety of organizational and ownership arrangements. The free-standing hospital is increasingly rare as multihospital or multi-institutional systems emerge. Hospitals are expanding services to include not only inpatient care but also a broad array of services such as ambulatory clinics, membership programs for the elderly, psychiatric services, and substance abuse programs.

Hospital Size

Hospitals can be categorized in a number of ways, including by size, ownership, and services provided. Of the 6,281 hospitals in the United States in 1988, 2,772 (44 percent) had 99 or fewer beds; 2,290 (36 percent) had 100–299 beds; 743 (12 percent) had 300–499 beds; and 476 (8 percent) had 500 or more beds.[27] Although a large percentage of hospitals are small (99 or fewer beds), these hospitals account for only 15 percent of the total number of beds.

Hospital Ownership

The categories of hospital ownership are voluntary (nonprofit, including hospitals under religious control), government (local, state, and federal), and proprietary.

Table 1-1 Overview of the Development of the U.S. Health Care System (1976–present)

	Pre-1776	*1776–1876*
Major health issues	Plagues Epidemics Sanitation Dietary deficiencies	Infections Sanitation Epidemics
Medical discoveries	1602 Harvey's circulation of blood 1650 Boyle's Law 1675 Hooke's discovery of cells 1714 Fahrenheit thermometer	1796 Smallpox vaccine 1805 Morphine isolated 1816 First stethoscope 1840 Henle's germ theory 1844 Anesthesia in surgery 1865 Antisepsis 1871 First city water filtration system 1870s Telephone, electric light, combustible engine, typewriter, commercially rolled cigarettes
Health care policy/laws		Health of the people is the responsibility of the states; sporadic attempts to legislate public health; spirit of laissez-faire
Federal government's role		1798 Congress created the Marine Hospital Service 1875 Surgeon General appointed
Professional growth—medicine	In colonies, clergy were doctors 1765 College of Philadelphia, first medical school in U.S.	1783 Harvard Medical School opens 1812 New England Journal of Medicine 1848 American Medical Association 1873 First state BME
Professional growth—allied health	Nursing performed by religious orders; midwives delivered babies	1861 Dorothea Dix establishes Army Nurses Corps 1862 Nightingale opens nurses' training school in London 1882 Clara Barton establishes American Red Cross
Delivery of care	Pts. treated in home; MDs treated by letter written to pts. far away; hospitals established to treat poor 1750 Pennsylvania Hospital	MDs had to practice surgery, obstetrics, as well as internal medicine; all treatment, even surgery, performed at home 1810 Mass. General Hospital became model for others 1872 American Public Health Association
Financial trends	Wealthy landowners paid MDs a yearly fee to provide care for family and slaves	Cost of medical school approx. $150/yr. for 2–3 yrs. 1840 MD's office visit: $.05–10 natural delivery: $4–30 1860 natural delivery: $5–50

continues

Table 1-1 Continued

	1876–1946	1946–present
Major health issues	Acute infections and illnesses	Acute illnesses Chronic diseases AIDS Addiction Aging population
Medical discoveries	1880s Discovery of microorganisms 1886 Steam sterilization 1889 Surgical gloves 1895 X-rays 1899 Aspirin X-rays for cancer therapy 1900 ABO blood groups described 1903 BP cuff, EKGs 1914 Pasteurization of milk 1921 Insulin 1936 Sulfa drugs 1937 First blood bank 1941 Penicillin	1940s Electron microscope 1949 Lithium for mental illness 1951 Fluoride for caries 1952 First pacemaker 1953 DNA discovered 1955 Salk polio vaccine 1956 External defibrillator 1958 CPR 1960 Lasers introduced 1961 Oral polio vaccine 1969 Rubella vaccine
Health care policy/laws	Spirit of responsible concern; NY State requires reporting TB 1906 Food and Drug Act 1912 US Public Health Service 1914 Harrison Anti-Narcotic Act 1946 Hill-Burton Act National Mental Health Act	1963 Community Mental Health Center Act 1965 Medicare-Medicaid 1966 Comprehensive Health Planning Act 1971 National Cancer Act 1972 PSROs established 1974 National Health Planning and Resources Development Act 1982 TEFRA (established DRGs) 1986 Health Care Quality Improvement Act
Federal government's role	Concern for public health 1878 Marine Hospital Service given power to cooperate with State Boards of Health 1879 National Board of Health Increased federal involvement after the Great Depression 1946 CDC established	Increasing amount of federal regulation, especially after Medicaid Late 60s Blank check attitude to improving nation's health Early 70s Cost containment 1972 Intern salary: $9778 1974 Cost of medical school: $12,650/student/yr. 1980 Quality assurance, cost containment
Professional growth—medicine	1883 Journal of the American Medical Association 1910 Flexner report on medical education 1936 American Cancer Institute	1949 National Institute of Mental Health Increased specialization; more MDs become board eligible or certified

continues

Table 1-1 Continued

	1876–1946	1946–present
Professional growth—allied health	1885 First visiting nurse service 1910 Public Health Nursing program at Columbia 1911 American Nurses' Association	Rapid increase in a wide variety of allied health professions
Delivery of care	As surgery became more complex, pts. had to go to hospitals; increased need for skilled nursing care; increased need to centralize expensive x-ray and lab equipment in hospital 1899 American Hospital Association 1918 American College of Surgeons started hospital surveys 1935 First hospital for drug addicts During Depression hospitals forced to give increased amount of free care; increase in group practices	Community outpatient mental health clinics 1952 Formation of JCAH Increase in large multihospital corporations; formation of PPOs, IPAs; increase in salaried MDs 1973 HMO Act
Financial trends	1902 $4/day hospital stay $40/month nursing salary By 1935 all but 4 states had workmen's compensation 1933 First Blue Cross plan organized 1940s Kaiser Permanente started	1972 Cost of medical education: $9700/student/yr. 1974 $80–187/pt day for hospital stay Increased involvement by business in health care finances; decreased cost shifting

Note: Data from *Two Centuries of American Medicine* by J. Bordley and A. McGehee Harvey, W.B. Saunders Company, 1976.

Most hospitals are nonprofit (53 percent), followed by government (32 percent) and proprietary (15 percent).[28] However, if one excludes government facilities, the percentage of proprietary hospitals in 1987 was 24.1 percent, up from 14.1 percent in 1977.

Hospitals can also be described according to specialty. In 1987 most hospitals were classified as short-term general and other specialty (89 percent), followed by psychiatric facilities (9 percent), long-term general and other specialty (2 percent), and tuberculosis and other respiratory disease (less than 1 percent).[29]

Hospitals are integrating vertically and horizontally in response to changes in the environment that have threatened their survival. Horizontal integration refers to the addition of organizations or services of the same type (e.g., one hospital acquiring another hospital). Vertical integration occurs when the organization decides to engage in a new enterprise or new type of program. For example, as mentioned earlier, many hospitals are adding new services such as substance abuse clinics, long-term care units, and psychiatric programs.

As a result of these organizational shifts, hospital systems grew rapidly in the late 1970s and early 1980s. In 1978, 1,455 hospitals were owned by multihospital systems; 628, by investor-owner systems; and 727, by nonprofit systems.[30] In 1982, 1,740 hospitals were owned by multihospital systems, an increase of 19.6 percent. The number of multihospital systems increased further to 303 by 1987.[31] Multihospital systems controlled 2,020 hospitals and 380,575 beds. Most of the systems were nonprofit or church related (79 percent).

Hospital Reimbursement

Hospitals are reimbursed for services rendered through a variety of mechanisms. Most of their revenues are from third-party payers, including local, state, and federal governments; commercial insurance companies; Blue Cross and Blue Shield plans; and in some cases health maintenance organizations (HMOs) and preferred provider organizations (PPOs). Because of the large number of third-party payers and the variety of payment mechanisms, sound financial planning and information systems for financial management are essential to hospital survival.

To control costs, many third-party payers are implementing new payment mechanisms and requiring utilization review and second opinions. For example, in California hospitals must contract with the state if they wish to serve Medicaid patients. Payment is a pre-negotiated flat per diem rate. Other payers who contract with hospitals are HMOs and PPOs. With the passage of the 1982 Tax Equity and Fiscal Responsibility Act (TEFRA) and the Social Security Amendments of 1983, Medicare replaced the cost-based retrospective payment system with a PPS based on DRGs. Medicare patients are assigned to a DRG and payment is based on the amount allowed for that DRG. The PPS provides incentives for efficient service delivery, since reimbursement is predetermined based on the DRG assignment and not on resource utilization.

There was some concern that hospitals might be tempted to reduce the number and quality of services to save money. Although the average length of stay (ALOS) declined for individuals aged 65 and over (from 10.7 days in 1980 to 8.6 days in 1987), it also declined for those aged 45–64 (from 8.2 days to 6.8 days). This decline in ALOS means that hospitals are serving more acute patients. Yet this increase in acuity is not due solely to the PPS. Overall, evidence to date does not indicate that the PPS has resulted in reduced quality of care.[32]

Hospitals are heavily regulated organizations. Not only must they comply with all relevant state, local, and federal requirements for businesses, but they must meet additional requirements because of the nature of their business—health care. Nonfederal hospitals in each state are state licensed and exist by the authority of the state under general statutes regarding corporations or under specific statutes or charters. Federal facilities (e.g., Veterans Administration hospitals) are an exception, since they are not regulated by the states. Hospitals also must meet Medicare and Medicaid conditions of participation if they wish to provide services to enrollees of those programs. In addition, most hospitals seek accreditation through the Joint Commission on Accreditation of Healthcare Organizations (Joint Commission) or the American Osteopathic Association (AOA).

THE HEALTH CARE TEAM

Hospitals employ a bewildering array of health professionals and allied and ancillary health personnel. Over 200 different occupational groups exist, and in some hospitals the number of job titles approaches the number of employees. Staffing patterns and levels in hospitals and other health facilities have changed in recent years. The driving forces behind these changes include the introduction of new technology, advances in medical practice, and, in some cases, new requirements by state and federal governments (e.g., the conditions of participation under Medicare and Medicaid).

The large number of distinct professional and occupational groups complicates human resource management. In contrast to the days when medical care was provided by the physician, possibly with the aid of a nurse, the provision of medical services today requires a team made up of diverse professionals. Often the members of the health care team come from disparate educational backgrounds and have been socialized into roles that do not easily mesh. Professionals have been characterized as desiring and expecting autonomy in the workplace, further complicating the development of cooperative and productive health care teams.

For the purpose of this discussion, human resources in the health care industry will be categorized as (1) management and administrative personnel, (2) professional and technical personnel, and (3) support personnel.[33] Occupations in the first two categories usually require the completion of special educational programs and licensure or certification.

Management and Administrative Personnel

Education for professional managers of health services emerged relatively recently. The first master's program was developed in 1934 at the University of Chicago. Graduate programs are found in various settings: schools of public health, business schools, and schools of allied health. Programs of study are typically two years in length and prepare the graduate to enter middle-management positions in a wide variety of health care settings. In 1989, 52 programs were accredited by the Accrediting Commission on Education in Health Services Administration (ACEHSA).

Undergraduate programs in health care management emerged in the 1960s in response to system expansion and an increased need for individuals trained to assume entry-level management positions. The Association of University Programs in Health Administration (AUPHA) has established standards for baccalaureate programs and applies these standards to programs seeking full AUPHA membership. In 1989, 24 programs were approved for full AUPHA membership. Five programs were associate members preparing for full membership status.

Recent trends in health care management include the increasing number of women entering both baccalaureate and graduate programs (from 8.1 percent in 1968–69 to 72.7 percent in 1984–85 for baccalaureate programs).[34] Executive and nontraditional programs are being developed for physicians and allied health professionals seeking to move from clinical to management roles.

Professional and Technical Personnel

As mentioned earlier a large number of occupational groups contribute to the delivery of health care. Although it is beyond the scope of this chapter to discuss all or even most of these groups, the key ones will be described in terms of education, number in practice, and trends in the field. For the purpose of this discussion, a distinction will be made between independent practitioners and dependent practitioners. The former are allowed by law to provide a delimited set of services without supervision or authorization by others; the latter provide services under supervision or after authorization by an independent practitioner.

Independent Practitioners

As discussed earlier in this chapter, medical education and the medical profession underwent major changes in the early twentieth century. The practice of medicine is now highly specialized, with over 80 specialties and subspecialties. Training programs are long, often requiring over seven years of postbaccalaureate study.

The number of active physicians increased from 326,200 in 1970 to 501,200 in 1984 and is projected to be 686,600 in 2000.[35] The number of practitioners per 100,000 population increased from 156 in 1970 to 217 in 1984 and is projected to be 259.9 in 2000. Whether these figures represent a surplus, shortage, or supply-demand equilibrium is subject to debate.[36] Several factors complicate the supply and demand analysis of physicians. Geographic distribution, distribution across specialties, utilization patterns, and medical care practice are just a few of these.[37]

Podiatrists, dentists, psychologists, and optometrists are also independent practitioners. Although the supply and the practitioner-to-population ratio are expected to increase for all these groups, the percentage change will vary considerably. For example, the physician-to-population ratio is projected to change 28.4 percent from 1984 to 2000, yet the change for dentists is projected to be only 3.4 percent. Additionally, admissions to dental schools are declining (from 6,301 in 1978–79 to 5,274 in 1983–84).

Dependent Practitioners

Professional nurses constitute the largest group of health personnel. In 1970 there were 750,000 active registered nurses (RNs), and in 1986 there were 1,592,600.[38] The estimate for 2000 is 2,079,400. The number of RNs per 100,000 population increased from 366 in 1970 to 613 in 1984 and is projected to be 775 in 2000.[39] Yet hospitals and other health delivery sites are having difficulty filling vacant RN positions.

Nurses may prepare to enter the field by completing any one of three educational programs. Diploma programs were the first ones developed and are usually two to three years in length and hospital based. The number of students enrolled in these programs dropped from 93,760 in 1965–66 to 60,213 in 1975–76; it dropped further to 30,179 in 1985–86.[40]

Baccalaureate programs typically are four to five years and are offered by colleges and universities. The number of students enrolled in these programs increased from 30,378 in 1965–66 to 100,680 in 1975–76 but declined to 93,340 in 1985–86.[41]

Associate degree programs were developed in the fifties with the support of the federal government. Since the establishment of the first program in 1952, the growth of these programs has been rapid. The number of students graduating from these programs increased from 11,564 in 1965–66 to 89,492 in 1975–76 and to 97,706 in 1985–86.[42]

Nurse training programs are accredited by the National League of Nursing. The key professional association is the American Nurses' Association. Registered nurses are licensed in all states. The first licensure act was passed in 1903, and by

1923 all states and the District of Columbia licensed nurses under nurse practice acts.[43]

Nursing practice, like medical practice, has become increasingly specialized. Among the specialty groups are nurse anesthetists, psychiatric nurses, and nurse practitioners. Specialties require training beyond the initial program of study and in some cases require a master's degree.

Current issues in nursing include the appropriate roles and tasks for professional nurses, the preferred educational program (diploma, associate degree, or baccalaureate degree), and the shortage of professional nurses. The full-time equivalent RN vacancy rate in hospitals increased from 4.4 percent in 1983 to 13.6 percent in 1986.[44] Of greater concern, however, has been the recent decline in admissions to nursing school, a drop of 30 percent since 1983.[45]

Several factors may be responsible for the shortage of RNs, including increasing opportunities for women to enter other professions (e.g., law and medicine), the changing utilization of RNs, job stress, and limited salary progression. Quite simply, women are seeking career opportunities in other fields, perhaps reducing the number entering nursing and the number remaining in nursing.

Practical nurses (licensed practical or vocational nurses) complete 9 to 12 months of training, usually in a vocational school or a community college. The first programs were established in 1917 as a result of the Vocational Education Act.[46]

Support Personnel

Other allied health personnel include workers in the medical laboratory, radiologic service workers, physical therapists, speech pathologists, occupational therapists, dental hygienists, and pharmacists, to list only a few. Although the educational and licensure requirements for individual occupations vary considerably, the general trend is for educational requirements to increase over time and licensure and certification requirements to become more restrictive. For example, physical therapy is attempting to move the degree required for entry-level practice from the baccalaureate level to the master's. Another trend is for occupational groups to seek more autonomy in practice. For example, dental hygienists in California are seeking to change licensure laws so that they can engage in a mode of independent practice[47] and pharmacists in Florida are seeking changes that would allow them to prescribe drugs in limited circumstances.

PAYING FOR CARE

Payment mechanisms within the health care sector are complex and constantly changing. At the beginning of the twentieth century, payment was usually made out of pocket by the individual receiving the service. In some cases government and religious organizations would directly provide services through hospitals and clinics.

During the Depression, the Blue Shield and Blue Cross plans were developed and the government began to subsidize health services for some indigent groups. For example, Title V of the Social Security Act provided support for maternal and child health programs. The importance of third-party payers increased steadily in the following decades. A third-party payer is a party—a government agency, insurance company, or employer—that reimburses providers for services delivered to others. In 1940, only 18.7 percent of the payments for personal health services were by third-party payers. In 1960, the percentage was 44.1 percent, and by 1981, it was 67.9 percent. For hospitals, it is now over 90 percent.[48]

ALTERNATIVE DELIVERY SYSTEMS

Health Maintenance Organizations

HMOs provide an alternative to traditional delivery and financing mechanisms. An HMO is an organization that provides a comprehensive set of health services to a voluntarily enrolled population for a fixed monthly or annual fee. Although the first HMO, the Ross-Loos Health Plan, was organized in 1929 and the Kaiser Permanente Medical Program was established in northern and southern California in 1945, few HMOs existed until their growth was stimulated by the passage in 1973 of the Health Maintenance Organization Act.[49] The federal government supported the development of HMOs through a program of grants and loans. HMOs were considered to be an efficient means of providing and financing health services. The federal government hoped the growth of HMOs would help contain health care expenditures by reducing the use of costly health services and by competing with the commercial insurers and the Blue Cross and Blue Shield plans.

Organizational Models

HMOs are usually based on a staff, group practice, or the independent practice association (IPA) model. Common to all three models are (1) a component responsible for plan management, including the development of the service and payment structure and the acquisition of service providers, service delivery sites, and plan enrollees; (2) service providers, including physicians and other health care personnel; (3) service delivery sites, including hospitals and ambulatory clinics; and (4) enrollees.

In the staff model, the plan employs the providers and owns and operates the facilities. Physicians and other providers are generally salaried and provide services only to HMO enrollees.

In the group practice model, the HMO contracts with a multispecialty group and other facilities (e.g., hospitals) for the provision of services. The HMO reimburses the group on a capitation basis, and the group then reimburses the physicians and other providers. In some cases, a distinction is made between a group model in which the plan contracts with a single medical group and one in which the plan contracts with several medical groups or providers. The former model is referred to as a group model and the latter as a network model.

In the IPA model, the plan contracts with multiple providers who maintain their own offices and may treat patients other than HMO enrollees. The plan reimburses the physicians directly, usually at a percentage of their usual and customary fees. In 1988 there were 231 (36 percent) group model HMOs (including network and staff models) and 417 (64 percent) IPAs.[50]

The growth of HMOs was rapid. In 1970 there were only 33 HMOs serving 3 million enrollees. By 1980 there were 236 HMOs serving 9.1 million enrollees, and by 1984 there were 306 HMOs serving 16.7 million. From 1983 to 1984, the number of HMOs increased 16.2 percent and the number of enrollees increased 22.4 percent.[51] More recently, however, the growth rate has declined, and the number of HMOs actually decreased from 1987 to 1988 by 6.8 percent.[52] Part of this decline is due to the acquisition of some HMOs by others and part is due to increasing costs, which result in premium increases and a weakened competitive position.

Preferred Provider Organizations

PPOs contract with employers or other groups of enrollees to provide coverage for a comprehensive set of health services. A panel of health care providers is established through contracts based on negotiated discounted rates or a fixed fee schedule. Unlike HMOs, PPOs do not require prepayment. Also PPO enrollees have a broader choice of providers. A PPO usually contracts with a large panel of providers, but the enrollees may seek services from providers other than those contracting with the PPO. To encourage enrollees to use the services of contracting providers, the PPO usually has a larger co-payment for services received from noncontracting providers. Individuals enroll in a PPO because service costs are lower when contracting providers are used. Providers contract with a PPO in order to secure a larger patient base. Finally, the PPO seeks to contract with providers at favorable rates or discounts in order to keep premiums low and thus ensure their position in the insurance marketplace.

PPOs are growing rapidly. From 1984 to 1986, the number of people covered by PPOs increased from 1.4 million to 16.5 million.[53] Most PPO enrollees are located in only three states: 35 percent in California, 17 percent in Colorado, and 9 percent in Florida. Growth of PPOs was especially rapid in California after the passage of Assembly Bill 3480 in 1982, which allowed private insurers to negotiate rates with institutional providers and offer benefits of such rates to the insureds who select those providers. The sponsoring agency of a PPO is usually a hospital (27.7 percent) or a Blue Cross or Blue Shield plan (27.7 percent).[54] Physicians, commercial insurers, and investor groups also sponsor PPOs. Because most PPOs were developed in the past five years and because they vary so widely in structure, it is impossible to predict what their course of development will be in the coming decade.

Other Alternative Delivery Systems

As hospital care increased in cost and as patients sought convenient service delivery options, new service delivery sites and approaches emerged. Outpatient surgical centers began to appear (the first was established in Phoenix in 1970). Urgent care centers, free-standing diagnostic clinics, birthing centers, and renal dialysis clinics were developed to provide service options that were affordable and convenient. Hospitals have responded by adding some of these services. The net effect has been a greater response to consumer desires by many health care providers.

THE FUTURE

Predictions regarding the future of the health care industry are risky. The industry is complex, rapidly evolving, and constantly impacted by changes in the larger environment. Yet, a few predictions can be safely made. Health care expenditures will continue to increase; it is the rate of increase that is subject to debate. If effective cost controls are implemented, the rate of increase may slow. If they are not, then expenditures will continue to account for an ever-larger percentage of the gross national product. In the next decade, hospitals and other health care providers will continue to adjust to an increasingly competitive marketplace. Less successful providers will fail or be acquired by their competitors.

Financing

Financing of health service has undergone dramatic changes in the past two decades and even more dramatic changes may occur in the 1990s. Factors related to anticipated changes in financing include (1) the need to provide coverage for the indigent, unemployed, and employed uninsured; (2) the need to develop financing methods that encourage efficient, high-quality service delivery; and (3) the need to develop an easily understood, unified approach to financing, thereby reducing the burden on both the patient and the provider.

Two states, Massachusetts and Hawaii, have recently enacted programs to expand health care coverage for their populations. Other states may take similar action if these programs are effective and affordable. At the federal level, the idea of national insurance is still promoted by many, although how to structure and finance such a program is the subject of much debate.

Technology

Although the role of technology was addressed earlier, technological advances will continue to be a driving force in the industry. Unfortunately, these advances may not always lead to positive results. In health care, in contrast to other industries, new technologies often increase rather than decrease cost. Thus, careful cost-benefit analyses are necessary in determining which technologies should be adopted. Additionally, careful evaluation of new technologies will remain a problem as groups which might benefit from them press for adoption before adequate testing is completed.

New technologies also impact human resources. As new equipment and new methods of prevention, diagnosis, and treatment are developed, health care providers will need to acquire new skills and knowledge. New specialties may develop and new occupations emerge. The health care team will continue to evolve as technological advances impact the field of practice.

Ethical Issues

A consideration of issues related to bioethics and managerial ethics is essential in contemplating the future of the health care industry. The rapid expansion of medical technology virtually guarantees that new issues in bioethics will emerge while the system is still grappling with current ones. Questions related to organ transplants, genetic engineering, surrogate parenting, the definition of death, wrongful life, and rationing of health care, to name only a few issues, must be addressed through forums that consider the economic, legal, and ethical ramifications of different courses of action.

Because of the unique nature of health services, managerial ethics assumes greater importance than for many other industries. Managers have to balance the responsibility that their organizations have to deliver services to those who need them against the need to remain financially sound. Should hospitals be expected to maintain trauma centers or emergency rooms that drain resources needed to maintain other services? No easy answers are available. One can only predict that issues in bioethics and managerial ethics will continue to be debated.

NOTES

1. J.V. Vincenzino, "Trends in Medical Care—Update," *Statistical Bulletin*, Metropolitan Insurance Companies, January–March 1989, 26–34.
2. U.S. Department of Health and Human Services, Public Health Service, Bureau of Health Professions, *Health United States, 1988*, DHHS Pub. no. (PHS) 89-1232 (Washington, D.C.: Government Printing Office, 1989).
3. P.R. Torrens, *The American Health Care System: Issues and Problems* (St. Louis: C.V. Mosby, 1978), 3–15.
4. O.W. Anderson, *Health Services in the United States: A Growth Enterprise Since 1875* (Ann Arbor, Mich.: Health Administration Press, 1985).
5. J.J. Hanlon and G.E. Pickett, *Public Health: Administration and Practice*, 7th ed. (St. Louis: C.V. Mosby, 1979).
6. Ibid.
7. R. Stevens, *American Medicine and the Public Interest* (New Haven: Yale University Press, 1971), 7.
8. Ibid., 24.
9. Hanlon and Pickett, *Public Health*, 22.
10. Torrens, *American Health Care System;* Anderson, *Health Services in the United States*.
11. Stevens, *American Medicine and the Public Interest*.
12. C.L. Haglund and W.L. Dowling, "The Hospital," in *Introduction to Health Services*, 3d ed., ed. S.J. Williams and P.R. Torrens (New York: Wiley, 1988).
13. Anderson, *Health Services in the United States*.
14. Torrens, *American Health Care System*.
15. Stevens, *American Medicine and the Public Interest*, 68.
16. Ibid.
17. R.W. Scott and J.C. Lammers, "Trends in Occupations and Organizations: Health Care and Mental Health in Sectors," *Medical Care Review* 42, no. 1 (1985): 37–76.
18. Torrens, *American Health Care System*.
19. Anderson, *Health Services in the United States*.
20. A.R. Somers and H.M. Somers, *Health and Health Care: Policies in Perspective* (Rockville, Md.: Aspen Publishers, 1977), 8.
21. L.D. Brown, *Health Policy in the United States: Issues and Options* (New York: Ford Foundation, 1988).
22. F.A. Wilson and D. Neuhauser, *Health Services in the United States*, 2d ed. (Cambridge, Mass.: Ballinger, 1985).
23. Torrens, *American Health Care System*.
24. Brown, *Health Policy in the United States*.
25. U.S. Department of Health and Human Services, Public Health Service, *Health United States, 1986*, DHHS Pub. no. (PHS) 87-1232 (Washington, D.C.: Government Printing Office, 1987), Tables 106 and 107.
26. Brown, *Health Policy in the United States*.
27. American Hospital Association, *Hospital Statistics*, 1988 ed.(Chicago: American Hospital Association, 1988).

28. Ibid.

29. Ibid.

30. D. Ermann and J. Gabel, "Multi-hospital Systems: Issues and Empirical Findings." *Health Affairs* 3, no. 1 (1984): 51–64.

31. American Hospital Association, *AHA Guide* (Chicago, American Hospital Association, 1988).

32. J.R. Lave, "The Effect of the Medicare Prospective Payment System," *Annual Review of Public Health* 10 (1989): 141–61.

33. R.S. Hanft, "Health Manpower" in *Health Care Delivery in the United States,* 2d ed., ed. Steven Jonas, 61–95. (New York: Spring, 1981).

34. U.S. Department of Health and Human Services, Public Health Service, *Minorities and Women in the Health Fields,* DHHS Publication no. (HRSA) HRS-DV 171 (Washington, D.C.: Government Printing Office, 1987).

35. U.S. Department of Health and Human Services, Public Health Service, Bureau of Health Professions, *Fifth Report to the President and Congress on the Status of Health Personnel* (Washington, D.C.: Government Printing Office, March 1986).

36. W.B. Schwartz, F.A. Sloan, and B.A. Mendelson, "Why There Will Be Little or No Physician Surplus between Now and the Year 2000," *New England Journal of Medicine,* 318 (1988): 892–96; Graduate Medical Education Advisory Committee, *Report of the Graduate Medical Education Advisory Committee to the Secretary of DHHS,* vol. 1, Summary Report (Washington, D.C.: GPO, 1981).

37. R.D. Thomas, "Projecting Physician Demand and Supply: The Importance of Nonmedical Factors," *Journal of Health and Human Resources* 1 (1988): 388–92.

38. U.S. Department of Health and Human Services, *Fifth Report to the President and Congress on the Status of Health Personnel.*

39. U.S. Department of Health and Human Services, *Health United States, 1988.*

40. U.S. Department of Health and Human Services, *Minorities and Women in the Health Fields.*

41. Ibid.

42. Ibid.

43. Wilson and Neuhauser, *Health Services in the United States.*

44. P.I. Buerhaus, "Not Just Another Nursing Shortage." *Nursing Economics* 5, no. 6 (1987): 267–79.

45. C. Wallace, "Is There a Nursing Shortage?" *LACMA Physician,* October 10, 1988, 36–40.

46. Wilson and Neuhauser, *Health Services in the United States.*

47. W. Frey and R. Gottschalle, "Round 3: California Dentists, Hygienists Still Skirmishing," *Healthweek,* July 17, 1989, 12.

48. Vicenzino, "Trends in Medical Care."

49. Anderson, *Health Services in the United States.*

50. California Association of Hospitals and Health Systems, *Hospital Fact Book,* 13th ed. (Sacramento: California Association of Hospitals and Health Systems, 1989), 46.

51. Interstudy, *National HMO Census, 1984* (Excelsior, Minn.: Interstudy, 1985).

52. P. Cotton, "More HMOs Likely to Show Profit, Invest in Upgrading," *Medical World News,* September 25, 1989, 72.

53. G. deLissovoy, et al., "Preferred Provider Organizations—One Year Later," *Inquiry* 24 (Summer 1987): 127–34.

54. Ibid.

Chapter 2

Hospital Accreditation

Cindy Orsund-Gassiot, CMSC

A HISTORY OF THE JOINT COMMISSION ON ACCREDITATION OF HOSPITALS*

The history of the Joint Commission on Accreditation of Hospitals [now Joint Commission on Accreditation of Healthcare Organizations] is a story of the health professions' commitment to patient care of high quality in the 20th century. The story began on a summer day in England in 1910. While riding back to London from a visit to a tuberculosis sanitarium, Dr. Ernest Codman was explaining his end-result system of hospital organization to Dr. Edward Martin. According to Dr. Codman, his system would enable a hospital to track every patient it treated long enough to determine whether or not the treatment was effective. If the treatment was not effective, the hospital would then try to find out how to prevent similar failures in the future. Dr. Martin responded that he thought Dr. Codman's system was one of the important reasons why an American college of surgeons should be established:

> An American College would be a fine thing if it could be the instrument with which to introduce the End Result Idea into hospitals; in other words to standardize them on the basis of service to the individual patient, as demonstrated by available records.[1]

Beyond establishing the concept of a linkage between an American college of surgeons and hospital standardization, this conversation was also the first expression of the principle that was eventually to guide the standardization program:

---

* The section, "A History of the Joint Commission on Accreditation of Hospitals," is reprinted with permission of the American Medical Association from *Journal of the American Medical Association*, 258 (August 21, 1987): 936–940, by James S. Roberts, MD; Jack G. Coale, MA; Robert R. Redman, MA. Copyright 1987, American Medical Association.

service to the patient. Dr. Martin's interest in improving conditions in hospitals was shared by other physicians and by hospital administrators in the United States and Canada. Conditions in hospitals were embarrassing to the professions. Most hospitals were little more than boardinghouses for poor and sick persons. Patients were not examined when they were admitted, and because histories and diagnoses were seldom recorded, medical records were useless. Most hospitals also lacked the equipment and services necessary for conducting proper preoperative and postoperative evaluation of surgical patients. Furthermore, few efforts were made to determine the results of patient care and treatment. Leading physicians believed that the basis of the most serious problems was the lack of organized medical staffs. Certainly, no efforts were made to determine a physician's competence to practice in a hospital, and no one was held responsible for the quality of care provided to patients.[2]

While conditions in hospitals were viewed as grim, many involved in medicine and hospital administration were optimistic about the future. The source of their optimism was the convergence of significant advances in the science of medicine and in management concepts, as well as the recognition of the value of hygiene in health care. Technological progress in the practice of medicine, particularly in the performance of surgery in hospitals, offered considerably safer care for patients. Management principles developed during the industrial revolution were also being applied successfully in all types of businesses, including hospitals. Interest in formulating standards of care and in developing systems to produce better products more efficiently began to spread. Dr. Codman's end-result system was just one example of the application of management principles to hospital care.

These several factors were the background against which the Third Clinical Congress of Surgeons of North America met in November 1912. At this historic meeting, Dr. Franklin Martin made a proposal that was to lead to the founding of the American College of Surgeons. Immediately following that proposal, Dr. Allen Kanavel set forth the following resolution at the request of Dr. Edward Martin:

> Be it resolved by the Clinical Congress of Surgeons of North America here assembled, that some system of standardization of hospital equipment and hospital work should be developed, to the end that those institutions having the highest ideals may have proper recognition before the profession, and that those of inferior equipment and standards should be stimulated to raise the quality of their work. In this way patients will receive the best type of treatment, and the public will have some means of recognizing those institutions devoted to the highest ideals of medicine.[3]

It is a tribute to Dr. Edward Martin's foresight that he managed to associate this first official expression of the need for hospital standardization so closely with the proposal that would result in the creation of the American College of Surgeons. There appeared to be a clear realization that the hospital standardization program must have the backing of a national organization if it were ever going to have a chance to succeed. Largely because of his efforts, hospital standardization became one of the stated purposes of the College when it was founded in 1913.

During the first few years of its existence, the College focused its energies on solving problems of vital concern to its survival and success. Hospital standardization quickly and unexpectedly became one of these problems. During the first three years of its existence, the College found it necessary to reject 60% of the applicants for fellowship because the 50 case records required from each fellowship applicant provided the College with an insufficient basis to determine clinical competence.[4] Shortly thereafter, John Bowman, PhD, the director of the College, used his influence with the Carnegie Foundation, New York, to obtain a gift of $30,000 to launch a hospital standardization program.

From October 19 to 20, 1917, 300 fellows from the Committees on Standards from every state in the union and every province in Canada, as well as 60 leading hospital superintendents, met in Chicago to discuss hospital standardization. During the conference, the participants described existing conditions in hospitals and discussed the kinds of improvements that would be necessary to ensure the proper care and treatment of patients. This conference, the papers and some of the discussions of which are published in the first issue of volume 3 of the 1917 *Bulletin* of the American College of Surgeons,[5] is of interest not only because it established the foundation for hospital standardization, but also because it created the concept that knowledgeable and experienced health care professionals should assess conditions in the hospital environment and work to achieve consensus on standards that would have the greatest positive effect on the quality of care provided to patients. That concept continues to underlie the accreditation process today.

On December 20, 1917, two months after the Conference on Hospital Standardization, the American College of Surgeons formally established the Hospital Standardization Program, and in March 1918, the College published a "Standard on Efficiency" in the *Bulletin*. Expecting to approve at least 1000 hospitals during the first year, the College staff began testing the program in April 1918.

The results of the field trials were announced by Bowman at a conference on hospital standardization in New York on October 24, 1919. Bowman told the audience that 692 hospitals of 100 beds or more had been surveyed and that only 89 hospitals had met the standards.[6] While these results are not surprising when one considers conditions in hospitals at the time, the results were nevertheless shocking.

Although the College made the numbers public, it burned the list of hospitals at midnight in the furnace of the Waldorf Astoria Hotel, New York, to keep it from the press. Some of the most prestigious hospitals in the country had failed to meet the most basic standards. However, 109 hospitals corrected deficiencies after their initial surveys and were subsequently approved. Although the field trials were disappointing, they dramatically demonstrated the need for a national hospital accreditation program, and they solidified national support for the program. Consequently, the College's Board of Regents adopted five official standards for the program at its December 1919 meeting.[7] These standards, which are collectively known as the *Minimum Standard* (Exhibit 2-1), said it was intended to

> safeguard the care of every patient within a hospital by insisting upon competence on the part of the doctors, and upon adequate clinical and pathological laboratory facilities to insure correct diagnosis; by a thorough study and diagnosis in writing for each case; by a monthly audit of

---

Exhibit 2-1   The Minimum Standard

1. That physicians and surgeons privileged to practice in the hospital be organized as a definite group or staff. Such organization has nothing to do with the question as to whether the hospital is "open" or "closed," nor need it affect the various existing types of staff organization. The word STAFF is here defined as the group of doctors who practice in the hospital inclusive of all groups such as the "regular staff," "the visiting staff," and the "associate staff."

2. That membership upon the staff be restricted to physicians and surgeons who are (a) full graduates of medicine in good standing and legally licensed to practice in their respective states or provinces, (b) competent in their respective fields, and (c) worthy in character and in matters of professional ethics; that in this latter connection the practice of the division of fees, under any guise whatever, be prohibited.

3. That the staff initiate and, with the approval of the governing board of the hospital, adopt rules, regulations, and policies governing the professional work of the hospital; that these rules, regulations, and policies specifically provide:

    (a) That staff meetings be held at least once each month. (In large hospitals the departments may choose to meet separately.)

    (b) That the staff review and analyze at regular intervals their clinical experience in the various departments of the hospital, such as medicine, surgery, obstetrics, and the other specialties; the clinical records of patients, free and pay, to be the basis for such review and analyses.

4. That accurate and complete records be written for all patients and filed in an accessible manner in the hospital—a complete case record being one which includes identification data; complaint; personal and family history; history of present illness; physical examination; special examinations, such as consultations, clinical laboratory, X-ray and other examinations; provisional or working diagnosis; medical or surgical treatment; gross and microscopical pathological findings; progress notes; final diagnosis; condition on discharge; follow-up and, in case of death, autopsy findings.

5. That diagnostic and therapeutic facilities under competent supervision be available for the study, diagnosis, and treatment of patients, these to include at least (a) a clinical laboratory providing chemical, bacteriological, serological, and pathological services; (b) an X-ray department providing radiographic and fluoroscopic services.

Source: Reprinted with permission from *Bulletin of the American College of Surgeons*, Vol. 8, p. 4, © 1924.

the medical and surgical work conducted in the hospital during the preceding interval; and by prohibiting the practice of the division of fees under any guise whatsoever.[8]

That these standards are as essential to the provision of quality care in hospitals today as they were in 1919 is no small tribute to the men who contributed to their development. In 1924, Dr. Franklin Martin said that the *Minimum Standard*, had "become to hospital betterment what the Sermon on the Mount is to great religion."[9]

With the adoption of the *Minimum Standard*, the accreditation process that continues today was set in motion. The following steps are included in this process: the development of reasonable standards that every organization should be expected to meet and that the health professions agree will have a positive effect on improving the quality of patient care; the voluntary request for survey and approval by a health care organization; the survey of the organization by professionals who assess compliance with the standards and provide consultation to support achievement of greater levels of compliance; and the subsequent efforts of organizations to use the standards and survey results to improve patient care.

The *Minimum Standard* was considered to be a beginning. The College knew that hospitals would advance and change, and it expected the Hospital Standardization Program to evolve with them. Ensuring that the standards and the accreditation process remain responsive to conditions in health care organizations and focused on issues that will protect and promote quality of care has proved to be one of the greatest challenges to the health professions.

The Hospital Standardization Program had a strong beginning, and the value of the program became broadly apparent. The case records submitted to the College by surgeons in approved hospitals provided an acceptable basis for evaluation, and the quality of care in these hospitals improved noticeably. As news of the program's success spread, more and more hospitals sought approval. The number of approved hospitals rose from 89 in 1919 to 3290 in 1950, over half of the hospitals in the United States.

By 1950, the size and scope of the program had increased significantly, and the College, which had already invested $2 million in the Hospital Standardization Program, was having difficulty in supporting the effort alone. In addition, the increasing sophistication of medical care, the growing number and complexity of modern hospitals, and the rapid emergence of nonsurgical specialties after World War II required that the standards be revised, expanded, and updated, and that the scope of the survey be extended. These considerations clearly suggested that the Hospital Standardization Program needed the support of the entire medical and hospital field. Consequently, the College solicited the support and participation of other national professional organizations in the creation of an independent organization that could devote all of its efforts to improving and promoting voluntary accreditation.

After considerable deliberation, the American College of Physicians, the American Hospital Association, the American Medical Association, and the Canadian Medical Association joined the American College of Surgeons on December 15, 1951, to form the Joint Commission on Accreditation of Hospitals as an independent, nonprofit organization. The Canadian Medical Association withdrew in 1959, to participate in the development of its own program, the Canadian Council on Hospital Accreditation. The College officially conveyed its program to the Joint Commission on December 6, 1952, and the Joint Commission began to offer accreditation to hospitals in January 1953.

In addition to carrying on the College's program, the Joint Commission preserved the traditions established by the College. The accreditation process remains voluntary, the standards continue to represent what health professionals agree is most conducive to the provision of quality care to patients, and the accreditation survey still provides an evaluation that achieves its most beneficial effects through a combination of evaluation, education, and consultation. Also, as in the past, the information obtained in the survey process is still held in confidence between the Joint Commission and the organization surveyed. [Under public pressure, the Joint Commission changed its policy in 1989 and now must release findings of surveys under certain circumstances.]

The Joint Commission today is directed by a 22-member Board of Commissioners. Seven commissioners are appointed by the American Medical Association; seven by the American Hospital Association; three by the American College of Physicians; three by the American College of Surgeons; one by the American Dental Association, which accepted an invitation to become a corporate member in 1979; and one is a private citizen appointed annually by the rest of the board.

Under the direction of the Board of Commissioners, the Joint Commission continued to expand the College's program, which was now called the Hospital Accreditation Program. It hired and trained a cadre of experienced surveyors and focused the survey on medical staff and patient care issues; and just as the College of Surgeons had done, it periodically revised the standards to reflect the evolution of hospital care.

In August 1966, the Joint Commission board made a major decision to undertake a complete revision of the standards to reflect an optimal achievable rather than a minimal essential level of care. This decision, which redefined the Joint Commission's role in health care, was made for two reasons. First the majority of hospitals in the country had achieved and were maintaining the minimum standards, and because of this, the standards no longer challenged hospitals to reach for the levels of quality care the Board of Commissioners thought could now be achieved. The second reason was even more compelling. Dr. John Porterfield, who was then the director of the Joint Commission, described it as follows:

> In the mid 1960s the Joint Commission found itself no longer the advanced and lonely leader. The Federal government wrote its conditions

for participation in Medicare. State after state with new and refurbished licensing authority wrote regulatory codes, where there had been few or none before. They did have some premise on which to build and it is more than coincidence that the federal conditions and, more particularly, the state codes bore a strong family resemblance to the Joint Commission's accreditation standards. From advanced leader, the Joint Commission seemed almost overnight to be struggling to stay even in the vanguard of progress. And it was challenged, most seriously, as being no longer necessary because now everybody was beginning to do what it had once done alone.[10]

When the government moved toward usurping the Joint Commission's role as the definer of the minimal acceptable level of hospital care, it became necessary and appropriate for the Joint Commission to become the definer of the optimal achievable level of care. In doing so, the Joint Commission was not only realizing the intentions of the founders of hospital standardization, but also assuming a role that was more compatible with the ideals of the health professions that supported voluntary accreditation.

The publication of the optimal achievable standards in the 1970 *Accreditation Manual for Hospitals* was a landmark.[11] In little more than 50 years, the one-page set of standards that specified a minimal essential level of performance had developed into a 152-page manual of state-of-the-art standards. The Joint Commission did not intend the term *optimal achievable* to mean the ideal. It meant the best that could be achieved at the time, given the legal and other concerns that must be accommodated in national standards to make them as effective as possible.[12] The publication of these standards was a clear indication of the tremendous progress hospitals had made since the beginning of this century and of the impact of voluntary accreditation on the quality of hospital care.

In the early 1960s, concern for the quality of care provided in other types of health care organizations that were proliferating throughout the country led the Joint Commission and other national professional organizations to discuss the possibility of developing new accreditation programs. The expansion of the Joint Commission to include programs for other types of health and health-related organizations seemed only natural after the successful leadership it had demonstrated in improving hospitals. The Joint Commission had experience and expertise, and it had national scope and acceptance. A principal organization for voluntary accreditation would also give unity and strength to new accreditation efforts and would afford the greatest opportunities for the coordination of efforts and consistency among approaches to accreditation.

Working with an ever-expanding number of national professional organizations, the Joint Commission developed standards and accreditation programs for a broader variety of health care settings. An accreditation program for long-term care facilities was established in 1965, for organizations serving developmentally disabled persons in 1969, and for psychiatric facilities, substance abuse programs, and community mental health programs in 1970. An accreditation program for ambulatory health care programs was established in 1975 and for hospices in 1983.

During the expansion, the Joint Commission established what are now called Professional and Technical Advisory Committees. One of these committees advises each Joint Commission accreditation program on standards development and survey procedures. Each committee is composed of approximately 15 individuals who are usually appointed as representatives of national organizations having expertise relevant to the particular accreditation program. In addition, approximately 15 experts on education and publications and 15 on health care safety serve on committees that advise the Joint Commission in these areas. All Joint Commission accreditation services are supported by education, publications, and research activities.

Through its Board of Commissioners, the various committees that advise the Joint Commission on a regular and ad hoc basis, the thousands of facilities that participate in the accreditation process and a standards development process that includes extensive review by the field, the Joint Commission maintains close working relationships and continuous communications with health professionals. Through these mechanisms, the Joint Commission monitors the health care environment and has access to the best advice available in health care. This is of incalculable value in the Joint Commission's efforts to maintain state-of-the-art standards and survey processes, as well as education programs and publications. These mechanisms also give the Joint Commission a large measure of assurance that current issues and trends will be fully discussed before important decisions are made.

In addition to its close working relationships with the health professions, the national professional organizations that represent them, and the wide array of accredited organizations, the Joint Commission has important relationships with government. These relationships began in 1965, when Congress passed Public Law 89-97, the Medicare Act. Written into this law was a provision that hospitals accredited by the Joint Commission were "deemed" to be in compliance with most of the *Medicare Conditions of Participation for Hospitals*[13] and, thus, deemed to meet eligibility requirements for participation in the Medicare program. Because a hospital that was certified for Medicare was also considered certified for Medicaid, hospitals accredited by the Joint Commission were similarly eligible for Medicaid participation. Consequently, hospitals that desired to participate in the Medicare and/or Medicaid programs could undergo either a certification inspection by a state agency or an accreditation survey by the Joint Commission.

Government oversight and responsibility were added to this system in 1972 through amendments to the Social Security Act, Public Law 92-603. These amendments required the Secretary of the Department of Health and Human Services to validate Joint Commission findings on a selective sample basis or on the basis of substantial complaint. The law also required the Secretary to include an evaluation of the Joint Commission accreditation process, as gleaned from validation surveys, in his annual report to Congress on Medicare.

Accredited psychiatric and tuberculosis hospitals were not accorded deemed status by the Social Security Act. Instead, the Act required that such hospitals be accredited by the Joint Commission to participate in Medicare and Medicaid. Because this requirement impinged on the voluntary nature of the accreditation process, the Joint Commission sought and finally succeeded in obtaining elimination of this mandate in the Deficit Reduction Act of 1984, Public Law 98-369.

The Joint Commission also has developed relationships with state governments. Today, 39 states and the District of Columbia have incorporated the Joint Commission's hospital accreditation requirements, in whole or in part, into their hospital licensure systems. In most of these states, however, licensure is not granted merely on the basis of accreditation, but rather on the basis of an acceptable review of Joint Commission findings by the state licensing agency. All of the affected states have retained the enforcement powers that accompany responsibility for licensing hospitals. Even though a hospital is considered licensable if it is accredited, the hospital must still comply with licensing laws and regulations.

Accredited hospitals have been considered to meet Medicare health and safety standards for over 20 years now, and the Joint Commission has considerable experience with state licensure programs. Through this time, there is no evidence that these arrangements have had any negative effects on Joint Commission standards and survey processes. On the other hand, there is considerable evidence that these cooperative relationships with government have had synergistic effects that benefit all concerned.

The combination of private sector and public sector responsibilities has served as a stimulus for the Joint Commission to improve its accreditation process. A two-year study of the Joint Commission, state agencies, and what was then the Department of Health, Education, and Welfare, was conducted by the General Accounting Office and reported to Congress on May 14, 1979, in publication HRD-79-37, *The Medicare Hospital Certification System Needs Reform*.[14] Although the report identified deficiencies in the procedures of all three organizations, it praised the Joint Commission for the consistency, effectiveness, and economy of its standards-setting, surveyor-training, accreditation-survey, and decision-making processes.

At the state level, cooperative arrangements with the Joint Commission have provided states with an alternative perspective on the strengths and weaknesses of the hospitals under their jurisdiction and have enabled them to concentrate their resources and enforcement efforts on problem facilities. These arrangements have reduced the number of surveys that hospitals have had to undergo and, consequently, there have been considerable savings of time, effort, and money for these hospitals.

No history of the Joint Commission's voluntary accreditation program effort would be complete without a discussion of quality assurance. The first national requirements calling for regular review and evaluation of the quality of care provided to patients in hospitals were part of the minimum standards of the American College of Surgeons. After the Joint Commission assumed responsibility for the College's program, efforts were undertaken to develop standards for the various services in modern hospitals. These standards paralleled the minimum standards with regard to their emphasis on review and evaluation of the quality of care provided. However, most in-hospital evaluations that were conducted were informal and subjective and were based on an individual practitioner's knowledge and experience in evaluating records and in observing the performance of others.

At the same time, those involved in quality assurance research were developing methods to make the review and evaluation process more structured and objective. While various approaches were proposed, all involved two common elements. These focused on the use of systematic review procedures and the development of objective and valid criteria for measuring the actual quality of care being provided. Both of these elements constituted the essence of a medical audit methodology that the Joint Commission began promoting in the early 1970s. As a result, retrospective outcome-oriented audits were conducted throughout the country. Medical audits even became requirements of the Professional Standards Review Organizations legislated in 1972, in Public Law 92-603.

While encouraging the medical audit as a method of reviewing quality of care, the Joint Commission also directed attention to enhancing and clarifying other quality assurance standards. Requirements concerning medical staff monitoring functions were consolidated and clearly defined as surgical case, pharmacy and therapeutics, blood and antibiotic usage, and medical records review. Standards were also adopted that called for review and evaluation of both the quality and appropriateness of care provided by medical and support service departments. Safety management, infection control, and utilization review standards were also strengthened. Finally, the Joint Commission adopted standards that asked hospitals to consider relevant results of quality assurance activities in reviewing the credentials and delineating the clinical privileges of medical staff members. This was the first explicit reference in Joint Commission standards to the important relationship between quality assurance activities and the delineation of clinical privileges.

Despite this quality assurance focus, most relevant hospital activities consisted of formal audit studies. In too many cases, these studies became paper exercises conducted to meet Joint Commission or Professional Standards Review Organization requirements. Because of this, the quality assurance effort was compromised and failed to effect the desired intent. Preoccupation with the audit requirement rather than quality of care had left hospitals at the periphery of meaningful quality assurance activities.

To address this problem, the Joint Commission developed a new quality assurance standard in 1979, which eliminated the numerical audit requirements and directed hospitals to develop a hospital-wide program that integrates all quality assessment activities. The purpose of the standard was to shift the attention of hospitals toward a systematic quality assessment process, the central element of which was the monitoring and evaluation of all important aspects of patient care to identify and correct patient care problems.

Since adoption of the new quality assurance standard for hospitals in 1979, the Joint Commission has established similar standards for all of the other types of health care organizations that it accredits. Through this standard, the Joint Commission intends to foster the integration of quality assurance mechanisms into the core management systems of accredited facilities. Clearly, quality assurance activities are increasingly linked to the processes of planning, budgeting, and tracking the utilization and cost of limited resources in many health care organizations today.

The evolution of voluntary accreditation has spanned most of the 20th century and is an integral feature of the era of modern medicine. Beginning with the commitment of the American College of Surgeons, the process has steadily gained the support of the hospital and medical fields. Today, the Joint Commission accredits approximately 5000 of the 6500 hospitals in the United States and 2800 other health care organizations. Approximately 1% to 2% of those who seek accreditation do not achieve this status—a reflection of the strong professional motivation of those seeking accreditation to meet the established standards.

Since the Joint Commission began, the voluntary accreditation movement has spread to Canada and Australia and in 1981, the Catalonia province of Spain implemented the first hospital accreditation program in Europe. Interest in voluntary accreditation and quality assurance systems in health care is now spreading rapidly to other countries.

Since 1917, the voluntary accreditation movement has been a consistent and persistent voice for quality in health care. The future holds it own challenges, but as in the past, meeting those challenges provides substance to the merits of voluntarism—of the willingness of the health professions to regulate themselves on the basis of their ideals, integrity, and commitment to patient care.

THE AGENDA FOR CHANGE

In 1985, the Joint Commission launched a set of initiatives called the "Agenda for Change." A fundamental objective of the Agenda for Change is the creation of indicator-based monitoring systems within all accredited organizations. Individual health care organizations will be expected to use clinical indicators developed by expert task forces convened by the Joint Commission in the quality improvement process. The systems for collecting and transferring the data have been computerized.[15]

Through this process, hospitals will routinely collect a limited set of important clinical and organizational process and outcome data, send them to the Joint Commission, and receive back aggregate, comparative data. Accreditation in the future will be based not only on compliance with the standards but on changes in outcomes as well.[16] The indicators are intended to help hospitals and clinicians improve patient outcomes by revealing problem areas that warrant further evaluation. They are not intended to be used as direct measures of quality, nor as a basis for accreditation decisions. However, future accreditation decisions will be influenced by how effectively hospitals use such feedback in their internal quality improvement programs.[17]

When implemented on a national level, the Joint Commission hopes the use of clinical indicators will increase the effectiveness of the performance-monitoring process.[18]

THE AMERICAN OSTEOPATHIC ASSOCIATION

The American Osteopathic Association (AOA) Committee on Hospital Accreditation is the accrediting agency for designated osteopathic hospitals. That is, the hospital must have designated in the name of the facility and printed on the hospital's stationery the word *osteopathic*. A hospital with a medical staff composed of both allopathic and osteopathic physicians may become accredited by the AOA but need not be designated as osteopathic.[19]

To achieve voluntary accreditation, osteopathic hospitals must meet standards published in the *Accreditation Requirements of the American Osteopathic Association*. The survey process, appeals procedure, and term of accreditation are similar to those of the Joint Commission on Accreditation of Healthcare Organizations.

THE SOCIAL SECURITY ACT: MEDICARE

Title XVII of the Social Security Act, Health Insurance for the Aged, is commonly known as Medicare. The legislation was passed in 1965 and went into effect in 1966. The Medicare program is operated by the Department of Health and Human Services.

Hospitals receiving Medicare reimbursement must satisfactorily comply with the Conditions of Participation, which are federal regulations delineating standards for health care delivery similar to the standards of the Joint Commission. As stated earlier, hospitals accredited by the JCAHO or the AOA are "deemed" to meet the Conditions.

Since the Conditions of Participation differ slightly from Joint Commission or AOA standards, medical staff services professionals should be familiar with them. State departments of health conduct Medicare validation surveys or may perform unannounced surveys of hospitals in response to a patient or family complaint. These surveys can be very stringent and thorough, so attention to the requirements of both the voluntary accrediting body and Medicare is a must.

NOTES

1. E.A. Codman, "An Autobiographic Preface," in *The Shoulder: Rupture of the Subraspinatus Tendon and Other Lesions in or about the Supracromial Bursa* (Boston: Thomas Todd, 1934), v–vi.
2. J.A. Hornsby, "Hospitals as They Are: The Hospital Problem of Today—What Is It?" *Bulletin of the American College of Surgeons* 1 (1917): 4–11.
3. L. Davis, *Fellowship of Surgeons: A History of the American College of Surgeons* (Chicago: American College of Surgeons, 1973).
4. C.P. Schlicke, "American Surgery's Noblest Experiment," *Archives of Surgery* 108 (1973): 379–85.
5. Hornsby, "Hospitals as They Are."
6. Davis, *Fellowship of Surgeons,* 221.
7. Ibid., 489–90.
8. F.H. Martin, *Fifty Years of Medicine and Surgery: An Autobiographical Sketch* (Chicago: Lakeside Press, 1934), 338.
9. G.W. Stephenson, "The College's Role in Hospital Standardization," *Bulletin of the American College of Surgeons* 66 (1981): 17–29.
10. J.P. Porterfield, "From the Director's Office," *Bulletin of the Joint Commission on Accreditation of Hospitals* 4 (1972): 1–2.
11. Joint Commission on Accreditation of Hospitals, *1970 Accreditation Manual for Hospitals* (Chicago: Joint Commission on Accreditation of Hospitals, 1971).
12. J.P. Porterfield, "Mechanisms for Hospital Standards; *Bulletin of the Joint Commission on Accreditation of Hospitals* 48 (1968): 1–4.
13. U.S. Department of Health, Education, and Welfare, *Conditions of Participation for Hospitals* (Washington, D.C.: Social Security Administration, 1966).
14. U.S. General Accounting Office, *The Medicare Hospital Certification System Needs Reform: Report to Congress* (Washington, D.C.: U.S. General Accounting Office, 1979).
15. Joint Commission on Accreditation of Healthcare Organizations, "Pilot Hospitals Report Experience," *Agenda for Change Update* 3 (October 1989): 9.
16. "Agenda for Change: The JCAHO's Point of View." *Code 3 Focus* (3M Health Information Systems) 6, no. 3 (1989): 2.
17. Joint Commission on Accreditation of Healthcare Organizations, "Clinical Indicators for Initial Testing," in *Agenda for Change Information Kit* (Chicago: Joint Commission on Accreditation of Healthcare Organizations, 1989).
18. Ibid.
19. American Osteopathic Association, *Accreditation Requirements of the American Osteopathic Association* (Chicago: American Osteopathic Association, 1988), 5.

Part II

The Medical Staff Players

And all the men and women merely players.

Shakespeare, *As You Like It*

Chapter 3

The Medical Staff Organization

Richard E. Thompson, MD

The medical professional and the hospital, cognizant of a growing interdependence, have voluntarily collaborated to institute a system of "self-government" which provides for an organized staff, with specific lines of authority . . . all designed to achieve and maintain high standards of medical care . . . [But] survey findings and third-party comments stress that voluntary controls are not being uniformly applied and that, in fact, many medical staffs are not functioning properly.

C. W. Eisele, *The Medical Staff in the Modern Hospital*

Medical staff organizational responsibilities are not limited to meeting requirements of the Joint Commission on Accreditation of Healthcare Organizations (Joint Commission) and of state institutional licensing agencies. Neither can the critical role of the medical staff organization be defined *only* in a legal context. In today's competitive health care environment, the organized medical staff is one key to fulfilling the promise of "quality" made by the hospital department of marketing and public relations.

DEFINITION

In some contexts, *medical staff* refers to a group of practitioners, as in "the medical staff needs to keep better patient records." But in the context of this chapter, *medical staff* and *medical staff organization* refer to an organizational structure and specific organizational functions that exist in order to relate practitioners to their health care center's governing body.

The test of this definition is "credentialing," which can be summarized as follows: (1) The individual practitioner applies; (2) the medical staff organization, through responsible individuals and committees, recommends; and (3) the governing body appoints or disappoints.

BRIEF HISTORY

Some are surprised to learn that the medical staff organization is nearly 80 years old, having its modern origins in a statement by the American College of Surgeons in 1919.[1] Once, the medical staff organization was simple, because the hospital was simple. There were doctors, nurses, patients, a hospital "superintendent," and a board of trustees. There was a "regular staff" (active staff) and a "visiting staff" (courtesy staff). There were two or three medical staff officers and a monthly meeting of the general staff to conduct business. In larger hospitals, departments (groups of specialists) also met separately—to "review and analyze their clinical experience . . . the clinical records of patients, free and pay, to be the basis for such review and analysis."[2] The Constitution and Bylaws of the Medical Staff was a document of only a few pages.[3]

Since 1919, rules regulating the medical staff have been subject to "approval of the governing board of the hospital."[4] But the trustees seldom, if ever, did anything other than rubber-stamp doctors' decisions. The doctor was the de facto captain of the ship. The hospital was sometimes referred to as "the doctors' workshop," and the physician's portion of the patient's medical record was called "the *order* sheet." The only person who commonly stood up to the doctor was the chief nurse.

But as the modern-day health care center evolved, so did new issues between the hospital and its medical staff.

The hospital superintendent became the president of the health care corporation, creating a new issue. "What is the extent of 'executive privilege'?" wondered staff members, especially in areas which physicians traditionally considered their territory.

Boards of trustees became boards of directors. Among other things, they were, and still are, encouraged to question reports from the medical staff as vigorously as they question the monthly report from the institution's chief financial officer. No more rubber stamp.

There, in a position of high authority, physicians saw, and still see, the chief nurse, now a vice-president of the health care organization.

And among the monstrous changes (monstrous in some physicians' eyes), was the increase in the constraining fetters of restrictive government regulation. And, of course, the increased role of lawyers.

The tendency of many physicians was to circle the wagons.

Instead of credentialing solely with patient protection in mind, physicians allowed it to be perceived that some were not above "economically contaminating" credentials recommendations to benefit current staff members. Thus the Law decided that the "learned professionals" exclusion should no longer be invoked to protect credentialing decisions from accusations of anticompetitive behavior (see Chapter 14).

Instead of objective peer review, physician leaders and committee members held lengthy meetings and produced minutes indicating that "after much discussion, the care was considered appropriate." Even when more objective reviewers knew better.

Instead of inviting assistance, such as from administrative support personnel, some physicians created suspicion by insisting on "executive sessions," a euphemism used to exclude anyone but doctors from meetings.

At the same time, a paradoxical—nearly laughable—scenario developed regarding physicians' attitudes toward their own leaders. The degree of *distrust* earned by staff leaders was directly proportional to the skill and efficiency these leaders displayed in carrying out organizational tasks which the staff had chosen them to perform.

One result of ineffective staff action was the evolution of a threatening, punitive notion of "corrective actions," taken "against" staff members after "investigation" and preparation of "charges." The staff, through fear of losing control, had effectively handed over its most sensitive, controversial job to lawyers.

Thus did the medical staff organization begin. Thus was its position seriously weakened, through the years, by apathy and fear. And thus does the medical staff organization arrive on the threshold of a new century badly in need of improvement and repair.

NINE SPECIFIC RESPONSIBILITIES

The medical staff organization must perform at least nine functions fairly, efficiently, effectively, and to the satisfaction of the health care organization's governing body.

1. *It must recommend to the governing body action on new applications.* Permission to use the hospital does not come from the medical staff; it comes from the governing body (see the section "Relationships" below). Using a procedure defined in bylaws and related documents, responsible staff leaders and committees recommend governing body action on applications for *membership privileges* (including assignment to a category and a clinical department) and individual *clinical privileges* (e.g., specific permission to admit or treat patients limited in clinical areas in which the applicant has demonstrated basic qualifications and satisfactory experience). There must be no general medical staff action on credential requests. (See Chapters 8 and 14.)

2. *It must evaluate practitioner performance based on comprehensive data.* The traditional notion is that only physicians can evaluate any aspect of a

physician's performance. This notion is valid only to the extent that "the complexity of clinical decision-making and the unique features of each patient care encounter dictate that individuals interpreting information about a physician's quality/cost performance possess a working knowledge of clinical medicine."[5] Today, traditional peer review and quality assurance committees are gradually giving way to the routine collection of valid performance data, often by nonphysicians. Practitioner judgment remains important at the step of drawing valid conclusions from data and determining the reasons for isolated incidents (see Chapter 9).

3. *It must recommend to the governing body action on applications for renewal or increase of membership or clinical privileges.* Membership and clinical privileges must be renewed periodically, ordinarily every two years. And staff members might, at any time, request an increase in membership or clinical privileges. These requests must follow the same route as initial applications for privileges.

4. *It must provide continuing medical education (CME) opportunities.* CME programs, case presentations, and so on, are ordinarily provided by clinical departments and sections (see "Anatomy of the Medical Staff" and "Medical Staff Bylaws" below).

5. *It must recommend to the governing body corrective actions.* Corrective actions, in the context of medical staff and governing body functions, are formal governing board actions that are ordinarily chosen on the recommendation of the medical executive committee and in response to unacceptable practices or behaviors of staff members. Corrective actions may relate to questionable clinical practices, disregard for rules, disruptive behavior, impairment, or unethical practices (see Chapter 14).

6. *It must pursue corrective adjustment.* Corrective adjustment is a term coined by the author[6] to refer to a personal *but official* approach to a staff member who needs to be convinced that practice habits or behavior must improve. Such efforts might be pursued by a department chairperson, a selected peer on behalf of the chairperson, or another medical staff official. The results of such efforts must be documented, and the efforts must be pursued to the satisfaction of the medical executive committee and governing body. (In other words, legal constraints should not inhibit or prohibit simple solutions for simple problems. But a distinction must be made between official corrective adjustment efforts and purely collegial discussions.)

7. *It must provide coordinated input to the chief executive officer and governing body.* The relevant department chairperson should be the primary input point for an individual practitioner's concerns. Use of the medical staff organization to provide such input is more likely to be favorably received than rump-group ultimatums or divided votes of the general staff.

8. *It must submit regular and special reports to the governing body.* Through the chief of staff and the medical director (if such a position exists), the governing body must receive information about the medical staff organization's activities and the recommendations of the medical executive committee.

   - *Regular* (monthly or quarterly) reports to the governing body would include such items as

     —the results of routine data-based evaluation of practitioner performance (much of this information should be positive)

     —the chief of staff's report, including activities and recommendations of the medical executive committee and news about individual staff members (appointments, honors, published articles, etc.)

     —the report of the medical director (if applicable)

     A portion of the chief executive officer's report may also relate to medical staff interests, activities, and concerns.

   - *Special* reports to the governing body would include items such as

     —a summary of key features of applications for initial appointment or privileges that the governing body is being asked to act on

     —information to support renewal of appointment and privileges for each current staff member

     —information to support requests from staff members for additional clinical privileges or for increased membership privileges (change in staff category)

     —a recommendation to take corrective action, with supporting information

     Reports to the governing body should be substantive and brief. They might initially be received by a performance oversight committee of the governing body (see Figure 3-1).[7]

9. *It must update medical staff bylaws and related documents.* The traditional emphasis has been on annual revision of medical staff bylaws and related documents. Bylaws changes must be recommended to the staff for adoption, then taken to the governing body for approval. Specific rules and procedural guidelines are often established and revised by the medical executive committee, subject to governing body approval.

At least two functions are notably (and purposely) missing from this list:

- *Establishment of economic ventures* is not, at this writing, ordinarily considered a function of the traditional medical staff organization. Rather, new legal entities are established for economic ventures between physicians and the

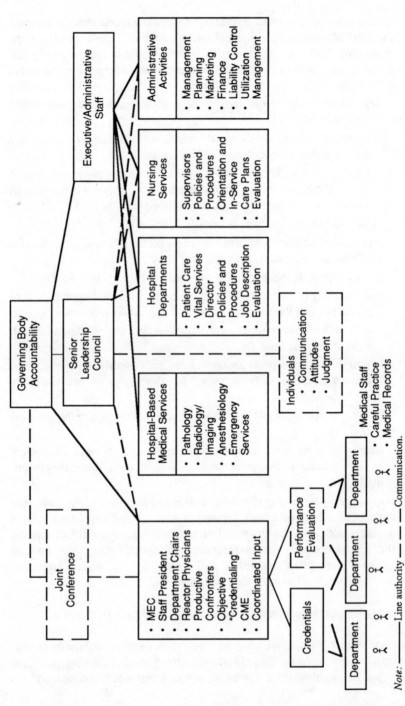

Figure 3-1 Hospital Organizational Components and Their Relationships. *Source:* Reprinted from *The Board Member's and CEO's Guide to Medical Staff Structure and Responbilities* by R.E. Thompson, p. 11, with permission of Senss Publications, © 1989.

Note: ——— Line authority – – – ——— Communication.

health care center. So far, this has seemed to work best for at least two reasons: (1) the group of physician investors may not (commonly will not) be the same as the total membership of the medical staff (practitioners with privileges to use hospital services for their patients), and (2) it is best for all if the traditional patient-protection activities of the staff, such as credentialing and peer review, do not become "economically contaminated." (The accuracy of this statement may eventually change. See "Trends and Anticipated Developments" below.)

Quality improvement is not listed as a separate function because it shouldn't be a separate function. *Medical staff quality improvement* is an umbrella term that refers to the sum total of medical staff organizational activities. To consider quality improvement a separate activity only stimulates the establishment of needless and time-consuming bureaucracies and paperwork. The quality improvement office or department should provide critical support for medical staff and governing body functions, but there shouldn't be a separate "program" primarily producing minutes, studies, and problem lists.

RELATIONSHIPS

Some believe there is controversy about the relationship between the medical staff organization, the governing body, and the chief executive officer. There is no real controversy, only confusion and some wishful thinking.

Figure 3-1 is a schematic representation of the medical staff organization's relationship to other organizational components of the hospital.[8] (The author has coined the term "hospital/physician governance unit" to refer to this relationship.)[9] The medical staff organization is part of the health care center's governance structure because of language in governing body bylaws such as the following:

> *Article X: Medical Staff.* The board of directors shall cause to be created a medical staff organization, whose members shall be physicians, dentists, and podiatrists privileged to attend patients at this medical center. Membership in this medical staff organization shall be a prerequisite to the exercise of clinical privileges in the medical center except as otherwise specifically provided in the medical staff bylaws.

The medical staff bylaws describe the details of the medical staff organization and the staff members' responsibilities and prerogatives (see "Medical Staff Bylaws" below).

The medical staff organization, then, is not "self-governing" in the sense of being autonomous. But the staff organization *should* be self-governing in the sense of maintaining self-control and self-discipline.

The role of the chief executive officer (CEO) is to pursue the governing body's policies, goals, and corporate culture. On a day-to-day basis, the CEO is invested with the authority of the governing body.

Physicians may not understand these organizational principles. One result of a lack of understanding can be accusations (usually unjustified) that the CEO has overstepped his or her jurisdiction, especially in matters relating to medical staff affairs.

The governing body should seek input from medical staff leaders when evaluating the CEO's performance. At the same time, it is primarily the responsibility of the governing body to help staff leaders, and followers, understand that the CEO's decisions and actions, although they should reflect medical staff advice, do not necessarily depend on medical staff consent.

The role of a medical director (or vice-president for medical affairs) must be carefully defined if such a position is to contribute to cohesion of the hospital/physician governance unit (see Chapter 5).

The relationship of the medical staff organization and its members to other components of the hospital, such as nursing, now often involves a mechanism similar to the senior leadership council depicted in Figure 3-1. Properly implemented, the senior leadership council is an effective additional management instrument, not an extension of governance.

ANATOMY OF THE MEDICAL STAFF ORGANIZATION

A medical staff organization should include the following basic parts:

- clinical departments and sections
- categories
- committees
  —medical executive committee
  —credentials committee
  —senior leadership council (not medical staff only)
  —other necessary committees (if any)
- staff leaders
  —chief of staff (staff president)
  —other officers
  —chairpersons of clinical departments
  —chairpersons of necessary committees
- administrative support

—medical staff services office or department
—chief executive officer
- information system (less emphasis on data and more on objective conclusions)
- governing body support
—adequate resources
—thoughtful response to recommendations
—appreciation

For help in understanding the following descriptions, refer frequently to Figure 3-1.

Clinical Departments and Sections

A clinical department should be defined, in the definitions section of medical staff bylaws, as a group of practitioners with the same or similar clinical expertise, interests, and concerns. A clinical department is the original medical staff working unit.[10] Examples might include departments of medicine, surgery, pediatrics, and so on.

A clinical section (or service) is ordinarily defined as a subdivision of a clinical department. Sections should be established only when necessary. Examples might include the gastroenterology section of the department of internal medicine and the urology section of the department of surgery.

Assignment of a staff member to a clinical department does not automatically restrict *clinical* privileges. Assignment to a department is a *membership* function that establishes the line of authority from the governing body to the individual staff member (see Figure 3-1).

Departments and sections were once, and are again becoming, more important organizational divisions than the variety of staff committees.

Functions of Clinical Departments

The following are the primary functions that each clinical department or section is responsible for (see "Individual Leaders" below):

- an appraisal of (1) initial applicants likely to be assigned to the department and (2) department members at reappointment time (note that credentialing and recredentialing are not departmental functions; making appointments and awarding specific clinical privileges are functions of the governing body)
- data-based reviews of the performance of department members
- continuing medical education

- corrective adjustment (not corrective action, which is a medical executive committee and governing body function)
- coordinated input provided to the chief executive officer and governing body
- submission of regular reports to the medical executive committee (departmental activities are then included in the committee's report to the governing body)

Departmentalization versus Nondepartmentalization

Medical staffs that are still not departmentalized probably have avoided departmentalization for two reasons:

1. The Joint Commission requires that clinical departments meet monthly. So some medical staffs do not have "departments," they have "services." They can thus argue that their "services" need not meet monthly, because it is only "departments" that need to.
2. Some believe that a small medical staff can perform medical staff functions with a monthly meeting of the general staff, with the executive committee function being performed by a committee of the whole.

Both of those reasons for not being departmentalized are now obsolete. Specialty-specific clinical information needs to be dealt with by responsible individuals, and the performance of those individuals (department chairmen, physician analysts, productive confronters, etc.) should be reported to and commented on at the department meeting.

Additionally, if a medical staff consists of more than ten active physicians, then there are probably "circuit-riding" consulting physicians also providing clinical services at the hospital. There are, in addition, hospital-based medical services such as pathology, radiology, anesthesiology.

It is a current requirement of the Joint Commission that clinical departments meet monthly. Even the smallest medical staffs should consider having at least two departments (medicine and surgery). Then, instead of having one overloaded key staff leader (the chief of staff), necessary tasks could be divided among two or three key staff leaders.

Staff Categories

The purpose of medical staff categories (active, courtesy, consulting, etc.) is to define the relationship of each staff member to the particular medical staff organization. For example, the categories determine answers to the following questions: Who can vote? Who is eligible to hold office or be a department chairperson? Who must comply with meeting attendance requirements? Which staff members must fulfill obligations arising from the social responsibilities of physicians, such as inclusion on the emergency department's specialty backup roster?

Unlike the old days, there is no direct relationship between category assignment and clinical privileges.

> *Example:* Dr. A, a family physician, is an *active* staff member. In fact, his fairness and leadership skills are so highly respected that he has twice been elected chief of staff. But his *clinical* privileges are limited to a hospital practice commensurate with his training and experience. He is required, for example, to request consultation for any of his patients who are in the coronary care unit.

> *Example:* Dr. B is a subspecialist in cardiology. She has been granted all possible *clinical* privileges in cardiology. But because she only rarely sees patients at the hospital, she is assigned to the *courtesy* staff. Thus, she may not vote or hold office and is not required to comply with meeting attendance requirements.

Once clinical privileges were determined by category assignment. But now individual-specific clinical privileges are awarded on the basis of individual qualifications and performance. The degree to which the individual is clinically active at the particular hospital determines his or her category assignment.

The number of categories needed in the medical staff bylaws will vary according to the organizational complexity and composition of the medical staff. For a small hospital with only a few physicians on the staff, only two or three categories may be needed. For larger hospitals, four or five categories may be needed. Some common categories are as follows:

- *Active* staff members regularly admit and treat patients. The medical staff leadership ordinarily comes from this group.
- *Courtesy* staff members only occasionally admit or treat patients at an institution. They may have maximum clinical privileges but will have only minimal membership privileges or obligations.
- The *associate* category is often the category to which new staff members are assigned for an initial period (e.g., one year). The associate staff member is expected to practice heavily at the hospital and would ordinarily be advanced to active staff status after the provisional period.
- Traditionally, *provisional* status was a category choice. This is no longer recommended. A statement in the bylaws should define the routine provisional period as applying not only to initial staff members but also to new clinical privileges granted to current staff members.

- *Consulting* physicians are specialists or subspecialists who see patients at the invitation of admitting physicians. They have minimal membership privileges.

Less common categories include these:

- *Scientific* or *academic* medical staff members primarily teach or work in nonclinical areas. (Note: The proper approach to using categories is not to simply place all medical school faculty members in one category. As with other physicians, faculty members on the staff should be assigned categories on the basis of their clinical activities. Thus, some faculty members might be assigned to the academic staff, some to the consulting staff, and some even to the active staff.)
- *Honorary* staff members are physicians the medical staff wishes to honor (e.g., a senior physician retiring from practice or a well-known physician from outside the community).

Other category choices are possible. The key to streamlining the organizational structure of the medical staff is to have as many clinical departments as are necessary to achieve the happy medium between "lumping and splitting" practitioners with similar clinical interests and expertise. There should also be only four or five committees and three to six categories (just enough to define the nature of each staff member's membership status within the particular institution).

Committees

The Medical Executive Committee

The medical executive committee is the highest authority of the medical staff, except that the meetings of the general staff (1) elect officers and (2) adopt medical staff bylaws and amendments thereto, which are then recommended to the governing body for approval.

This organizational structure, in which an executive group acts for the total membership, is not unique to medical staffs. For example, under at least some state statutes governing condominium associations, general meetings of owners only select a board, approve and amend bylaws, and, at least in some cases, have specific rights (e.g., the right to vote on budget increases over certain specified limits). The condominium board (analogous to the medical executive committee) ordinarily acts on behalf of the owners in such matters as establishing rules (subject, of course, to guidelines in condominium bylaws).

The medical executive committee ordinarily meets monthly. Duties and responsibilities of the committee should be specified in the medical staff bylaws, as in the following example:

> The duties of the medical executive committee shall be:
>
> 1. To represent and act on behalf of the medical staff subject to such limitations as may be imposed by these bylaws;
> 2. To coordinate the activities of and policies adopted by the medical staff, departments, and committees;
> 3. To receive and act on reports and recommendations from the departments, committees, and officers of the staff concerning performance evaluation activities and other responsibilities;
> 4. To recommend to the governing body all matters relating to appointments, reappointments, staff category and department assignments, and clinical privileges;
> 5. To pursue, with the governing body, corrective actions to their necessary conclusions;
> 6. To make recommendations on medico-administrative and hospital management affairs, including patient care needs such as space, staff, and equipment;
> 7. To obtain medical staff cooperation in order to retain the accreditation status of the hospital as determined by the Joint Commission on Accreditation of Healthcare Organizations;
> 8. To participate in identifying community health needs and in setting goals and implementing programs to meet those needs;
> 9. To resolve interdepartmental disputes, when necessary and if possible.

The ninth final task on the list should be especially emphasized. Suppose, for example, a member of the family practice department has privileges to care for patients with medical problems. The chairperson of the internal medicine department believes that the family physician manages diabetic patients inappropriately because he waits too long to call in specialty consultation. But when the chairperson of the internal medicine department shares her concerns with the chairperson of the family practice department, disagreement is apparent. If a solution cannot be found working together and with the practitioner in question, then both chairpersons should present a brief report of the situation to the medical executive committee, which must resolve the issue one way or another.

The exact composition of the medical executive committee should be spelled out in the medical staff bylaws. At this writing, such committees are ordinarily composed of some combination of voting members (officers, clinical department chairpersons, and sometimes members at large chosen by the general staff) and nonvoting ex officio members (CEO, administrator of nursing services, etc.).

Sometimes the chairpersons of the credentials committee and the performance evaluation committee (see Figure 3-1) are members of the medical executive committee.

Credentials Committee

The credentials committee evaluates completed applications for initial appointment, clinical privileges, reappointment, and renewal of clinical privileges, as well as any requests for additional privileges from current staff members.

After confirming the validity of requested information and evaluating the fairness and objectivity of the relevant department chairperson's appraisal, the credentials committee traditionally forwards its recommendation to the medical executive committee, which makes credentials recommendations directly to the governing body (Figure 3-1). (For details, see Chapter 8.)

Performance Evaluation Committee

A variety of groups now pursue a plethora of quality agendas with differing objectives. The medical staff organization's "quality" agenda must focus on confirming each staff member's *qualifications* (through credentialing) and *performance* (using modern data-based evaluation methods). It should be understood that "performance evaluation" is done instead of, not in addition to, reviews by topical committees. That is, instead of a blood use committee and a drug and antibiotic committee and several other committees all reporting directly to the medical executive committee, clinical information is gathered from a variety of sources, sorted by physician, and dealt with by the chairpersons of the clinical departments to which the physicians are assigned. (Each department chairperson may be assisted by physician analysts and "productive confronters.")[11]

The difference is substantive, not merely semantic. Exhibit 3-1 is an example of peer review done the old-fashioned way, with physicians confusing traditional case review with the need for developing physician-specific performance awareness data. In many hospitals, obsolete quality assurance and peer review methods have been replaced by data-based performance awareness—physician-specific data generated by the clinical department to which the physician is assigned.

The information flow begins with abstracting and proceeds through an evaluation step (once accomplished by committees, now ordinarily accomplished by the department chairpersons and others they may appoint to assist them). The information is then used in various ways, such as in deciding whether to reappoint, and in determining corrective adjustments or corrective actions if there is a problem with physician performance or behavior. (See Chapter 9 for complete details.)

See Figure 3-1 for placement of the performance evaluation committee. It is the link between the clinical departments and the medical executive committee in the case of issues concerning performance.

Exhibit 3-1 An Example of Traditional But Unacceptable Peer Review

---

From the Minutes of a Meeting of the Department of Medicine

Dr. Smith talked about gastrointestinal bleeding. He said that a couple of years ago, 25 cases were looked at and in 12 (50 percent) no source of bleeding had been found by the time of discharge of the patient from the hospital. Last year, he took a look at 23 more cases. All these patients had bleeding severe enough to require transfusion. By the time of discharge from the hospital, the cause of bleeding had not been found in 16 (70 percent) of these. No particular conclusions were drawn after discussion, except that we are apparently not getting any better at finding the source of gastrointestinal bleeding.

From the Minutes of a Meeting of the Department of Internal Medicine (Under "Case Review")

Admitted 9/20 and discharged 9/25. Eighty-year-old white female with acute upper GI bleeding, anemia secondary to the bleed, insulin-dependent diabetes, electrolyte imbalance, urinary tract infection, dehydration, chronic obstructive pulmonary disease, arteriosclerotic heart disease, and ulcerations of the feet with a CVA (cerebrovascular accident . . . stroke) and right-sided hemiparesis (paralysis). The question was why the patient was *re*admitted two days after having been discharged with a diagnosis of electrolyte imbalance and massive GI bleed. The committee felt that since the previous admission was missing, they could not reach a conclusion on this case.

The composition of the performance evaluation committee may be similar or identical to an old medical staff "quality assurance" committee. The term *performance evaluation committee* is suggested, however, because the older term is less directly descriptive and may leave the impression that this committee should do "studies" and "appraisals." Properly implemented, the committee will oversee the performance evaluation activities of clinical departments.

Senior Leadership Council

Traditionally, a formal organizational link between the medical staff and other hospital components was missing. One short-lived attempt to forge such a link was the effort to establish "joint practice committees" composed of physicians and nurses. A senior leadership council is not a committee of the medical staff (see Figure 3-1). It is a communication forum for senior leaders of the medical staff, administration, and nursing. Usually on a quarterly basis, each medical staff department, nursing department, and direct patient care hospital department has its turn to provide a brief issues-oriented report to the council about interests and concerns that are multidisciplinary in nature. The purpose is to find and implement solutions to problems which cannot be effectively solved by one department working unilaterally. Since the activities of hospital patient care personnel must be responsive to the physician's "order sheet," participation of staff leaders in meetings of the senior leadership council is extremely important.

Confusion Relieved!

Note that the structure described so far includes three clearly defined functions:

1. The performance oversight committee of the governing body *receives reports* about professional performance.
2. The performance evaluation committee of the medical staff *oversees* the performance evaluation activities of clinical departments.
3. The senior leadership council, which is not an extension of any authority, functions as a multidisciplinary communication forum that facilitates *sharing and jointly implementing* solutions and improvements.

This clear division relieves the frustration and confusion that commonly existed when these three functions were sometimes inappropriately intermingled in a "quality assurance" committee.

Other Necessary Committees

The only committee of the medical staff required by the Joint Commission is the medical executive committee. The only committees necessary to provide sufficient authority and coordination of medical staff organizational activities are those described above. Other committees related to clinical activities may still be necessary, such as an ethics committee, tumor registry committee, and research protocol committee (sometimes called the "institutional review committee").

Staff leaders and members must participate in some functions requiring the input of several disciplines, such as safety and infection control. These functions may be the responsibility of separate multidisciplinary committees or part of the agenda of the senior leadership council. Other committees may be extraneous.

Staff Leaders

Chairpersons of Clinical Departments

The modern medical staff organization features the following leadership positions.

Chief of Staff (or Medical Staff President). The chief of staff is the chairperson of the medical executive committee, presides at general staff meetings, and acts as liaison with the chief executive officer, the nursing department, and the governing body. Traditionally the chief of staff is considered the chief executive of the medical staff.

A list of the chief of staff's duties should be contained in medical staff bylaws. Below is an example of such a list.

The Chief of Staff shall

1. act in coordination and cooperation with the CEO in all matters of mutual concern within the hospital
2. call, preside at, and be responsible for the agenda of all general staff meetings
3. serve on the medical executive committee as its chair
4. serve as ex officio member of all other medical staff committees
5. be responsible for the enforcement of medical staff bylaws, rules, and regulations
6. appoint committee members to all standing, special, and multidisciplinary committees, except as otherwise provided
7. present the views, policies, and needs of the medical staff to the governing body and CEO
8. interpret the policies of the governing body to the medical staff and report to the governing body on performance and maintenance of quality and efficient patient care
9. assist department chairs in understanding and fulfilling their responsibilities

Chief of Staff–Elect and Immediate Past Chief. The chief of staff–elect serves a learning year prior to assuming the office of chief of staff. The immediate past chief is a valued experienced adviser. In addition, these individuals might be given defined responsibilities in the medical staff bylaws.

Chairperson of the Credentials Committee and Chairperson of the Performance Evaluation Committee. These individuals should be experienced staff leaders with a reputation for being fair, objective, and analytic. Like all medical staff leaders, they must be good communicators.

Clinical Department Chairpersons and Section Chiefs. Running a monthly meeting is now the *least* important task of clinical department chairpersons and section chiefs. Following is a sample list of the responsibilities of these positions.

A clinical department chairperson or section chief must

1. counsel, advise, or admonish individual members of the department or section when there are questions concerning clinical performance, disregard for reasonable rules, lack of respect for co-workers, inefficient practice, suspected impairment, or practice outside the limits of the clinical privileges that have been awarded

2. act as spokesperson for the department or service vis-à-vis such groups as the medical executive committee and other medical staff committees, departments, and sections; the hospital administration; nursing and other hospital departments, and, on occasion, the governing body

3. act as primary spokesperson for the department or section vis-à-vis outside agencies, where applicable, such as during the hospital's survey by the Joint Commission

4. analyze information, including but not limited to information pertinent to applications for membership and privileges by individuals who are members of or are likely to be assigned to the department or section, performance evaluations, the capital improvement needs and the staffing needs of the department or section, and the relevance of departmental or sectional policies and procedures

5. evaluate causes for and participate in responses to untoward incidents involving members of the department or service

6. serve as a coordinating point by providing information about hospital and medical staff affairs to members of the department or section

7. plan and conduct meetings of the department or section with the help of relevant support personnel

8. develop and follow a departmental policy and procedure manual

In numerous specific instances, the success of staff organizational functions depends on the availability of a staff leader who simultaneously embodies authority, respectability, and relevant clinical expertise. That's usually a description of the clinical department chairperson.

Chairpersons of Necessary Committees

If committees other than those mentioned above are necessary, the committee's tasks, and those of its chairman, should be specified in the medical staff bylaws and related documents.

Selection of Staff Leaders

As with any organization, some specific method of selecting leaders is described in the bylaws and related documents. Traditionally, medical staff leaders were elected by popular vote. That's still one way to do it. However, over the years, the medical staff has weakened itself through careless leadership selection. The traditional joke is, "Harry went on vacation and while he was gone we elected him chairperson." Sometimes department chairpersonships are simply rotated. And sometimes, most unfortunately, a medical staff has made itself vulnerable through leadership selection mistakenly viewed as protective (see Exhibit 3-2).[12]

Exhibit 3-2   Example of an Inappropriate Method for Selecting a Medical Staff Leader

---

(An actual letter, with identifying information removed)

Dear Colleague:

The ocean waves toss, pummel, and polish the pebbles on the beach until they are smooth, worn down and compliant. So too in recent years hospital management has persuaded and manipulated medical staff officers into complaisance and docility.

To counteract this malignant effect we need a chief who is smart, tough, blunt, hard, fair, and yes, even abrasive. We need a chief who has vast experience of meetings and committees, both of the hospital medical staff and of the _____ County Medical Society. We need a chief who is willing and eager to attend even more of these tedious but important meetings. In the times ahead when government bureaucracy and hospital management are making increasing penetration into the practice of medicine we need to elect a resolute and steadfast leader.

Please come to the Medical Staff meeting and vote for _____ as Chief of Staff Elect.

Sincerely,

_____ , M.D.

Source: Reprinted from *The Medical Staff Leader's Complete Practical Guidebook* by R.E. Thompson, p. 151, with permission of Senss Publications, © 1988.

Since a weak medical staff also weakens the hospital, and since staff officers and department chairpersons are responsible to the governing body as well as to staff members (see Figure 3-1), the issue of governing body participation in selecting staff officers and department chairpersons has arisen. It is not at all unusual now to find some sort of process whereby staff members indicate individuals they would accept as leaders, then have the names presented to the governing body for appointment or ratification. Traditional-minded staff members, of course, oppose governing body participation in the selection of staff leaders. Actually, if staffs had exercised care in selecting leaders, the issue need never have arisen.

In modern medical staff bylaws, language similar to the following may be found:

Officers and department chairpersons shall be members of the active staff. Department chairpersons shall be certified in the relevant specialties. In selecting leaders, attention shall be paid to the responsibilities involved and to the interests, respect, cooperation, and skills (including written and oral communication skills) required to best provide medical staff participation in hospital affairs.

One key to avoiding legal jeopardy for the hospital, staff leaders, and those who work with the staff is to help physicians understand procedures that must be followed when they are acting on behalf of the medical staff and not simply on their own behalf.

Administrative Support

Effective assistance must be provided to staff leaders. The quality assurance department (or medical staff services department in some hospitals) must provide physician-specific performance data to staff leaders and work with them to interpret it properly. The medical records department must abstract information for use by staff leaders. In fact, a variety of offices must contribute information to be used by staff leaders (e.g., infection control, utilization management, risk management, the finance office, the data processing department, etc.).

The CEO must, of course, consider medical staff organization activities his or her personal responsibility and not delegate these important functions "down the line."

The heart of support for medical staff functions is the medical staff services department or office. Even more important than having bountiful space, fancy equipment, and a central location, the office must be run by a qualified individual who has an in-depth knowledge of the medical staff and governing body structure, functional methods, medical staff bylaws, and so on. This individual must be an effective communicator and possess a sense of balance, perspective, and humor. He or she must be willing to attend to details and be a good organizer of information, such as that contained in physicians' files. In addition, he or she must exhibit a high degree of professionalism. Chatting about sensitive work to friends could be disastrous for all. (See Chapter 6 for detailed information about the medical staff services professional.)

Information System

Scan again the responsibilities of the department chairman above. Note that effective accomplishment of medical staff organization functions requires a foundation of *information*. Next note that *information* and *data* are not synonyms. "Information = data *plus* objective, valid, accurate conclusions."[13]

Believe it or not, the most critical element of an information system is not electronic data processing capability. That is a critical, but not the most critical, element. Whichever method of data processing assistance is employed—no matter how sophisticated, no matter how much money is spent—data will still only be data. Converting valid data to reliable information requires attention to the *human judgment* elements of the information system. This means the system is *incomplete* if it lacks staff leaders interested in honing leadership skills—clinical analysts with a reputation for both clinical skills and fairness and skilled "productive confronters" who can effectively explore the ramifications of clinical data with staff members.[14]

Governing Body Support

Long-lasting and divisive hard feelings can result if concerned staff leaders, trying to do their job, feel "hung out to dry" by the governing body and CEO. The following constitute good evidence of reasonable governing body support:

1. *Good Communication.* This does not mean creating another committee that must meet monthly and generate minutes, such as a "joint conference committee." Neither does it mean that each individual physician should expect personal attention. It does, however, mean cross-reporting among staff, administrative, and governing board leaders. It means having courage to share governing body and executive decisions with staff leaders. Communication also means effective questioning by the governing body members of reports from the medical staff—and members knowledgeable enough to evaluate the answers they are given.

2. *Appropriate Composition of the Governing Body and Governing Body Committees.* Physician leaders should participate in governing body meetings and on relevant governing body committees. This does not mean that the general staff "elects" members of the board! And turnabout is fair play. How about a governing body member on the medical executive committee? (See "Trends and Anticipated Developments" at the end of this chapter.)

3. *Adequate Resources.* The governing body must approve expenditures adequate for effective administrative support of staff activities (see "Administrative Support" above).

4. *Thoughtful Responses to Recommendations.* The governing body will not always be able to do what the medical staff organization requests. If a recommendation from the medical executive committee is not carefully questioned by the governing body, and if a denial is not accompanied by a brief statement of the reasons, then the integrity of the hospital-physician governance unit may be jeopardized.

5. *Expressions of Appreciation.* It is not easy to be an effective staff leader. And lack of effective staff leadership can make the governing body vulnerable. There is much to appreciate, and governing body members should show that they recognize this.

6. *Combined Retreats.* Governing body–medical staff leadership retreats are not guaranteed to be successful. But well-planned retreats, with focused

objectives, can be very productive. The social aspects of retreats are important, but some of the best retreats are not far from home, lengthy, or hugely expensive.

MEDICAL STAFF BYLAWS

Medical staff bylaws are rules governing the responsibilities and prerogatives of the staff as a whole and of individual staff members. Through the years, thousands of physicians have signed an agreement to abide by medical staff bylaws. But many have had little understanding of, or interest in, what they were agreeing to abide by. It is as if a baseball player tried to play the game without understanding that "four balls gives you first base" or that "three strikes and you're out." Fortunately, staff members increasingly recognize the importance of understanding and following bylaw provisions.

The author of this chapter is not an attorney. (For answers to legal questions, see Chapter 14.) The following is intended merely to provide a practical understanding of some common medical staff bylaw issues.

Bylaw Contents

Medical staff bylaws can be relatively simple. (Please keep in mind that *simple* and *easy* are not synonyms.) For the last two decades, the norm has been long, complex bylaws that constantly undergo revision. But now the trend is to create bylaws more like the U.S. Constitution—general rules carefully stated (with the details of implementation in other documents) and requiring only 10 or 15 amendments every hundred years (other than language improvements to clarify the intent of existing provisions).

Here's a sample outline of such a medical staff bylaws document (a different order may be preferred, but these are the necessary components):

1. *Preamble.* The preamble describes what the document is all about.
2. *Definitions.* The key to avoiding a needless argument when there is no real disagreement is to spend time defining terms accurately. So many words and phrases can be used in many different ways that modern medical staff bylaws may include three or four pages of definitions.
3. *Purpose.* This section explains what a medical staff is supposed to do and why.
4. *Appointment Provisions.* This section describes who is eligible for staff appointment and what specific application and appointment procedures must be followed. (As a general rule, *what* must be done is put in the bylaws;

how it must be done [detailed procedural descriptions] is put in bylaw-related documents. For details, see Chapter 8.)

5. *Categories.* This section lays out the various categories of staff (active, courtesy, etc.). For example, it describes the different membership prerogatives and responsibilities of staff members who use the hospital a lot or a little or physicians whom the staff merely wishes to honor.

6. *Individual-Specific Clinical Privileges.* Medical staff bylaws ordinarily state that staff members may exercise only those clinical privileges that the applicant applies for, the medical executive committee acts upon, and the governing body grants. Details of procedure are found in the medical staff membership and privileges (credentialing and recredentialing) policy and procedure manual. Specifics may be described, such as temporary privileges of various kinds, a universally applicable provisional period, rules governing the hospital practice of dentists and podiatrists, and so on. (For details, see Chapter 8.)

7. *Other Practitioners.* This section contains the rules and procedures for considering requests to use hospital services from practitioners who are not traditional medical staff members, hospital employees, or contract group physicians. Such requests now come from many kinds of practitioners, including clinical psychologists, certified nurse anesthetists, chiropractors, and so on. Most medical staff bylaws now contain provisions for allied health professionals, medical associates, and medical assistants (or some similar category). (For details, see Chapter 8.)

8. *Officers, Meetings, Clinical Departments and Sections, Department Chairpersons and Section Chiefs, and Committees.* Perhaps one-third of the content of medical staff bylaws relates to the question, How is the staff organized to accomplish necessary organizational tasks? For details, see "Anatomy of the Medical Staff" earlier in this chapter.

9. *Marginal Practice, Unacceptable or Disruptive Behavior, Disregard for Rules, Impairment, and Unethical Practices.* This section describes how the medical staff and the governing body intend to deal with "out of bounds" clinical practice, disrespect, or other unacceptable behavior. This section of the bylaws, traditionally titled "Corrective Action," may now provide for a "kinder, gentler" approach to solving some issues with medical staff members.[15]

10. *Rules and Procedures.* Medical staff bylaws should contain a brief statement referring to the existence of bylaw-related documents, such as those described on the following pages.

11. *Amendment and Adoption.* Rules for adopting amendments to existing medical staff bylaws must be specified. Bylaws may also include a separate provision for adopting a totally new bylaw document.

12. *Miscellaneous Provisions.* Bylaws probably contain provisions for staff members to be granted a leave of absence and immunity from liability in good faith credentialing and performance evaluation activities. They may contain other miscellaneous provisions. Medical staff bylaws may—indeed should—contain a brief statement about the position and degree of authority of a medical director (vice-president for medical affairs) with respect to the medical staff organization.

See Exhibit 3-3 for a bylaw evaluation checklist.

Medical Staff Bylaw–Related Documents

Once, all rules governing the medical staff organization were contained in just three documents: the hospital (governing body) bylaws, the medical staff bylaws, and the medical staff rules and regulations. Today, governing body bylaws and medical staff bylaws should be accompanied by several documents containing detailed procedures and specific rules. In this context, the term *procedure* does not refer to legally binding regulations. Rather, procedure manuals should contain specific forms, guidelines, sample letters, step-by-step instructions, flow diagrams, organizational charts, and so on.

The purpose of these materials is to provide effective guidance for medical staff leaders and those who work with them. In addition, medical staff members find clearly stated rules easier to accept and follow. And finally, use of these documents can provide the consistency that is such a critical component of legal safeguards.

Modern medical staff bylaw–related documents include the following:

- *Rules and Procedures, General.* Rules and procedures applicable to all staff members regardless of clinical specialty. This manual should have two parts:
  - —*Part 1: Clinical Rules and Procedures.* This section should contain traditional rules about clinical activities. Such rules concern completion of patient records, scheduling of surgical cases, automatic stop orders for certain drugs, and so on.
  - —*Part 2: Organizational Rules and Procedures.* Details that once cluttered up the bylaws can be placed here, for example, specified meeting times, nominating procedure details, standardized agendas for general staff meetings and for monthly meetings of clinical departments, and so on.
- *Medical Staff Membership and Clinical Privileges Policy and Procedure Manual.* This manual should contain a step-by-step account of credentialing and recredentialing (reappointment) activities, sample letters, forms and worksheets, and policies and interpretative statements.

Exhibit 3-3 Bylaw Checklist

Do your bylaws, rules, and regulations:	By-laws	Rules and Regula-tions	Policies and Proce-dures
1. Provide formal procedures to evaluate the following:			
a. Applications and credentials of practitioners applying to the medical staff			
b. Appointments to the medical staff			
c. Reappointments			
d. Delineation of clinical privileges			
2. Provide a credentialing process:			
a. Define characteristics of a completed application			
b. Define time periods related to application completion and processing			
c. Define required qualifications for members of the medical staff			
3. Define requirements of the provisional period			
4. Provide policies and practices for clinical departments			
5. Provide assistance in obtaining rehabilitation services for impaired medical staff members			
6. Not restrict or deny voting rights, within the scope of licensure, to members of the active staff with degrees other than MD			
7. State how a member must report any malpractice action			
8. Outline details for dealing with substandard practice, unacceptable or disruptive behavior, disregard for rules, impairment, and unethical practice			
9. Provide for adoption and approval by both the governing body and medical staff			
10. Provide for a medical executive committee			
11. Provide for members to pledge provision of continuous patient care			
12. Provide a fair hearing and appellate review process for medical staff members and other members with clinical privileges			
13. Provide a process for corrective action			
14. Define how often meetings are held and state attendance requirements			
15. Describe the organization and officers of the medical staff			
16. Provide effective communication channels between the hospital administration, governing body, and medical staff			
17. Include a statement of prerogatives and responsibilities for each medical staff category			
18. Relate specific roles of members with clinical privileges in the care of inpatients, emergency room patients, ambulatory care patients, and home health care patients			
19. Describe the credentialing process for allied health professionals			
20. State that a physical exam and medical history be done no more than seven days before or 48 hours after admission for each patient admitted by an MD or DO or, in the case of maxillofacial surgery, by an oral surgeon who has been granted such privileges by the medical staff			

- *Clinical Department Policies and Procedures.* A policy and procedure manual should exist for each clinical department listed in the medical staff bylaws. Among other things, each manual should contain rules, both clinical and organizational, that apply uniquely to members of the appropriate clinical department.

The contents of bylaw-related documents mentioned so far have essentially the same impact as bylaw provisions. That is, the statement of agreement signed by a staff member is ordinarily taken as agreement to be governed by these necessary supplements to medical staff bylaws as well as by the provisions of the bylaw document itself.

In addition, supplementary documents may exist which do not contain additional rules and policies but which are intended merely as helpful guides for medical staff leaders (who must correctly implement bylaw provisions) and for nonleaders (who must, in fairness, understand what is expected of them). Following are two examples:

1. *Summary of Key Features.* Using excerpts of bylaw language, applicants and staff members can be provided a summary of the highlights of bylaw provisions in a few pages. Note that such a summary must not be used as a substitute for the entire bylaw document. Such a summary also can be useful for orienting governing body members, who should be familiar with the contents of medical staff bylaws.
2. *User's Guide to Medical Staff Bylaws.* Unlike the summary of key features, this document would not simply repeat bylaw language. Rather, the user's guide should contain diagrams, descriptions, clarifications, examples, and so on, designed to assist those responsible for *applying* the provisions of the medical staff bylaws to specific situations. The user's guide should be placed in a three-ring, loose-leaf binder so that additions can be made as interpretations are agreed upon and clarifications are developed.

Creating a simple bylaw document, accompanied by a variety of documents containing further definition and detail, can result in the following benefits:

- The information is separated into several reference documents that are much easier to use than a single lengthy document.
- Common pitfalls are avoided, pitfalls that can be created when bylaw provisions are inconsistently implemented for want of clear, step-by-step delineations of procedures to be followed.
- The bylaws document is only infrequently in need of revision (except for improvements in language that are found through experience to clarify meaning).

Revising Medical Staff Bylaws

When medical staff bylaw revision is found to be necessary, care should be taken to avoid the following common errors:

- having an attorney prepare bylaw changes with the input of only a few staff leaders and then defending the changes against the objections of the general staff
- allowing physicians to believe that they can draft bylaw language without the assistance of an attorney
- pursuing a piecemeal revision of an existing document without examining all related bylaw provisions that might be affected by the seemingly simple changes
- converting an obsolete bylaw document suitable for the early 1970s into a new but still obsolete bylaws document suitable for the early 1980s
- quitting after legal issues have been considered but before considering important organizational restructuring with equal vigor
- quitting after creating the bylaw document but before developing related documents

Using a procedure similar to the following can both shorten the bylaw revision process and improve the product (the legal counsel's participation in the process is assumed):

1. Decide exactly what's wrong with the existing bylaws. Don't overlook general shortcomings, such as lengthiness.
2. Present conclusions (and justifications) about needed improvements to the general staff. This helps to develop early the understanding that is necessary before a staff will adopt bylaw changes. At the meeting, describe the process that will be followed and invite interested staff members to provide written comments or suggestions to the bylaw committee chairperson.
3. Create an informal and relatively large "bylaw development group." Include the bylaw committee and the medical executive committee, but also include interested or concerned physicians who may not happen to hold a formal leadership position. Include anyone involved in preparing existing bylaws and the legal counsel, the CEO, and a governing body representative (inclusion of the latter is optional).
4. After an initial meeting to identify and discuss key issues, choose someone to prepare a "menu" draft, with no pride of authorship, for discussion.
5. Distribute this draft to the bylaw development group, then meet to discuss it.

6. Prepare a second draft. Distribute it, then meet to discuss it. Approval by the legal counsel of the directions being taken must be obtained no later than this step. Unless the legal counsel is doing the drafting, he or she may not have been at the earlier meetings. Legal issues cannot, of course, be decided without the legal counsel. But the development group, in its first two or three meetings, may take up organizational issues (length of officer terms, frequency of general staff meetings, composition of the medical executive committee, exact listing of clinical departments, etc.) without taking up the legal counsel's time.

7. Prepare, discuss, then fine-tune a third draft, and take it to a first reading meeting to which the general staff is invited.

8. After further fine-tuning the document, present it to the general staff for adoption.

9. As soon as possible, present the adopted document to the governing body for approval.

10. Prepare or revise bylaw-related documents.

If it appears that the revision process is requiring more than six to eight months, then the causes of the delay should be sought and dealt with.

TRENDS AND ANTICIPATED DEVELOPMENTS

What will the health care center's medical staff organization look like five years from today? The most honest answer is: Nobody knows. But some trends are obvious, and some safe predictions can be made if one assumes continuance of the trends. There is no authority for the following statements; they are opinions of the author of this chapter.

1. *There will be fewer committees.* The "cyclical referral syndrome," in which an issue is passed from committee to committee without being resolved, is being replaced by the expectation that responsible leaders will exert leadership. Of course, the committees discussed in this chapter will be necessary as checkpoints to assure that individuals do not take unfair advantage of their positions or authority.

2. *Medical executive committees will be smaller.* The founding fathers of this country felt, in spite of their fear of monarchy, that executive responsibility and authority must reside in an individual, not a committee. Perhaps the executive of the medical staff in five years will not be an individual, but if not, it will probably be an executive council of no more than five members.

3. *Clinical department chairpersons will be paid.* Even in community hospitals (whatever *they* may look like five years from now), volunteer clinical department chairpersons possibly will have disappeared. Questions of what amount a clinical chairperson should be paid and who should pay it are in dispute. But there seems to be increasing agreement that current and increasing expectations of department chairpersons cannot be satisfactorily fulfilled if chairperson positions are staffed by volunteers.

4. *The role of the chief operating officer of the medical staff will differ from setting to setting.* The position and role of the medical director (vice-president for medical affairs) will continue to evolve, but five years from now the job description of this position will not be standardized. In some settings, this position may carry more formal authority than at present. In other settings, the medical director may still serve a statesmanlike role, working with, and as a liaison between, the executive staff and the medical staff.

5. *Patient-oriented credentialing will be the rule.* Having weathered the "era of economic contamination," credentialing and recredentialing will resume their original purpose—patient protection. One reason will be altruism. But another reason will be the success of the law in discouraging abuse of the credentialing process to gain competitive advantage.

6. *Data-based evaluation of physician performance will be regional in scope.* Since its inception, peer review has been hospital specific. That may change. Professional review organizations (PROs) will probably constitute a historical footnote rendered unnecessary by further bundling and capitation of payments for medical services. But the health care industry itself, perhaps through evolution of the Joint Commission's Agenda for Change or some yet uncreated vehicle and driven by public demands for accountability, may have lost confidence in the internal peer review process. Clinical data from one location may be shipped to another location for confirmation of the stated conclusions, thus applying the second-opinion concept to peer review.

7. *Medical staff service professionals will be administrative specialists.* Most medical staff offices and departments will be directed by certified (and re-certified) medical staff service professionals who will command organizational positions, respect, and salaries commensurate with how well the organization appreciates their value.

8. *Medical staff bylaws will be more concise.* Simple, clear bylaw documents, supplemented by descriptions of details in related manuals, will replace the bulky bylaw documents of old.

9. *The "two bylaws" model may be replaced.* There may be only governing body bylaws. Current provisions that concern the medical staff would be expanded somewhat to include descriptions now in the medical staff bylaws.

Details would be placed in governing body bylaw–related manuals of policies and procedures.

Health care centers may employ physicians as they do nurses, although this is not likely. It's also possible that "unit management" may be the rule. Specialists would relate less to the medical staff as a whole than to a hospital unit, where they would be equal participants with middle managers and nursing supervisors. This is also unlikely—a mere five years from now. Another unlikely possibility: separate incorporation of the traditional medical staff (this concept is discussed in Chapter 4). Still another: MediClump, the physician group that has a contract to provide medical services for MediBest, a health maintenance or preferred provider organization, may obtain a contract from the hospital to evaluate qualifications (credentialing) and performance (peer review). That's a viable alternative, since the Medi-Clump physicians would likely bring better methods and more experience and enthusiasm to these tasks than the traditional medical staff, separately incorporated or not. Of course, the judgments of MediClump, in the context of such a hospital contract, would still be subject to the final judgment and decision-making authority of the hospital's governing body, with whom MediClump had the contract.

Remembering that we are talking about only five years from now, the most likely possibility is increased effectiveness of a streamlined traditional hospital medical staff, with shorter medical staff bylaws and responsible individual leaders properly compensated.

10. *Medical staff members will appreciate their organization more.* Staff members who have no desire to be organizational leaders will nonetheless appreciate and cooperate with the efforts of their leaders and fulfill necessary medical staff organizational functions. Part of the reason will be positive: an increased understanding of the issues. Part of the reason will be negative: an appreciation of the fact that the medical staff could become extinct if it does not fulfill its responsibilities.

11. *More trust will exist among medical staff members and administrators.* Medical staff members and leaders, governing body members, and the CEO will be more open with each other as suspicion of lack of integrity generated by today's interpretation of "competition" is replaced by an appreciation that everyone must depend on everyone else for the accomplishment of goals. One result may be governing body representation on the medical executive committee, credentials committee, and performance evaluation committee.

12. *Information sharing will be prevalent.* Summary results of performance evaluation activities will be shared with the public. The public already is

demanding data comparing the performance of physicians whose names are suggested by physician referral services. That demand will not lessen.

13. *Regulation may increase.* State and federal statutes may dictate more precisely the structure of the medical staff. For example, a law in New York requires the existence of a medical director.

14. *Staff leaders will remain part of governance.* Executive leaders of the health care center and governing body advisers will increasingly appreciate having, at the governance level, carefully selected, respected clinicians who demonstrate a commitment to the mission of the institution.

In fact, the safest prediction of all is that no matter which of several structural forms the medical staff might assume, it will not simultaneously be given the ultimate trust and authority (fiduciary duty) reserved for the governing body.

NOTES

1. American College of Surgeons, *The Minimum Standard for Hospitals* (Chicago: American College of Surgeons, 1919).

2. Ibid.

3. T.R. Ponton, "Medical Staff Bylaws," in *The Medical Staff in the Hospital*, 2d ed., ed. M.T. McEachern (Chicago: Physicians' Record Company, 1953), 319–28.

4. American College of Surgeons, *Minimum Standard for Hospitals*.

5. Richard E. Thompson, with David R. Thompson. *Peer Review: An Objective Analysis and Suggestions for Change* (Wheaton, Ill.: Senss, 1987), 19.

6. Richard E. Thompson, *The Medical Staff Leader's Complete Practical Guidebook* (Wheaton, Ill.: Senss, 1988), 48–54.

7. Richard E. Thompson, *The Board Member's and CEO's Guide to Medical Staff Structure and Responsibilities* (Wheaton, Ill.: Senss, 1989).

8. American College of Surgeons, *Minimum Standard for Hospitals*.

9. Ibid.

10. Ibid.

11. Richard E. Thompson, *The Hospitalwide Accountability System* (Wheaton, Ill.: Senss, 1988), 108–13.

12. Thompson, *Medical Staff Leader's Complete Practical Guidebook*, 151.

13. Thompson, *Hospitalwide Accountability System*, 25–29.

14. Richard E. Thompson, with David R. Thompson, *Productive Confrontation: What, When and How* (Wheaton, Ill.: Senss, 1987).

15. Richard E. Thompson, "Kinder Gentler 'Corrective Action': Easing Physician Fears While Simultaneously Improving Effectiveness of 'Peer Review,' " *North Carolina Medical Journal* 50 (September 1989): 502–7.

Chapter 4

The Independent, Self-Governing Medical Staff

Howard L. Lang, MD

It is a time honored dictate—and plain common sense—that if you are to be held responsible for something, you must have control of it. The medical staff is responsible for providing high-quality medical care, and the organizational structure best suited to enable physicians to provide that care is the professionally independent, self-governing medical staff model.

It is through self-governance that a medical staff can protect itself against management or board actions that place the hospital's economic interest over the patient's need for high-quality medical care. Although the medical staff wants to keep the hospital financially sound, the welfare of patients is more important than other considerations, whether they be considerations of the hospital management, the governing board, or even the welfare of physicians.

ESSENTIALS OF SELF-GOVERNANCE

Self-governance may be defined as ruling by right of authority, exercising a directing influence without outside interference. To be truly independent and self-governing, the medical staff should adhere to the following essentials.

Initiating, Developing, and Adopting Medical Staff Bylaws, Rules, and Regulations

The medical staff bylaws, rules, and regulations provide the structure for self-governance that permits the medical staff to discharge its responsibilities in matters of medical care quality.

An independent medical staff legal counsel (not the hospital legal counsel) should aid the medical staff in the development of the medical staff bylaws. After they have been adopted by the medical staff, the bylaws are reviewed by the board of the hospital and approved (approval should be withheld only on reasonable grounds). The hospital board's responsibility in reviewing the bylaws is to assure itself that the medical staff is conducting its activities in a fair and unbiased manner consistent with legal requirements.

Amending Medical Staff Bylaws, Rules, and Regulations

The medical staff must approve any amendments to its bylaws, rules, and regulations, as must the board of the hospital.

Since the bylaws constitute a contract between the board and the medical staff, neither body may unilaterally amend them. The board has no right to unreasonably impose its wishes on the medical staff, and it should not assume the authority to unilaterally revise, either directly or indirectly (such as through the corporate bylaws), the medical staff bylaws. If a hospital board has evidence that the medical staff is not promulgating appropriate bylaws, it has other remedies available to correct the situation.

It is exceedingly important that the medical staff periodically reviews and revises its bylaws to keep pace with the ever-changing environment in which the staff functions.

Selecting and Removing Medical Staff Officers

The medical staff's ability to elect its own officers is at the very core of self-governance. The self-governing medical staff has the right and the responsibility to develop criteria and standards for the selection, election, seating, and removal of its officers.

Some have written that the chief of the medical staff is a member of the institution's management hierarchy, that he or she is responsible to the hospital administrator, and that his or her authority flows from the governing board. This is categorically false. The chief of staff derives his or her authority from the medical staff and represents the medical staff to the administration.

The primary duty of the chief of staff and other medical staff officers is to ensure that the medical staff is in a position to maintain its patient advocacy role and that actions taken are in the interest of the patients.

Medical Staff Membership

The medical staff is responsible for developing reasonable criteria and fair procedures for recommending the granting, delineating, and removal of clinical privileges. Such criteria and procedures must, of course, be compatible with state and federal laws.

In these times of economic competition among hospitals, each medical staff must take steps to ensure that the governing board does not base credentialing decisions on the effect that an applicant or a present medical staff member might have on the hospital's bottom line. Quality and competency must be the factors considered in credentialing. Any trend toward economic-based credentialing standards should be condemned.

Establishing Patient Care Standards

It is the right and responsibility of the self-governing medical staff to initiate, develop, establish, and enforce professional standards for appropriate medical practices in all medical staff departments and peer review and quality assurance committees. Remember that by law, only physicians can practice medicine; the hospital governing board may not. Although the board is certainly concerned with quality medical care and has oversight duties, the establishment of patient care standards and the regulation of professional practice are rightful responsibilities of the medical staff.

Independent Legal Counsel

Receiving advice from the medical staff's own legal counsel (as opposed to the hospital's) is necessary to ensure the staff's legal and organizational integrity. This is not to imply that hospital attorneys are malevolent. It is simply that their perspectives and loyalties are different than those of the medical staff. Having independent legal counsel is especially important as the functions, responsibilities, and liabilities of the medical staff become greater and more complex.

In addition, there may be times when the hospital's interests conflict with those of the medical staff or when the hospital acts contrary to the medical staff bylaws. In those circumstances, the medical staff may assert its separate status, obtain its own legal counsel and, through the applicable rules of the jurisdiction, seek correction of any wrongful act.

In today's competitive environment, hospitals compete with each other and, at times, with the physicians who compose the medical staff. Securing independent legal counsel can guarantee that the medical staff receives information and advice from an attorney whose undivided loyalty is to it. If the medical staff does not have separate legal advice, it might be prevented from knowing or protecting its rights.

CONCLUSION

Increasingly, physicians are threatened with the loss of authority at key decision points in patient care; yet responsibility for the quality and outcome of that care rests squarely on their shoulders. Physicians must resist this erosion of their professional authority.

Physicians on the medical staff no longer have the luxury of being concerned solely with issues that affect their individual practices. Physicians must now involve themselves with the collective concerns of the hospital medical staff and seek ways to deal with those concerns.

All good things in medicine flow from a medical staff's commitment to quality patient care. Through self-governance, physicians on medical staffs will benefit not only their patients but also the hospitals and the communities they serve.

Chapter 5

The Hospital Medical Director

Charles R. Mathews, MD

HISTORICAL PERSPECTIVE

Most physicians practicing today have fond memories of less complicated times, before diagnostic-related groups (DRGs) and professional review organizations (PROs), before preferred provider organizations (PPOs); of times when *marketing* was not a health care verb and malpractice liability and competition were on the periphery of professional awareness.

The relationship of physicians to their hospitals seemed similarly uncomplicated: A lone secretarial type usually manned the minuscule medical staff office, processing the one- or two-page applications for medical staff membership and keeping a calendar of the meetings.

In those untroubled years, physicians and "administration" coexisted in a stance of polite nonintimacy, while they reaped their portions of the green harvest of Medicare charge–based reimbursement. Practitioners performed their healing arts in their hospital "workshops," filling the beds (often straining the bed capacity), while the administrators kept the shop running. The infrequent contacts between the two groups usually arose from requests by the physicians for more equipment or services, which were usually forthcoming since third-party payers picked up the tab.

Into the seventies, the organizational structure of the typical medical staff was relatively straightforward, governed by a pyramidal hierarchy consisting of committee chairpersons, heads of clinical departments, and a chief of staff at the apex. In the community hospitals, top medical staff leaders typically were elected and hold office for one or two years.

In most hospitals, the time-tested laissez-faire model persisted into the early eighties, at which time a number of forces converged to irreversibly alter the delivery of health care services in hospital and nonhospital settings, including the physicians' office practices.

HOSPITAL TRUSTEE ACCOUNTABILITY

Beginning with the landmark *Darling*[1] case in 1965, the courts and the various regulatory and accrediting bodies have increasingly held hospital governing boards accountable for the quality of care delivered in their institutions. Trustees are no longer simply public-spirited citizens, contributing time and fund-raising abilities to their hospitals of choice. They now typically assume fiduciary roles that encompass the responsibility for the practitioners' performance in patient care. Rarely, however, are trustees medically sophisticated, and they must rely upon the medical staff not only to deliver an acceptable level of care but to document and report to the governing body the quality and appropriateness of such care. Although the governing board has historically, of necessity, delegated the monitoring of quality (quality assurance) to the medical staff, the pattern of "arms length" delegation became unacceptable in the accountable eighties.

HOSPITAL REIMBURSEMENT

The institution of the prospective payment system, with its DRGs, in 1983 signaled the end of the financial cornucopia for hospitals. The Medicare and other third-party spigots were tightened, resulting in an abrupt change in hospital admission patterns. As the medical staff learned that "groupers" were not a variety of fish, length of patient stay dropped dramatically. Many procedures theretofore performed comfortably within the walls of the hospital suddenly became outpatient procedures. Case mix changed: The patients admitted were sicker and required greater intensity of care. To monitor Medicare admissions, a professional review organization (PRO) appeared in every state by congressional mandate. Initially, the PROs monitored only the financial aspects of the admissions, but subsequently the monitors included quality of care. At the same time, there has been progressive "ratcheting down" of the reimbursements, with the result that hospitals consistently lose money on their Medicare admissions.

PROBLEMS OF TRADITIONAL MEDICAL STAFF LEADERSHIP

Time Commitments

Physicians have typically assumed leadership positions on the medical staff during their most active practice years. Always onerous, the increasing responsibilities and time commitments have made it very difficult in all but the smallest hospitals for a practitioner to perform the functions of a chief of staff or departmental or committee chairperson, without the skilled assistance of a full-time or part-time physician executive: the medical director (also known as vice-president for medical affairs and by other titles).

Dual Roles

The dual roles of elected medical staff leaders are often not fully appreciated by the governing board, nor by the elected leaders themselves. In one capacity, the chief of staff is the "president" or chief executive of the medical staff. As such, the chief of staff exercises the authority and assumes responsibility for the functions of the medical staff. The chief of staff also represents the interests of the staff vis-à-vis the hospital administration and to the governing board.

At the same time, whenever the chief of staff, departmental or committee chairpersons, or any other officers of the medical staff are performing their official functions, they are acting on behalf of the governing board and as such are in effect "officers" of that board, with derivative authority and accountability.

Lack of Continuity

Elected medical staff leaders characteristically serve for a very few years. One year, sometimes two, is the usual term for a chief of staff. Typically, by the time he or she has acquired the information and know-how necessary for effective functioning, the term of office is over. The physician then usually returns to his or her neglected practice, rarely surfacing thereafter in the medical staff hierarchy. The physician's administrative expertise and experience are lost, and the successor begins the acquisition process anew.

Information Base

The sheer quantity of information needed to manage the affairs of a medical staff in the hospitals of the eighties and nineties seems to be growing exponentially. In view of the limited terms of office and the demands of their medical practices, elected leaders cannot acquire the information base necessary to effectively carry out the many functions of medical staff leadership.

Lack of Managerial Abilities

Rarely have elected medical staff leaders had significant training or experience in managerial functions, yet these skills are essential for the orderly management of the medical staff. Some leaders seem to have been born with executive skills, and others acquire them over time. But the basic method is "on the job training," not an ideal mechanism given today's enormously complex hospital health care delivery systems.

Potential Conflicts of Interest

As practitioners, medical staff leaders have built-in potential conflicts of interest. Official decisions that they may be called on to make will often impact their practices, their referrals, or their economic interests. The dilemmas are common and will call into question the decision-making processes of the medical staff. In addition, there are frequent instances when the interests of practitioners are opposed to those of the institution, in which case the medical staff leader must act to protect the former.

Authority and Accountability

The derivative authority and the attendant accountability of the medical staff leadership concern the quality and appropriateness of patient care. The various monitoring mechanisms involved in this awesome responsibility include quality assurance, utilization review, and risk management. Also impacting upon the leadership are the multiple accrediting and regulatory bodies, including the Joint Commission on Accreditation of Healthcare Organizations (Joint Commission), the PROs, and the several state licensing and regulatory agencies. Practicing physicians rarely have the time, the store of information, the skills, or the will needed to fulfill the medical staff's delegated responsibilities regarding quality of patient care.

THE HOSPITAL MEDICAL DIRECTOR

The demands of leading and regulating the medical staff have exceeded the ability of practicing physician volunteers to meet those demands. This has led to the emergence, in many hospitals, of the medical director, whose role is to act on behalf of the medical staff leadership.

Initially found solely in the larger hospitals, by 1987 only hospitals of 100 beds or less had failed to hire medical directors in significant numbers.[2]

Characteristically, medical directors have been chosen from within their own hospitals (over 75 percent had practiced in the hospital in which they served). Though a wide spectrum of specialties are represented, medical directors usually have an internal medicine, surgery, or family practice background. Over 85 percent are board certified.[3]

The major role of the medical director is to function as a liaison between the medical staff and administration. The rationale is that a physician is best equipped to facilitate communication,

> particularly in areas with direct bearing on the quality of patient care. Having a physician skilled in management reassures the medical staff that administration is genuinely concerned about the unique demands physicians face in their profession. At the same time, the hospital's chief administrative officials need assurance that complex policy questions which directly affect clinical issues are being handled by a competent full time manager who is knowledgeable about medical procedures and also aware of modern management techniques.[4]

In the role of communicator and liaison, the medical director is the "lightning rod" attracting bolts of lightning from all points of the compass.

Functions of the Medical Director

In addition to the liaison role, the medical director performs a number of functions, which will vary according to the institution.

Medical Staff Organization

The medical director acts in place of, and on behalf of, the medical staff officers in the management of the medical staff organization. The medical director is comparable to the military "adjutant" who acts on behalf of the commanding officer. He or she is responsible for the operations of the medical staff office, which is usually under the direct supervision of a medical staff services professional.

Credentialing and Privileging

Close supervision of the processes of medical staff credentialing and privileging, of appointment and reappointment, is usually a major responsibility of the medical director. In the eighties, nothing is taken for granted: All diplomas, licenses, certifications, and clinical experience must be independently verified. Privileges must be granted only on the basis of documented training and clinical competence. It is also the medical director's responsibility to see that the process is not delayed and that there are no extraneous or anticompetitive factors affecting the granting of privileges.

Quality Assurance, Risk Management, and Utilization Review

These essential, interrelated hospital–medical staff functions are major responsibilities of the medical director and occupy most of his or her time. The medical director must be sophisticated in these fields and closely attuned to the day-to-day operations of the system. When incidents or "fall outs" require corrective action, the medical director must set the process in motion and follow through using the appropriate channels.

Medical Staff Development

It is not acceptable in the current milieu to have a medical staff grow by simple expansion. Its current composition must be assessed in light of how well it meets the needs of the hospital and the community. Its growth must be directed according to a specific plan approved by the governing board. Primary care physicians and other specialists must be sought and encouraged in accordance with the plan. There may be specialties overrepresented on the medical staff. Additions in these specialties could strain the existing hospital facilities, and applications would be put on hold.

The medical staff itself should have no part in the development or execution of a medical staff development plan to avoid anticompetitive implications. The medical director, however, if not in practice, is in a unique position to assist the process. As a hospital employee acting on behalf of the governing board, the medical director is free from the anti-competitive taint and will have the best grasp of the needs of the hospital. He or she should play a prominent role in physician recruitment efforts.

New Hospital Services

As hospitals shift their operations to meet socioeconomic and regulatory changes, the medical director should work with the hospital and medical staff planners to identify and develop new patient services and to reduce or eliminate the "losers" in DRG and third-party reimbursements.

Corrective and Disciplinary Action

Although the medical director rarely has the authority to order medical staff corrective actions, he or she is almost invariably at the center of the corrective action process. The medical director will have tracked each problem from its appearance in an incident report or from a quality assurance committee, and will have overseen its referral to the appropriate medical staff officials. He or she will usually coordinate any hearings and appeals, working closely with attorneys for the medical staff and the hospital. It is not rare, unfortunately, for the medical director to find him- or herself a co-defendant in the litigation that may follow an unsuccessful appeal by a physician who has been disciplined or has had an application for privileges denied.

Public Relations

The medical director is usually known in the community and can be an effective spokesperson for the hospital and medical staff in relations with the nonmedical world. The medical director is often a liaison with various public interest groups and can coordinate the presentation of informational seminars and outreach programs.

Problems and Challenges of the Medical Director

Organizational Challenges

The medical director does not fit into the traditional hospital organization. He or she is employed by the hospital, but the typical organizational chart shows no lines of authority but rather dotted lines to either side that show a reporting relationship to the hospital chief executive officer (CEO) and a liaison relationship with the medical staff leadership. Even after several years of experience, there may be no consensus on the medical director's niche.

Credibility

The medical director is usually on the hospital's payroll and his or her major reporting responsibility is to the hospital's CEO. In the eyes of some physicians, the medical director is therefore a "company man," not a real doctor who can be trusted to represent the viewpoint of the medical staff. This perception will be reinforced when the medical director, on occasion, represents the hospital on issues that may affect the interests of some practitioners. On the other hand, the medical director, by sometimes representing the medical staff, may be perceived as uncommitted to the institution. The question of loyalty can be very delicate, and the medical director often requires savoir-faire in order to maintain bilateral credibility.

Clinical Practice Challenge

According to a 1987 survey, 45 percent of hospital medical directors maintain a clinical practice, and the average amount of time spent on those practices is 15 percent.[5] Although a clinical background is probably essential, there are potential pitfalls for medical directors who continue to practice.

The commitment of time and expertise is the major consideration. Participation in the management of one of today's complex hospital organizations, including its medical staff, will usually require substantially more than a 40-hour workweek on the part of the medical director. There is simply too much going on, scheduled and unscheduled, for the medical director to have the time for a practice "on the side." His or her managerial performance or clinical practice (or both) will suffer.

In smaller hospitals, 200 beds or less, it may be impractical to employ a full-time medical director, and in those hospitals the medical director may be able to carry out his or her functions on a part-time basis.

Competition is another pitfall. Physicians may generally approve of a medical director who maintains a practice. However, an obvious problem arises when hospital decisions are made that may negatively impact the practices of the medical director's fellow practitioners. Impartiality and the avoidance of any perception of bias are essential for the practicing medical director.

Authority

Many of the medical director's challenges are related to questions of authority within the hospital's organizational structure. The more influential the medical director, the more there will be a resultant shift of authority away from the administration and, potentially at least, to the medical staff. This can be a major problem for the administration. To maintain an effective working relationship, the possession of good management skills by all of the players is necessary.

Since the medical director's actual authority is derivative, exercise of that authority is dependent upon the degree of backing he or she has from the CEO and from the hospital board. A rough, informal measure of the strength of such backing can be made by measuring the distance (both literal and figurative) between the offices of the CEO and the medical director.

Authority is basically of the following three types.

Hierarchical Authority. This type of authority is intrinsic to the office held. The pope, the president, the director of the PRO, the chief of staff, the chairman of the hospital board, and the hospital CEO all possess hierarchical authority. The medical director's hierarchical authority usually ranges between minimal and none.

Sapiential Authority. The medical director who survives several years in office is heavily endowed with authority based on knowledge acquired. He or she knows the members of the medical staff, including their clinical abilities, personality traits, egocentricities, staff lunchroom cluster patterns, and affairs of heart. On the other side, the medical director has a continuing relationship with the administration and personally knows of the president and the swarms of vice-presidents, assistant vice-presidents, department managers, and others in the administrative clique.

An essential component of sapiential authority is the medical director's "corporate memory." Chiefs of staff, department chairpersons, and other medical staff leaders are transitory, whereas, in the unstable milieu of hospital politics, the medical director is *relatively* long serving. He or she has been to the meetings, knows where the files are, and remembers who did what to whom when. The medical director knows where the bodies are buried.

Texts of the bylaws, rules and regulations, and protocols and procedures, including yesterday's revisions, are permanently installed in the medical director's cerebral memory bank and subject to instant recall; no Biblical scholar has a better command of holy writ. On the down side of this, medical staff leaders tend to cease opening the bylaws and rules manuals, instead calling out, "Ask Charlie, he knows."

Tact, silence, and a thoughtful bearing are useful for reinforcing authority based on acquired wisdom. Both the medical staff and administration know that the medical director knows (or they may think that he or she knows, which is almost as effective).

Charismatic Authority. Webster defines *charisma* as (1) a divinely inspired gift, grace, or talent, as for prophesying, healing, etc.; (2) a special quality of leadership that captures the popular imagination and inspires unswerving allegiance and devotion.

Although divine inspiration would surely be helpful to the medical directors—and some have been known to pray for it—an informal poll revealed none had achieved a sufficient level of sanctity.

As for the second definition, the medical director must indeed have that "special quality of leadership." (The remainder of the second definition is irrelevant. No medical staff or hospital administration has ever been characterized by "unswerving allegiance and devotion.")

The importance of charisma in this sense explains why most medical directors have been selected from within the ranks of the hospital medical staff, where they have a track record and where they have filled leadership roles within the medical staff organization.

Future of the Hospital Medical Director

Any hospital without a functioning medical director will be at an increasing disadvantage in the nineties. The integration of the medical staff into hospital operations will be a hallmark of those hospitals that survive the medical economic disruptions of the century's closing decade. Central to this integration—the key figure—is the medical director. Whereas in 1985 75 percent of hospitals of over 200 beds had full-time medical directors,[6] it can be anticipated that the figure will be close to 100 percent by mid-decade. In all but the smallest hospitals, the position will be full time.

The demands of the greatly expanded roles of hospitals will require medical directors to have structured training, including established courses in academic or quasi-academic settings. On-the-job training will no longer suffice, even for those "quick studies," who must master, among other things, organizational management, finance, economic analysis, and strategic planning.

A background in clinical practice will continue to be important for the perspective it gives to the medical director and for the purpose of establishing his or her credibility with the medical staff. However, the proportion of clinicians who become physician executives can be expected to decrease as younger physicians with appropriate academic credentials go directly from their training programs into managerial positions.

The organizational status of the hospital medical director will be more clearly defined, with the delegation of the "hierarchical" authority necessary for carrying out tasks. The concerns of the medical staff regarding such authority are best alleviated by specific language in the hospital or medical staff bylaws that delineates the authority and functions of the position.

The tripartite model of board-administration-medical staff, the "three-legged stool," will be outdated in the nineties. As a part of the evolving redefinition, the medical director will usually have the responsibility of reporting directly to the hospital governing board rather than through the CEO.

Looking toward the end of the decade into the twenty-first century, the availability of a pool of well-trained physician executives is expected to bring about a situation in which most hospital CEOs are physicians. Medical directors will continue to be necessary but their role will be modified in health care corporations headed by physicians.

In summary, the hospital medical director will be increasingly important during the coming socioeconomic health care convolutions. The role will be expanded and redefined. Continuing requisites for the job will be broad shoulders, a thick skin, and a sense of humor!

NOTES

1. *Darling v Charleston Community Memorial Hospital*, 211 N.E. 2d 253 (Illinois Supreme Court 1965).

2. American Medical Association, "The Role of the Medical Director," *Hospital Medical Staff Section Newsletter* 4 (June 1987): 1.

3. Ibid.

4. Joyce Riffer, "Hospitals Shift toward Paid Medical Directors," *Hospitals* 60 (February 20, 1986): 98.

5. American College of Physician Executives, *1987 Compensation Survey* (Tampa, Fla.: American College of Physician Executives, 1987).

6. American Medical Association, "Role of the Medical Director."

Chapter 6

The Medical Staff Services Professional

Ruth A. Buck, CMSC

HISTORY OF THE PROFESSION[1]

Twenty years ago, the medical staff secretary's major responsibility was to keep the list of physicians who regularly admitted patients to the hospital. Housed in a closet in a back hallway, in an unused patient room, or next to the newborn nursery, the medical staff secretary provided clerical support, made coffee, scheduled meetings, listened to physician complaints, and guarded the cherished history of the medical staff. This individual might have been found in a corner of the medical records department or, if lucky, in the administrative suite, in which case his or her contact with physicians was limited by the proximity of the office to that of the "enemy"—the hospital administrator.

Wherever the medical staff secretary of the 1960s called home in the hospital, he or she was closely linked with the medical staff and could be relied upon to assist physicians with their nonclinical but hospital-related duties. The medical staff roster the medical staff secretary maintained began to take on a semblance of accuracy and could be correlated with the credentials files located near the secretary's area. The scope of work was broadened to include not only scheduling meetings for medical staff committees but producing and maintaining minutes for these meetings.

The history of the profession can be tracked by focusing on the development of the organized medical staff. In those early days before the issue of the hospital's liability for the acts of its medical staff was so clearly defined within the context of medical malpractice suits, a physician's qualifications would be read from a one-page application form that outlined educational background and that application would then be voted upon by a yea or nay vote cast by a roomful of physicians at a general staff meeting. There was no verification of individual credentials, no reference letters on file, and no consideration of training and experience as the basis for delineating clinical privileges. With the exception of state licensure, little was known about applicants. In short, there was no "process" at all.

85

In its early attempts to organize, the medical staff adopted bylaws that were simplistic and general but that met the needs of the organization at the time. The major components described the composition and requirements for membership, the parameters of self-governance, and the purpose of the organization as a collegial body. Little thought was given to the content until an obstacle was encountered or a problem was magnified by inappropriate language in the bylaws. Twenty years ago, the bylaw document was hardly the working document it is today. The medical staff secretary's role in all this was keeper of the document. From time to time, he or she was expected to produce updated versions as bylaws were amended to address issues as they arose.

Changes in the health care industry throughout the 1970s forced hospitals to take a long, hard look at the medical staff. Veteran medical staff secretaries now began to be titled *medical staff coordinators*. In situations where permitted, the medical staff coordinator began to guide the medical staff through the arduous procedures known as the fair hearing and appellate review process. Sometimes the coordinator made suggestions about rewording the medical staff bylaws in order to achieve a stated objective. As attention became focused on the peer review process, it was the medical staff coordinator who was asked to create the proper documentation to carry the medical staff and hospital through an accreditation survey successfully. With growing expectations placed on the performance of the medical staff leadership, the role of the medical staff coordinator began to expand. The coordinator's familiarity with regulatory requirements and medical staff bylaws and his or her ability to coordinate the varied activities of the medical staff became valuable assets to the leaders of the medical staff organization. The leaders relied on the coordinator to provide guidance and administrative support for a wide range of responsibilities. The coordinator's high visibility and high level of acceptance with physicians were among his or her most valuable attributes. Over the years the experience gained by the medical staff coordinator in the medical staff office was augmented by more formal education. In many cases in the early 1980s, the medical staff coordinators were certified by the National Association Medical Staff Services and thus were acknowledged as individuals who had highly developed skills and who were expert in medical staff support services.

Today's medical staff services professional (MSSP) wears many hats, has many titles. The MSSP administers the medical staff's most important quality assurance function: credentialing and reappointment. With an innate sense of diplomacy, the MSSP bridges the communication gap between the physicians and the hospital staff. The MSSP assists the medical staff in establishing a quality-and-appropriateness-of-care mechanism that is workable and that will meet Joint Commission on Accreditation of Healthcare Organizations (Joint Commission) standards. Guided by the medical staff leadership, the MSSP is responsible for making certain that the results of peer review activities are used in the reappointment process. The MSSP is both a confidant of the general membership and an assistant to the leadership. The successful MSSP is constantly challenged to discover new ways to address issues that impact the hospital and medical staff. Whatever the title, the MSSP is an effective facilitator and interpreter of hospital and medical staff policy.

THE EVOLVING ROLE OF THE MSSP

With a solid background in the field of medical staff affairs, the veteran MSSP is an educator, assistant, advisor, and advocate. The MSSP provides continuity, knowledge, and experience and is undoubtedly one of the medical staff's most important resources. The MSSP is charged with the responsibility of helping to ensure compliance with licensing and accrediting agency requirements. In this capacity, the MSSP assists the elected leadership by making the statutes and standards available to the proper authorities within the organization. The MSSP can track the progress that each organizational component is making towards compliance and can be a catalyst for change where necessary or where directed by the medical staff leadership.

The MSSP is a systems expert, devising and implementing the practical mechanisms by which the credentialing, peer review, and reappointment processes are managed. The MSSP is a developer of forms that expedite the workload of the medical staff leadership. With a learned ability to scan a credentials application, the MSSP can identify potential questions or "red flags" for discussion with the appropriate committee or department chairperson. Working with the quality assurance department, the MSSP integrates the results of peer review into the reappointment profile, placing before the department chairperson all of the information needed to make a reasonable assessment of an application for reappointment to the medical staff.

As an advisor, the MSSP is able to guide the medical staff leadership through routine functions like monthly department meetings and more sensitive functions, like those surrounding physician impairment. Recognizing that the decisions always remain with the physicians, the MSSP can be an effective sounding board for problems and can help bring issues into perspective quickly. The MSSP is also able to advise the leadership on matters of priority in an expeditious manner.

As an educator, the experienced MSSP can instruct the medical staff leadership in the responsibilities of their elected positions. The MSSP may call upon noted authorities to provide meaningful educational sessions at the hospital. The MSSP can rely upon his or her own special knowledge of the medical staff organization— its committee and department functions—to bring a newly elected leader up to date on current issues. The MSSP may initiate a formalized training session or orientation within the hospital, using hospital staff to assist in this process, or he or she may be a catalyst for physician attendance at relevant continuing education programs on topics such as bylaws, credentialing, and peer review.

The MSSP is a valuable assistant to the elected leaders. With busy clinical practices and other demands on their time, physicians must depend on the full-time medical staff services staff to keep unnecessary paperwork at a minimum while directing their attention to the most critical issues. Under the most favorable circumstances, it is difficult for the elected leader to keep tabs on all that is going on within the medical staff, and so the MSSP is called upon to report on the activities of the clinical departments and to identify issues before the various committees. Since the MSSP frequently attends more meetings than even the most zealous physician member, he or she is completely comfortable in this role. By allowing the MSSP to be the focal point of all medical staff activities, physicians can avoid duplication of effort and wasted energy. As an assistant to the committee chairpersons, the MSSP prepares the agenda, is an efficient recordkeeper, and is fully responsible for implementing the follow-up resulting from the committee's deliberations. The MSSP can write all of the correspondence and meet with the hospital staff to discuss medical staff issues if this responsibility is delegated by the leadership.

Because elected leaders come and go (sometimes as frequently as every year) with each new term of office, there can be a serious lack of continuity within the medical staff organization. Here the MSSP fills the gap. With the benefit of knowledge of earlier discussions and previous decisions, the MSSP helps the medical staff carry out its responsibilities without interruption or needless repetition. Physicians find this particularly useful, especially if they are appointed or elected to positions for which they are ill-prepared.

The MSSP frequently serves as the main resource person for medical staff affairs. Whether there is a need to obtain information from other hospitals about testing for HIV positivity in a high-risk patient population or to compile samples of credentialing criteria for suction lipectomy, the MSSP is able to retrieve, display, and interpret reference information, drawing on the networking capabilities of the national professional association. Physicians, whose time is better spent deliberating on the issues at hand, find this background work a tremendous timesaver.

The MSSP who is thoroughly conversant with the medical staff bylaws and departmental rules and regulations can be called upon by physicians to assist in application of specific sections and interpretation of the bylaws. As physicians apply for medical staff appointment, the medical staff services department tries to familiarize them with all the relevant points of the bylaws, for example, meeting attendance requirements, due process provisions, medical recordkeeping, and prerogatives and responsibilities of the various categories of medical staff membership. A department chairperson may be able to resolve a dispute over emergency room coverage requirements, for example, if he or she calls upon the MSSP to produce the pertinent rules and regulations for discussion at the monthly meeting.

Throughout the facility, the image of the physician can be distorted by employees who have had varying degrees of successful interaction with members of the medical staff. Because the MSSP has an inherent understanding of the frustrations that accumulate in a physician's mind, the MSSP views the physician as the cornerstone of all patient care administered within the hospital's confines. More importantly, the MSSP has learned to channel those frustrations in the proper direction. In the medical staff services department, the physician's needs are accommodated wherever possible. In short, the MSSP is truly an advocate for the physician, using his or her knowledge of the hospital's organizational dynamics to accomplish whatever an individual, a department, or a committee wishes to have happen.

THE PROFESSIONAL ASSOCIATION

History and Perspective

In 1971 in southern California, a group of medical staff secretaries, curious about the similarities and vagaries of their jobs and anxious to share their special knowledge, held a meeting. Unwittingly, they formed the foundation for the National Association Medical Staff Services (NAMSS). Although the actual details of that first meeting are lost to history, it is known that the twenty-two women shared a common concern about the changing role of the organized medical staff. They were witness to an overall decline in the prestige of the medical profession as the incident of malpractice litigation and statutory regulations increased in the early 1970s. With Joint Commission standards and federal regulations placing more emphasis on the administrative duties of the elected leadership, the medical staff secretary, as the position then was titled, sensed the emergence of a new profession that would consist of individuals who could function as resources for the medical staff leadership, coordinators of duties who could provide the medical staff with much-needed continuity, and full-time advocates for the physicians and medical staff within the facility's hierarchy.

As the job of medical staff coordinator developed, so did the focus of the professional association, and within seven years of that first meeting the association was incorporated nationally. In its formative years, supported by a voluntary board of directors, the NAMSS helped to shape the medical staff services profession through adoption of a code of ethics (see Exhibit 6-1), networking, continuing education, and role modeling.

Today, the NAMSS represents over 2,000 members across the country, with local affiliate organizations in 75 percent of the states. The work of the voluntary board has been supplemented by full-time staff, with an executive director who guides the decision-making process. The NAMSS certifying examination for medical staff coordinators has become a benchmark of excellence and a measure of knowledge

Exhibit 6-1   Code of Ethics of the National Association Medical Staff Services

---

Recognizing the position of trust, responsibility and accountability held by the medical staff services professional, we resolve to be guided by the highest principles of the National Association Medical Staff Services.

We further resolve to promote quality patient care through the support of the medical staff and its functions; to assure confidentiality of all medical staff documents and activities; to place service before material gain; to exemplify loyalty and conscientiousness; to maintain dignity in any situation and to appropriately represent the profession.

We further resolve to be responsive to needs, receptive to change, and to perform our duties in the most cost effective manner.

We further resolve to share knowledge, foster educational opportunities and to encourage personal and professional growth through continued self-improvement and application of current advancements in medical staff services practices.

---

in this highly specialized field. These services are supplemented by a professional journal, a national conference, and teaching seminars.

The NAMSS As a Viable Force in the Health Care Industry

Through the early years of its existence, the NAMSS focused largely on its own development as a professional organization. Once established as the representative body for MSSPs, the NAMSS began to widen its area of influence within the industry. In 1987 the NAMSS board established the association's direction for the next three to five years by developing a long-range strategic plan. The main mission, as stated by the board within the context of the plan, is to improve the skills and general competence of practicing medical staff coordinators and managers.

The NAMSS has been dedicated to helping its members understand and change the organizational structure of the health care industry. Its overall focus has been on promoting a positive and professional image for the members of the NAMSS and for the association itself, thus securing higher levels of recognition, especially among hospital administrators and physicians. As the NAMSS strives to fulfill its mission through improvements in education, professionalism, and managerial skills among the membership, the improvements directly benefit the physicians whose needs are served by qualified MSSPs. And where the members can hone their skills and broaden their knowledge, they increase their own value to the medical staff and the hospital administration.

By monitoring changes in the industry that may impact on it members, while at the same time taking into consideration the immediate needs of its members, the NAMSS has kept ahead of most trends. For example, the NAMSS has expanded its membership base in recent years to encompass the needs of credentialing specialists who are employed in nontraditional health care facilities, such as health maintenance organizations. In many ways, the needs of the medical director, quality assurance coordinator and risk manager are being met through NAMSS initiatives.

To whatever extent possible, the NAMSS has forged links with other health care professional associations so that networking may occur at the organizational level. In 1987, the then president-elect of the NAMSS was appointed to serve on the task force for hospitalwide clinical indicators that is working with the Joint Commission to help realize Dr. Dennis O'Leary's Agenda for Change. The special expertise of MSSPs with a long history in medical staff quality assurance and a deep sensitivity to the need for a coordinated and comprehensive mechanism for evaluating care has brought a slightly different perspective to the work of the Joint Commission—the perspective of the medical staff without the clinical bias.

CERTIFICATION AND EDUCATION

In some cases, the NAMSS approach has been to improve the professionalism of its members. In order to provide validation for the technical expertise of its constituents, the association developed the first and only certifying examination for MSSPs, and in 1981 the hard work of a dedicated group of women who composed the NAMSS Certification Committee resulted in the administration of the first certification examination for medical staff coordinators. This was a major step in the effort to apply meaningful standards for individual professional achievement in the field of medical staff services. Since then, many avenues have been explored to improve the certification program as well as to increase its recognition and acceptance by other factions in the health care field.[2] Starting in the early 1980s, certification has gradually become more accepted as a measure of knowledge by hospital administrators, personnel directors, and physicians in leadership positions. Attesting to this trend is the growing number of newspaper ads seeking certified medical staff coordinators to fill vacant positions in medical staff services departments.

Today there are over 1,100 certified medical staff coordinators, who must maintain their credentials through relevant continuing education (the requirement is for 30 hours over a three-year period). Certification is rapidly becoming accepted as a standard measure of competence, and with an increasing number of applicants sitting for the examination each year, the NAMSS is encouraged to believe that its members see this as a tool for achieving personal success.

In 1985 the first ad hoc education committee was formed, and planning was begun for a comprehensive and systematic educational track to include undergraduate as well as continuing education opportunities for members. The now independent Education Council has published a textbook, outlined a core curriculum for medical staff services science, established standards for faculty and course content, and granted official recognition to undergraduate programs in several colleges offering an associate degree in medical staff services science. The council will continue its work in improving educational opportunities and developing standards for educational excellence.

THE FUTURE

The future looks bright for the MSSPs. As awareness of hospital executives is heightened regarding the importance of having a qualified person to assist with critical medical staff organization functions, the value and status of MSSPs will increase. With the development of additional academic programs in medical staff services science, competent practitioners will be available to fill the numerous vacancies now evident from newspaper advertisements seeking qualified individuals.

NOTES

1. Cindy Orsund-Gassiot and Patricia J. Starr, *Principles of Medical Staff Services*, 2d ed., ed. National Association Medical Staff Services, Education Council (Chicago: National Association Medical Staff Services, 1987).
2. Sharon H. Wix, "Certification Council," *Overview* 12 (March-April 1985): 4.

The Medical Staff Services Department

Joyce Gardner, CMSC

As the role of the medical staff services professional has evolved, medical staff services departments (MSSDs) have been created in many hospitals. At a minimum, a medical staff office (MSO) will be found today in all but the smallest institutions. Medical staff services units range from one-person offices to departments of ten or more, but the required functions will remain the same across all organizational structures. Managing medical staff services may be the main duty of a part- or full-time position, it may be assigned to the incumbent by specific language in a job description, or it may be vaguely implied in an unwritten plan. This chapter will discuss the organization of the MSSD, including the various staff members and their responsibilities, staffing levels, and the relationship of the department to the medical staff and other hospital departments.

THE MEDICAL STAFF SERVICES DEPARTMENT

The MSSD or MSO should be placed near the top in the overall hospital organizational structure (see Figure 7-1). An MSSD will usually be a department that reports directly to administration at a high level. In the case of an MSO, the office is usually organized within the administrative department itself. In smaller hospitals, the MSO may be a part of the medical records department or the quality assurance department. In some larger organizations, there may be a separate administrative entity that encompasses utilization review, quality assurance, and medical staff services administration. As the competition for health care dollars increases and hospitals seek to cement relationships with their medical staffs, MSOs may become components of "professional services" units, which are responsible for physician practice support and marketing, among other functions.

In MSSDs with three or more employees, the responsibilities may encompass the areas of continuing medical education, graduate medical education, physician referral and marketing, and staffing and supervising the medical library. MSSDs in

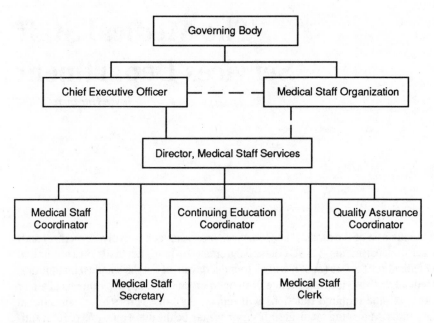

Figure 7-1 Placement of the Medical Staff Services Department within the Hospital Organization

some hospitals perform the functions of quality assurance, utilization review, and risk management as well as various other functions of the organized medical staff.

An MSSD requires a department director, whose title may be Director, Medical Staff Services; Administrative Director, Medical Staff Services; Administrator, Medical Staff Services; or some other appropriate title that clearly indicates the individual's role and responsibilities are administrative.

Role Descriptions

To carry out the assigned functions, an MSSD must have adequate personnel with various levels of experience, competence, and compensation. Each employee must have a position or job description that enables him or her to carry out assigned functions. The positions will generally fall into one of the following categories.

Medical Staff Services Director

This is the administrative position that has responsibility for supporting all activities of the medical staff organization. The director must act as a liaison between the medical staff, the administration, nursing, and the governing body. In addition, the director has responsibility for all aspects of management. The higher the position is on the administrative ladder, the greater the responsibilities. The director will require knowledge about such topics as accreditation standards, legal standards and procedures, medical terminology, state and federal regulations, and principles of management and supervision.

Medical Staff Coordinator

The medical staff coordinator is the senior person assigned to assist the director of medical staff services in carrying out his or her functions in the larger department. In smaller facilities, which often lack a medical staff services director, the coordinator may have the major responsibility for assisting the medical staff organization in carrying out its functions. The primary responsibilities include coordinating the functions of the medical staff and acting as a liaison between the medical staff, nursing, and administration. The medical staff coordinator will generally be responsible for credentialing; maintaining medical staff bylaws, rules, and regulations; and following up on policy matters that come through the medical staff committee and department structure.

Medical Staff Secretary

The medical staff secretary reports to the director in larger facilities and to the medical staff coordinator in smaller institutions. The secretary is responsible for preparing agendas for meetings of the staff and its committees, recording the minutes of the meetings, and preparing the minutes for distribution. He or she may use shorthand, longhand, speedwriting, or an electronic recording device for recording the minutes. The secretary also prepares correspondence on matters arising from discussion at medical staff meetings, assuring a continuous flow of information.

Medical Staff Office Clerk

The medical staff office clerk requires fewer skills than the coordinator or secretary. The clerk performs general office duties such as opening and routing mail, answering the telephone, preparing copies, filing, and typing routine correspondence.

Continuing Education Coordinator/Secretary

The continuing education coordinator (or secretary) has the responsibility to coordinate the activities of the continuing medical education program or committee. (In a university or teaching hospital setting, there may be more than one coordinator.) Duties include planning and promoting continuing education courses (based in part on the results of the hospital's quality assurance programs), reviewing program evaluations to assess their effectiveness, and providing overall assistance with the continuing education efforts of the hospital. The coordinator is also responsible for maintaining attendance records indicating the continuing medical education hours medical staff members have earned. The state licensing body may require physicians to submit evidence of continuing education before the state license to practice can be renewed. Therefore, physicians rely on timely, accurate records of participation in continuing education activities.

Graduate Education Coordinator/Secretary

The graduate education coordinator (or secretary) has administrative and clerical responsibilities for the graduate medical education programs. Duties include recruiting and retaining house staff, assisting with curriculum planning, preparing rotation schedules for the various services, and scheduling graduation programs. The graduate education coordinator may also have other responsibilities, such as assistance with visas and other immigration matters when foreign medical graduates enter the hospital's training programs.

Educational Requirements

Educational requirements for these positions vary. The director of medical staff services will most likely have a bachelor's degree and in some cases a master's. An associate degree in medical staff service management, business administration, or a related field is desirable for the medical staff coordinator position. A high school diploma is a prerequisite for most entry-level positions within the organization. A characteristic that is mandatory for all medical staff services positions is emotional stability. The ability to deal calmly in explosive situations is paramount for successful employment in an MSSD or MSO.

Staffing Levels

Health care reimbursement policies in effect since 1983 have increasingly pressured administrators to contain costs at all levels of the organization. Medical staff services is a non-revenue-producing department; that is, it produces no direct revenue for the institution and can be subject to budget cutbacks. Additionally, administrators frequently do not understand the extensive amount of work involved in adequately supporting the medical staff organization. One writer has noted

> In the tasks of supporting the appointment and reappointment process only, the number of full-time equivalent positions (FTE's) must be based on the size of the medical staff, regardless of the number of active staff.

Hospitals with medical staffs that include large numbers of courtesy or consultant staff must realize the extensive amount of staff work required to maintain current paperwork in each physician file and the effort expended in documenting current competence from other hospitals where these individuals practice. . . . Add to this function the responsibility for organizing meeting agendas, taking minutes, preparing follow-up items, and other activities associated with holding meetings, and FTE needs increase. The more committees, departmental meetings, and subsection meetings, the greater the number of staff required to support the functions adequately.[1]

Many MSSDs and MSOs are understaffed.

Organization

An MSSD or MSO may be organized in one of several ways. In the small hospital with a one-person MSO, the organization will be very simple: the individual will function as credentials coordinator, receptionist, secretary, and QA coordinator (in some hospitals) and will perform myriad related duties. In a large, complex MSSD, a formalized organizational structure needs to be in place to assure a consistently high level of performance.

Functional Organization

The MSSD may be organized functionally (i.e., according to the functions of the department). The medical staff services director performs specialized functions, and the director may organize the department according to other specialized functions. For example, a credentials coordinator may be assigned the specific function of credentialing. All matters relating to initial appointment, reappointment, and clinical privileges would be referred to the coordinator. Quality assurance likewise is a specialized function and might be assigned to a quality assurance coordinator (or nurse). Clerical support is more flexible and crosses functional lines between specialties. Functional organization of the MSSD is analogous to the organization of the departmentalized medical staff, which is structured according to function and includes the components of medicine, surgery, obstetrics/gynecology, pediatrics, and so on.

A word of caution concerning functional organization: When functions become so specialized that there is little overlap of responsibility for tasks, inefficiency can result. Unless the MSSD is very large, less definitive lines of responsibility are preferable.

Whether it is organized according to function or whether a few people share all the tasks, effective management will result in harmonious interactions between the

MSSD and the medical staff, other hospital departments, and outside agencies or individuals. The organizational chart and the job descriptions for MSSD personnel provide the framework for assigning responsibility, breadth of authority, and performance of tasks. However, they cannot ensure effective management, which can only result from attention to specific duties and responsibilities by individuals with well-honed organizational and management skills.

RELATIONSHIP OF THE MSSD TO ADMINISTRATION

The MSSD must establish and maintain open lines of communication between the administration and medical staff. Although this may at first seem relatively simple, we must examine where the MSSD is positioned.

The medical staff, which the MSSD serves, has little or no administrative authority within the hospital organization. The medical staff's power is derived from its ability to persuade the hospital's administration to make decisions on certain issues or matters affecting it. The administration of the hospital, on the other hand, has total control of the employment status of MSSD personnel (i.e., their compensation and personnel evaluations are in the hands of the administration). Although the loyalty of MSSD personnel may be to the medical staff organization, the department must maintain rapport with the administration of the hospital to protect professional integrity.

Conflict between the MSSD and the administration may be unavoidable. When conflict occurs, assessment, discussion, and resolution should be handled in a mature, professional manner. Administrators feel pressure from many sources: federal and state government, third-party payers, consumers, trustees, and business. They, in turn, may pressure the MSSD to expedite medical staff appointments and to minimize quality issues. The MSSD often is placed on a tightrope. On the one hand, it must assist the medical staff in maintaining quality patient care. On the other hand, it must assist the administration in maintaining financial viability. The loyalty of MSSD employees may occasionally be divided between the medical staff and administration. The department may be required to demonstrate loyalty to the hospital while maintaining the confidence and respect of the medical staff. In some extreme situations, the loyalty issue might leave MSSD employees hopelessly torn, in which case resignation may be the best solution. MSSD personnel should be prepared to face this eventuality.

RELATIONSHIP OF THE MSSD TO THE MEDICAL STAFF

The relationship of the medical staff to the medical staff office personnel and the medical staff services director is highly complex. The medical staff organization is dynamic, political, changing, and powerful. Through its officers, the medical staff is self-governing; however, its self-governance is voluntary and frequently unstable over time. Many hospitals have an elected chief of staff *and* a nonelected medical director. The two positions are distinguished by constituency and perceived base of power.

The Chief of Staff

The chief of staff is elected by his or her peers to represent the staff to the hospital administration, the governing body, and the community. The chief of staff may be perceived as a "good old boy," that is, perceived by the staff to be "one of them" in the staff's struggle with the administration over reduction of costs at the risk of quality patient care and adherence to regulations promulgated by outside agencies (e.g., the Joint Commission and state agencies such as professional review organizations).

The chief of staff is often a private practicing physician with a patient base that is dependent on referrals from others (if he or she is a specialist) or a network of specialists to whom he or she refers patients. While maintaining a private practice, the chief of staff (whose term of office is generally limited to one or two years) will not be eager to alienate those members of the staff upon whom his livelihood may depend. The chief of staff's power base is the medical staff who elected him or her as their representative.

The Medical Director

A medical director, unlike a chief of staff, who is elected, is employed by the hospital to administer the affairs of the medical staff. A medical director may be hired when the hospital has met constant and successful resistance from the medical staff in implementing necessary administrative changes to comply with outside regulations.

The medical director may be an "outsider," that is, a physician who has not practiced in the community and is not attuned to the political or economic needs of the community's physicians. The medical director sees his or her role as essentially administrative, and the medical directorship is less collegial in nature than the chief of staff position. In addition to medical staff administrative functions, quality assurance, utilization review, and risk management, the medical director may have administrative responsibility for graduate and continuing education programs. The medical director's power base is very often the governing body and, at a minimum, the hospital administration.

If the elected chief of staff and the hired medical director do not form an alliance, the MSSD will be caught in the middle. Resolution of the problems arising from divided loyalty will be an intense challenge, requiring the MSSD personnel to demonstrate political astuteness, diplomacy, and the ability to work collaboratively with both of these two centers of power.

On the other hand, the MSSD will develop relationships with members of the medical staff that will be very rewarding. The MSSD exists as a resource for physicians, and they learn to rely on the knowledge and expertise of MSSD personnel to assist them in all areas of practice. If, for example, they need an article from the library on a specific subject, they may go not to the library but to the MSSD. The role of counselor, advisor, and advocate is familiar to the successful MSSD, because it has learned to walk the extra mile to assist members of the medical staff.

RELATIONSHIP OF THE MSSD TO OTHER HOSPITAL DEPARTMENTS

The MSSD does not exist in a vacuum, separate and apart from other hospital departments. The MSSD will interact and interface with all other departments throughout the institution, and MSSD personnel will need to establish rapport and maintain communication with them. As physicians learn to bring their complaints and frustrations to the MSSD, the department's personnel must have a firm understanding of the relationship of the MSSD to other departments. Examples of departments and types of interaction are described below.

Nursing

Nursing employees are not always totally familiar with medical staff standards, regulations or policies. Thus, questions regarding physicians' roles and responsibilities may be directed from nursing to the MSSD. For example, if a nurse wonders whether a particular physician has the right credentials to perform a procedure on a patient care unit, he or she will direct the question to the MSSD. Nurses learn to depend upon the knowledge and advice of the MSSD in many such situations.

Nursing supervisors are trained to follow a chain of command to resolve patient care issues. The chain of command will include the MSSD (see Figure 7-2).

Medical Records

Some physicians are notoriously bad about timely completion of medical records. Hospital policies address situations in which physicians are delinquent in completing medical records. The names of these physicians appear on a delinquent chart or off-staff list. In cases of delinquency, a physician's admitting, consultation, or surgical privileges are suspended until the records are completed. The MSSD

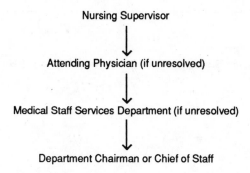

Figure 7-2 Chain of Command To Resolve Patient Care Issue

may be assigned responsibility for enforcing the off-staff list and may also be authorized by the medical staff and the administration to restore a physician's privileges when the records are complete and up to date.

Physicians sometimes complain that medical records department personnel harass or discriminate against them. The MSSD must maintain effective communication with both the medical records department and the aberrant physicians in order to accomplish the institution's goal of timely completion of medical records. The MSSD must also be skillful at calming the medical staff members who feel harassed.

The MSSD also frequently interacts with the medical records department in conjunction with the medical staff's quality assurance program. Since this program is based upon review of medical records, these records are frequently checked out of the medical records department and brought to meetings for discussion. The MSSD will also depend on medical records to provide statistics and other information in order to complete medical staff reappointments, staff evaluations, and other functions of the medical staff organization.

Admitting or Patient Registration

The admitting or patient registration department looks to the MSSD to provide timely information regarding members of the medical staff. Only practitioners who have been granted privileges may admit and treat patients in the hospital. The MSSD is the recognized source of this information. Therefore, communication between the MSSD and the admitting department must be frequent and effective.

Interactions between the MSSD and the other hospital departments occur frequently. The above serve only as examples of the types of daily cooperation to be expected.

NOTE

1. Julie L. Hopkins, ed., "Staffing up to Par!" *QRC Advisor* 5 (February 1989): 1–2.

Part III

Medical Staff Roles

"And one man in his time plays many parts,"

Shakespeare, *As You Like It*

Chapter 8

The Credentials Process

F.C. Dimond, Jr., MD

The credentials process includes the initial medical staff appointment, the delineation of clinical privileges, and the periodic reappraisal and reappointment of medical staff members.

WHY CREDENTIAL?

The main purpose of the credentials process is to ensure that any individual who wishes to provide patient care services within a hospital or other health care facility is qualified and competent to do so. Put simply, if an individual always performed only what he or she was qualified to do and did it well, there would be no need for a credentialing process. In the real world, however, this process is critical, with the burden on the medical staff and governing body to ensure a careful matching of credentials to privilege delineation and any associated staff membership.

Doubters of the merit of the process have but to review any number of significant court cases noting the impact on physicians and hospitals. A sampling of these cases follows.[1]

- *Darling v. Charleston Community Memorial Hospital*, 33 Ill.2d 325, 211 N.E.2d 253 (1965). The hospital was required to pay damages when a patient's leg had to be amputated due to complications following treatment for a fracture of the leg. The physician, a noncontractual member of the medical staff, was a general practitioner who had not treated a major leg fracture for three years. The physician settled the suit against him. The court found that the hospital's duty extended to assuring proper treatment and that the hospital was negligent in not having reviewed the physician's work and not having required consultation.
- *Purcell v. Zimbelman*, Court of Appeals of Arizona; 500 P. 2d 335 (1972). This case involved postoperative injuries, including loss of sexual function, loss of

a kidney, a permanent colostomy, and urinary problems. During an exploratory operation, an incorrect diagnosis of cancer was made rather than the correct diagnosis of diverticulitis, and a "pull-through" procedure was done. Inasmuch as the "lesion" was above the peritoneal reflection, a pull-through wasn't indicated, even for cancer. The physician had twice before done the same procedure unnecessarily, and in both cases a malpractice suit was filed against him and the hospital. There were also two other suits against the physician for alleged injuries from other surgical procedures. All four malpractice actions occurred prior to the operation on Zimbelman. The court found that the hospital failed in its duty to the patient and that the hospital must assume responsibility for the care of its patients and for supervising the competence of its staff doctors.

- *Gonzales v. Nork and Mercy Hospital,* No. 228566, Superior Court of California, Sacramento County, B. Abbot Goldberg, Judge (November 19, 1973). The patient incurred unexpected injuries from a laminectomy performed by an independent practitioner of the medical staff with orthopedic privileges. There was evidence that other patients had been similarly injured by the physician. The hospital first became aware of the physician's substandard practice when his malpractice insurer canceled his policy as a result of malpractice claims and losses relating to his performance of laminectomies. The court found that the hospital has a duty to protect its patients from malpractice by members of its medical staff, that its duty is to acquire essential knowledge (i.e., when it knows or should have known that malpractice was likely to be committed). Mercy Hospital was found to have no system for acquiring such knowledge. Another finding in the evolution of this case was the marked inconsistency between the physician's progress notes and the nursing notes.

- *Johnson v. Misericordia Community Hospital;* 301 NW 2d 156 (Wisc 1980). The hospital was held liable to a patient on whom surgery was negligently performed by an incompetent, newly admitted medical staff member. The court declared that the medical staff was "an arm of the hospital" and that a reasonable inquiry during the "credentialing" process would have disclosed the surgeon's deficiencies and lack of training. Thus, the court held the hospital independently liable on a theory of negligent peer review.

- *Elam v. College Park Hospital,* 132 Cal. App.3d 332 (CA 4th Cir, May 27, 1982). A patient was injured as a result of surgery performed by a podiatrist. Prior to the surgery that gave rise to this lawsuit, the hospital became aware of a malpractice case filed against the podiatrist. The court held that the hospital was thereby put on notice and had a duty to investigate the podiatrist's competence. Having failed to investigate, the hospital breached that duty and was held liable for the consequences of the podiatrist's negligence. The court announced a general rule that a hospital owes a direct duty to the patient to review carefully the competence of applicants and members before allowing them to become or remain members of the medical staff. The podiatrist was an independent contractor and not a contracted agent of the hospital.

GRAY AREAS

The credentials process applies to all individuals seeking clinical privileges, whether or not they are applicants for medical staff membership, applicants for clinical privileges without medical staff membership, or independent or contractual practitioners. Each step of the credentials process and its specific requirements must be spelled out in the medical staff bylaws or in a policy approved by the medical staff and followed. Gray areas that occasionally cloud the credentials system include the following:

- Administrative bypassing of the medical staff credentials process in the case of contract physicians or other practitioners who are hired through a hospital contract (e.g., contract emergency department physicians).
- Granting temporary privileges to nonapplicant physicians or other practitioners based only on a license check and the verbal approval of a chief of staff, department chief, or administrator, none of whom may even know the individuals. Although inadequate scrutiny may occur in the case of any specialty or physician, it is most common in the case of emergency department physicians. Such physicians are often members of a large group contracted to provide emergency department services to the hospital, and sometimes they have not been individually credentialed by the hospital but show up 15 minutes before their shift in the emergency room requesting temporary privileges.
- The dangerous tendency to grant privileges to the new applicant physician in town (because he or she has opened an office and needs to "start making a living") even though the hospital is still gathering information on qualifications and competence.
- Granting privileges to the foreign medical graduate from a remote country who indicates that his or her medical school has been closed down for many years and needed records are unavailable or that his or her training hospital or training program has suffered a similar fate.

The medical staff bylaws must define the credentialing process. None of the above situations can pose problems or become realities if the medical staff bylaws are written properly and followed. The administrator of the facility cannot bypass the credentials process because the bylaws require the same assessment for all staff members, contractual or independent, and the bylaws are supported through governing body approval. The bylaws should be very specific in requiring basic credentials information from nonapplicants who may receive temporary privileges (which should be strictly limited to begin with), and the bylaws should be enforced (except in the rare case of a life-saving situation).

An applicant for staff membership should be given temporary privileges only after all required information is in and processed and the application is awaiting anticipated governing body approval. As with all medical staff applications, the burden of proof for credentials lies with the applicant. Thus, for example, the foreign medical graduate must prove his or her status when school or training records are unavailable. In the case of the latter, it's a local choice, but some hospitals accept, in lieu of missing records, evidence of licensure following completion of a required examination and a review of a specified number of cases. If such evidence is accepted, a serious proctoring program should be undertaken (and of course this alternative route should be supported in the medical staff bylaws).

THE PRE-APPLICATION PROCESS

Many hospitals across the country have adopted a pre-application process in which a candidate for medical staff membership is sent a list of the hospital's membership criteria that has been approved by the governing body. If the candidate does not meet these criteria, an application form is not sent. This saves time in processing applications, for it screens out candidates obviously not qualified for staff membership (e.g., candidates lacking the required amount of professional liability insurance coverage and not intending to obtain it).

Criteria for Membership

The requirements for medical staff membership and privileges are stated in the medical staff bylaws. They usually include

- type of practitioner (e.g., physician, dentist, podiatrist)
- appropriate professional licensure
- appropriate educational and/or training credentials
- practice in one of the clinical services provided for the community by the hospital or into which the hospital is expanding
- professional liability insurance coverage in the amount required by the governing body

Occasionally medical staff bylaws require the applicant to agree to reside and maintain an office within a stated distance from the facility and with no fixed potential intervening traffic barriers, such as a bridge. This requirement is made to ensure the practitioner's availability to care for patients in a timely manner, including emergencies. However, the distances or described boundaries have sometimes been drawn or changed to reduce or eliminate competition. Hence, when setting up such a requirement, the hospital should seek legal counsel.

More and more frequently, the medical staff asks about specialty board certification as a criterion for medical staff membership. Although there is only limited court support for this, requiring certification is both reasonable and desirable. However, it probably is not acceptable to most medical staffs at this time.

The two main requirements are very clear. First, the requirement for board certification must be clearly related to quality of care. Otherwise it may be construed by some as an attempt to freeze out competition for patients. Second, the requirement must be consistent with state law, determination of which may require a legal opinion.

Other considerations related to board certification as a medical staff membership requirement include the following:

- The requirement must start on the date the governing body approves the medical staff bylaws change. At the same time, the decision must be made as to whether all non-board-certified staff members are to be automatically "grandfathered" in.
- If the "grandfathering" occurs, is it to be permanent or is there to be a reasonable period during which these individuals must become board certified?
- How will a specialty board requirement for periodic recertification be factored in?
- If there is a practice requirement between the completion of a physician's formal training and when he or she can sit for the board exams, would this prevent the facility taking in a highly qualified physician pending his or her taking the exams? And if the physician does not become certified, will he or she have to leave the staff?
- To help ensure the same level (standard) of certification, would physicians have to be certified only by boards approved by the American Board of Medical Specialties? Would another board certification system for physicians be considered?
- What would be the certification system used for all the different categories of nonphysician medical staff applicants or members?
- Although it rarely happens, a physician can be granted clinical privileges without medical staff membership. If this happened, the noncertified physician who had only privileges could practice in the hospital at the same level as a certified physician (thus seemingly negating the professed quality relation

of certification and staff membership), and furthermore the noncertified physician would not have to assume any medical staff responsibilities. However, based on current Joint Commission on Accreditation of Healthcare Organizations (Joint Commission) requirements, the nonstaff physician could not admit patients on his or her own in Joint Commission–accredited hospitals. Otherwise, the Joint Commission merely states that "specialty board certification is an excellent benchmark for the delineation of clinical privileges."[2]

- Although some hospitals may like to advertise the number of board-certified specialists on staff, this must be done carefully in order not to suggest guaranteeing a higher standard of care than other neighboring facilities. If this is interpreted by patients as a guarantee of better care, they may be more prone to sue when their higher expectations are not met.
- A physician is granted clinical privileges based on education, training, experience, and demonstrated competence. It could be difficult to relate board certification *only* to privilege delineation.

APPLICATION FOR MEMBERSHIP AND PRIVILEGES

Application Form

The first serious dialogue between the applicant and the medical staff and governing board complex is the filing of a completed, signed medical staff application form (with any required attachments). The form requests all routine background and current information and, in addition, poses some critical questions. Routine information includes the following:

- Full name of applicant, date and location of birth, current home and office address and telephone numbers, date of application, professional (practice) affiliation.
- Undergraduate education: name and location of school, dates attended, and degree received.
- Postgraduate education: name and location of school, dates attended, and degree received.
- Residency (includes internship if not a recent trainee) or fellowship: hospital, location, dates of training, specialty.
- All previous and current hospital and other health care affiliations: names, locations, dates.
- Membership in professional associations, societies, academies, colleges, and faculty or training appointments.

- Specialty board certification status: name of board, date of board certificate. If not certified, whether or not applicant is a current candidate for examination should be indicated. Terms such as *board qualified* or *board eligible* should not be used on the application form, which should be stated on the form so that these terms are not written in. The candidate should be asked to supply a letter from the board confirming his or her candidacy status, and the specialty board itself should be contacted directly by the medical staff services office.
- All state licenses, with the expiration date of each.
- The federal Drug Enforcement Administration (DEA) registration certificate number and the date of expiration should be listed. Similarly any state narcotics certificate number and expiration date should be indicated when the state has such a requirement. (A hard copy of the certificates should be required.)
- At least three professional references who have personal knowledge of the applicant's *recent* professional performance and experience. Peers who have not personally observed the clinical work of the applicant, as well as relatives and business associates, are not acceptable.
- All previous practice information: solo practice, partnerships, locations, dates.
- List of continuing medical education for the past two years.
- Professional liability coverage: carrier, amounts, dates of coverage.
- Past and present professional litigation and liability history, including any open cases.
- Staff categories: list of categories per medical staff bylaws.
- Clinical privileges requested. This information will be contained in privilege request form appended to the application and consistent with the specialty in which the applicant proposes to practice.
- Optional items
  —Publications and major speeches, with subjects, locations, dates.
  —A small recent photo (attached in the designated place on the application). The bylaws or the letter to the applicant should state that the photo will help identify the applicant at the time of any required interview or confirm identification by training or education program personnel requested to comment on the applicant. The photo is an excellent requirement but must be used properly.
  —A list of a specified number of patients treated or procedures performed and any related records.
  —Any required fee for processing the application and whether or not it is applied toward annual medical staff dues for successful staff applicants.

Critical Questions for the Applicant

The following are critical questions that must be included in the application for the purpose of detecting previous professional problems:[3]

1. Have you even been requested to appear before any licensing or regulatory agency (e.g., the State Board of Medical Examiners, the Drug Enforcement Administration, the Professional Review Organization (PRO), or the Inspector General) for a hearing or complaint of any nature?
2. Has any professional license of yours ever been denied (on application), suspended, revoked, limited, or otherwise acted against?
3. Have you ever been denied (on application) or surrendered a narcotics tax stamp?
4. Has any professional license of yours ever been denied (on application), suspended, revoked, or limited?
5. Has your DEA registration ever been denied (on application), suspended, revoked, or limited?
6. Have your clinical privileges (including admitting, consulting, and assisting) or staff membership at any health care facility ever been denied, suspended, limited, revoked, not renewed, or otherwise acted against?
7. Have you ever been denied membership or renewal thereof, had your membership revoked or otherwise acted against, or been subject to disciplinary action by any medical or professional organization or by any licensing agency of any state, district, territorial possession, or country?
8. Have you ever been convicted of a felony or misdemeanor (other than minor traffic offenses)?
9. Has any liability insurance carrier canceled, refused coverage, or increased rates because of unusual risk?
10. Are any actions pending with respect to items 1–9 above?
11. Have any judgments been made against or settlements been obtained from you in professional liability cases?
12. Are any professional liability cases pending against you?
13. Have you ever been under treatment for drug addiction or alcoholism? (If so, list any rehabilitation programs, with dates.)
14. Have you ever received psychiatric treatment or care? (If so, list any treatment programs, with dates.)
15. Are you currently under care for a continuing health problem?
16. Have you ever discontinued practice for any reason (other than for a routine vacation or formal education or training) for one month or more?

If any of the answers to the questions above are yes, the applicant should be asked to furnish details.

A health status question such as the following should also be included:

> Do you feel that your health status is adequate enough to permit you to provide the patient care services for which you are requesting clinical privileges? Yes___ No ___

If the answer is no, the applicant should be asked to furnish details. The applicant could also be asked to enclose a copy of his or her most recent comprehensive physical examination report or include authorization for release by the examining physician.

The application usually includes an "Immunity from Liability" section as well as a series of pledges by the applicant to:

1. adhere to generally recognized standards of professional ethics of his/her profession;
2. not participate in fee-splitting or "ghost" surgical or medical care;
3. participate, as required, in peer evaluation activities;
4. provide continuous care for his/her patients and delegate the responsibility for diagnosis or care of patients only to a practitioner who is qualified to undertake that responsibility;
5. obtain appropriate informed consent as required for the intervention contemplated;
6. abide by the medical staff bylaws, rules and regulations and hospital policies affecting the medical staff;
7. complete adequately, and in a timely fashion, the medical and any other required records for all patients he/she admits or in any way provides care for in the hospital;
8. seek consultation whenever necessary;
9. maintain the required amount of professional liability insurance coverage;
10. reasonably assist the hospital in fulfilling its uncompensated or partially compensated patient care obligations within the areas of his/her professional competence and credentials; and,
11. reasonably cooperate with the hospital in its efforts to comply with accreditation, reimbursement, and legal or other regulatory requirements.[4]

The application should conclude by indicating that one or more interviews may be required and asking if the applicant would be willing to be interviewed at the hospital if requested. The applicant should sign the form. Somewhere on the application form, perhaps below the signature area, should be a highlighted note to the effect that failure to complete any part of the form or the inclusion of false information will delay the application processing and may render the applicant ineligible for staff membership. The bylaws should support this.

A copy of the current medical staff bylaws, rules, and regulations and a *relevant* privilege request form should accompany the application form for staff membership.

PROCESSING THE APPLICATION

Once the application form is received and the applicant is seriously pursuing staff membership, a new applicant processing checklist should be started, which permits the medical staff services professional to know at a glance what information is already provided and what is missing (Exhibit 8-1). This page will usually be located on the backside of the front cover of a multipart credentials file folder (it should have at least six sections) and is used to track the status of the application by item, date requested, and date received, along with any follow-up dates.

The processing checklist automatically includes and focuses on application items that require written *source* verification. These include state licenses, postgraduate

---

Exhibit 8-1   Checklist for Review of Medical Staff Applicant Information Status

Information requiring favorable *source verification* before granting membership and privileges:

- Current professional licensure
- Postgraduate degree
- Successful completion of residency program
- Successful completion of fellowship program, as applicable
- Specialty bond status: _____ certification, _____ candidate
- Professional liability insurance coverage
- Other hospital or health care facility status
- Professional references (3)
- National practitioner data bank

Other required information provided by applicant or through other sources:

- Malpractice claims history, open and closed
- Disciplinary actions through: _____ licensure board, _____ professional society, _____ specialty board, _____ other hospitals, _____ health-related status, _____ PRO
- Submission of case records for medical review (optional with hospital)
- Executive Committee interview of applicant (optional with hospital)

degrees (medical, dental, etc.), residency and fellowship training, specialty board status (to verify any statement made by the applicant as to certification or candidacy for examination), professional liability insurance coverage, and other hospital affiliations. The references provided by the applicant should be sent a letter asking specific questions about the applicant's qualifications.

Red Flags

Some points need to be specifically considered in reviewing the completed application form and in relation to source verification. Look for "red-flag" items:

1. Any incomplete item that is pertinent to the application requires a letter telling the applicant that the application is on hold. This is particularly true in the case of the critical questions section, particularly with regard to liability and health issues. Telephone calls to the applicant usually are not productive, and there is no hard copy record of the information exchange. If a second letter is needed, it should be sent by certified mail to document arrival and ensure a signed receipt. The second letter should also indicate a final date by which the information must be received if the application is not to be placed in the dead file.

2. When the application reveals an unexplained time gap in the training and practice sequence since completing postgraduate education (e.g., medical school), this gap requires serious attention. The applicant must explain why there was a long period of inactivity or the application cannot be processed.

3. Any indication of a voluntary or involuntary loss of one or more privileges at another hospital or a restriction or loss of a license or DEA registration certificate, past or present, is another red flag that requires clarification before further processing of the application. If both the other facility or agency and the applicant refuse to cooperate in providing the needed information, then the application should go into the dead file and the practitioner be so notified. The medical staff bylaws should define what constitutes a completed application and also include language specifying that unresolved questions about an applicant make an application incomplete.

4. Since it takes time to build a practice, frequent changes in location in a short span of time requires investigation of the applicant. Practitioners may have a sound reason for moving from one state to another. On the other hand, a move may be related to problems with the state licensing agency, litigation problems, felony convictions, or health problems, none of which were mentioned on the application form. The health problems may relate to an impaired physician status that has not been resolved.

5. The practitioner who has a number of lawsuits pending or settled requires additional investigation. Professional liability claims are not necessarily an indication of a problem, but extra checking should be undertaken to determine that a pattern of substandard practice was not the cause. Obtaining source information on the applicant's professional liability coverage may require the applicant's written permission unless the bylaws or the application form or the cover letters accompanying it provide otherwise. The insurer, however, can still insist on written permission to release the information.

6. The practitioner previously impaired by alcohol or drug abuse may apply for membership and privileges. Documentation of rehabilitation and a period of monitoring help to verify recovery and provide evidence that the problem has been corrected (see Chapter 12).

Telephone Calls Concerning Applicants

Occasionally insight about the above problems can be gained through an administrator-to-administrator (or physician-to-physician) phone call, but unless a dated memo of the conversation is made, there will be no hard information on which to help base a decision. When phone calls are made to discuss an application problem or a negative reference letter, specific questions should be asked of the physician or administrator contacted. Included might be questions about the receipt of reports of poor medical practice; poor relationships with peers or hospital staff members that have been detrimental to patient care or hospital operations; and mental or physical illness or substance abuse problems that have interfered with the ability to practice quality medicine. Names of other informants who might be contacted can be obtained at the time the phone calls are made to previous hospitals and peer references.

Verifying Information on the Application

In seeking information from other hospitals, training programs, and peer references, it is important that needed information be requested correctly. The best chance of obtaining the needed information is through use of a form that requires a minimum of writing on the respondent's part (Exhibit 8-2). When developing a form keep these points in mind:

1. When indicating that the individual is applying for procedural privileges, include a list of the specific procedures requested by the applicant and ask if he or she has performed them and how satisfactorily. It is not at all

Exhibit 8-2 Checklist for Information To Request in Reference Letters

1. Nature of relationship to the applicant.
2. How long the respondent has known the applicant.
3. Whether the respondent has direct knowledge of the quality of medicine practiced by the applicant.
4. Whether the applicant's privileges have ever been denied, suspended, reduced, revoked, or terminated.
5. Whether the applicant has been the subject of any disciplinary action by a licensing board, hospital, professional society, and so on.
6. Whether the applicant has exercised the privileges requested and how satisfactorily and whether the applicant is still qualified to exercise them (referring the respondent to a copy of the privilege request form).
7. Knowledge of any health problem that would interfere with the applicant's ability to exercise the privileges requested.
8. Whether the respondent has any reservation about recommending the applicant for appointment and about granting privileges requested (if so, the respondent should explain why).

Rating based on applicant's demonstrated performance compared with that reasonably expected of a practitioner with the same level of training, experience, and background.

	Poor	*Fair*	*Good*	*Superior*	*No Knowledge*
Basic medical knowledge					
Professional judgment					
Sense of responsibility					
Ethical conduct					
Competence and skill					
Ability to work and cooperate with others					
Recordkeeping					
Physician-patient relationship					
Ability to understand and speak English					

uncommon, especially in the case of training program graduates, to learn that certain procedures for which privileges are being requested were never performed by the individual in the program or else that the necessary training was not provided in the program.

2. Inquire about the individual's health status to determine if there is a known health problem that might prevent the applicant from exercising the privileges being requested.

3. Ask if the applicant has the ability to work with other members of the health care and hospital team. As with other items on the form, a simple grading of

three or more levels of performance can be provided in order to make it easier for the respondent.

Additional Sources of Information on Applicants

Other potential sources of information on physician applicants that should be used include the Federation of State Medical Boards (which is a data bank containing disciplinary action information as reported by all of the state boards of medical examiners and other sources) and the National Practitioner Data Bank. This latter data bank should eventually contain a wealth of information, especially information concerning licensure and inadequate performance. For completeness of information sources, the American Medical Association's Physician Masterfile should be obtained for physician applicants.

Because the DEA registration expiration date cannot be verified through origination source verification, it is recommended that the medical staff applicant's (or member's) registration certificate be copied by the medical staff services office personnel. This usually is not a problem in the case of a small staff or a single-hospital region, but it can be somewhat impractical when there are several hundred staff members or when many of the staff members (e.g., consultants) rarely come to the hospital. In these situations, a timely copy will have to be submitted by the practitioners to the medical staff services office.

The Credentials File

Once the application has been received and processing starts, a multipart credentials file should be instituted. How it is set up is a matter of individual choice. However, some basic advice may help to make the use of the file more efficient. Place in one section all one-time items, such as the application form, the letters of reference, and so on. In another section, include recurring date-related documents that need to be immediately accessible, such as state licenses, the DEA registration certificate, and professional liability coverage documents. For these items, there is usually a tickler file in the computer for renewal purposes, but a hard copy is still required for the file. In another section, place staff reappointment and reprivileging information. A separate section of the file must be reserved for peer review findings (both good and bad) and related actions. Separating out the peer review findings simplifies the review process for the credentials committee and other committees and individuals, such as a department chief who has to review the file at the time of reappointment. It is important to incorporate the ultimately favorable review findings in the case of a physician who does not make it through the quality assurance screening process, because it shows that the system is fair and verifies that the physician's performance was evaluated. The individual folder section tabs should be labeled for quick reference.

DELINEATION OF CLINICAL PRIVILEGES

Privilege delineation, properly performed and monitored, continues to be the most important function performed by the medical staff and governing body. If each medical staff member had clinical privileges based precisely on training, experience, and proven clinical competence, and if each member performed properly only those procedures allowed by his or her privileges, there probably would be little need for the extensive quality assurance programs in place today. Individual privilege delineation protects the patient, the medical staff, and the facility. It helps ensure higher quality and lower risk and thus contributes to lower costs.

Privilege delineation is basically performed in three ways: (1) using a laundry list approach, (2) using a category approach, or (3) using a combination of these. Within a staff, departmentalized or not, a combination of the laundry list and category approaches may be used depending on the desires of certain departments or specialist groups. In general, surgical specialists are more apt to favor the laundry list approach and nonsurgical groups the category approach. In either case (surgical or nonsurgical group), the non-specialty-specific procedural privilege approach, which crosses multiple specialties, is strongly recommended (see below).

When the category approach to clinical privilege delineation is used, care must be taken to ensure that the privileges are actually delineated in a way that makes the limits of practice very clear. Some specialty organizations have published sample categories, but when read carefully it is obvious that within each category level the physician actually delineates what his or her practice will be.

Although determination of staff membership and the delineation of clinical privileges are two separate processes, they are interrelated and simultaneously culminate in a governing board decision. Probably the only exceptions are when a staff member requests a change in privileges following satisfactory completion of required training or when a staff member involuntarily suffers a reduction in privileges. However, neither of these exceptions concerns staff applicants.

The credentials file should not be cluttered with excessive privilege delineation forms. This most frequently happens with two types of laundry privilege lists: the bound booklet type and the loose-leaf multipage type. In both cases, the entire set of forms is sent to each staff applicant for completion on the assumption that some practitioners will request procedures in more than one specialty area. In both cases, the credentials files bulge with many unused pages of privilege delineation forms. There are at least three ways to prevent this situation:

1. Only the specialty privileges ordinarily associated with the applicant's type of practice should be provided. Sufficient blank spaces or lines should be available for the applicant to list other privilege requests.

2. In addition to the specialty-specific privileges listed (either by category or laundry list), there should be a supplemental procedure list that covers all procedures that are not absolutely peculiar to one type of practice. This list should be given to all applicants and to all staff members at the time of reappointment. This system offers multiple advantages in that it indicates who is doing what procedures in the hospital; helps identify procedures that need evaluation or practitioners who need monitoring; identifies procedures for which no standards of care have been set; and, best of all, only requires revision of one form when some procedural privilege has to be deleted from or added to the list. It is not uncommon to find physicians performing procedures (e.g., endoscopy) that they have been performing in the hospital for years without having ever been granted privileges to do so. Granting the privileges closes a risk gap.

3. The privilege lists sent out to applicants or used for reappointees should be limited to hospital-specific privileges. For example, privileges for obstetrics, radiation therapy, or cardiac surgery should not be listed if these services are not offered by the hospital.

Other concerns regarding privilege delineation forms include the following:

- For each privilege, the applicant or reappointee must clearly indicate whether the privilege is or is not being requested. This is a further reason for not sending out the bulky forms described in the previous section. Blanks are dangerous because it can't be determined if the physician has requested a certain privilege or procedure and, if so, whether the privilege or procedure has been approved.
- Reviewing, recommending, or approving groups must indicate whether the requested privileges are individually recommended or approved. Again, blanks are dangerous and challenge the credibility of the process.
- It must be made clear whether an assistant or a consultation is required for any particular privilege. The better forms add columns for checking these requirements when needed.
- All required individuals (e.g., the chairpersons of the credentials committee, department, and executive committee and the governing board representative) must sign the document approving or disapproving the privileges.

In addition to its thorough check of medical staff credentials files, the Joint Commission currently checks credentials files for two specific items related to standards requirements, which probably is the only reason to have the items in these credentials files. First, it must be indicated whether a practitioner has admitting privileges. Probably the only physicians who won't have admitting privileges are certain hospital-based specialists. Some nonphysician staff members, however, may have co-admitting privileges. Work the admitting privilege into the reprivileging as innocuously as possible to meet the Joint Commission standards at the time of the next reappointment.

Second, there must be peer input when any nonphysician is applying for clinical privileges or appointment or reappointment to the staff. The peer input requirement for initial staff appointment and privileging is usually satisfied through the professional references. For reappointment and reprivileging, the easiest way to comply is to have one or more peers sit with the credentials committee (but not necessarily as members) and provide input. The committee minutes must show that the peer input was considered in deciding on the committee's final recommendations. When there is no peer on the staff, it may be necessary to have an outside noncompetitive peer consultant review a number of cases and make recommendations to the credentials committee either in person or (preferably) in writing. The Joint Commission surveyors have not accepted these requirements only in the medical staff bylaws as satisfying the intent of the standards.

PROVISIONAL STATUS

The provisional period is usually defined by the medical staff bylaws as the first 12 months of staff membership. Some medical staffs have formalized this period by establishing a "provisional staff" category. The provisional period is necessary because the applicant has been accepted for staff membership and has been granted specific privileges based on paper credentials. The period of observation is needed to confirm (or discomfirm) that the decision was justified. From a fairness standpoint, it is necessary that the *initial* provisional period be the same for all newly appointed staff members. The bylaws must, however, provide for an extension of the period in two cases: (1) the provisional member has not used the hospital enough during the initial period to permit a review of performance, or (2) the member's performance is questionable and additional review is needed prior to rendering a final decision.

Although the initial provisional period is the same length for all new staff members, the number of cases or procedures to be proctored during the period may vary depending on the individual's previous experience and the opinion of the proctors. The word *proctoring* sometimes bothers the medical staff, and other terms may be used, such as *observing, monitoring, sponsoring,* and so on. Whatever it's called, several rules apply and the whole process itself should be spelled out in the medical staff bylaws (this is preferable) or in a policy approved by the executive committee of the medical staff.

To begin with, the bylaws or policy should delineate how the proctors are to be selected (the selection is ordinarily done by the department chairperson in a departmentalized medical staff and by the chief of staff in a nondepartmentalized staff). Among the rules should be the following:

- The proctor must not be a relative or a practice partner or associate of the practitioner being proctored.
- Proctoring shall include both *direct* observation and review of the related records for both nonsurgical and surgical types of practice.
- Proctoring will include the most sophisticated type of procedure to be done. For instance, performing varicose vein surgery, varicocelectomies, and hemorrhoidectomies does not equate with surgery for aortic aneurysm or femoropopliteal bypass surgery when proctoring a physician granted vascular surgery privileges. Similarly, an inguinal hernioplasty and appendectomy do not equate with surgery of the common bile duct for general surgery proctoring purposes.
- A written report should be submitted promptly for each case or procedure proctored (Exhibit 8-3). The report form should not require a lot of writing and should be easy to complete. Reports should be placed in the appropriate credentials file after review by the department chief.
- Reports should be reviewed in an ongoing manner rather than waiting until the end of the provisional period. This is to assure that any patient care performance problem is detected as soon as possible. When a problem is detected, the

---

Exhibit 8-3 Checklist for Information To Include in a Proctoring Report Based on Direct Observation and Record Review

1. Whether or not admission of the patient was justified.
2. If an invasive procedure done, whether or not it was indicated.
3. If an invasive procedure done, whether or not an appropriate technique was used.
4. If an invasive procedure done, whether or not there were complications.
5. Whether or not use of ancillary services (lab, X-ray, etc.) was appropriate and indicated.
6. Whether or not drug use was appropriate and indicated.
7. Whether or not the medical record was completed in timely manner.
8. Whether or not the medical record appropriately reflects the patient's progress while hospitalized.
9. If consultation was indicated, whether or not it was requested and available in a timely manner.
10. Whether or not the practitioner interacted appropriately with the medical staff and other professional staffs.
11. Overall impression of proctor on the quality of care provided by the practitioner.

physician being proctored should be notified immediately and steps should be taken to rectify the problem.

- As an alternative, when the practitioner being proctored does not admit or treat enough "sophisticated" cases in the hospital, cases from another hospital may be substituted, provided the proctor has privileges in both hospitals.

At the end of the initial proctoring period, one of several actions should be taken, the practitioner should be notified, and the information should be placed in the credentials file. Possible actions include the following:

1. The practitioner's performance has been satisfactory, and he or she is advanced to the appropriate nonprovisional staff category.
2. The practitioner's caseload or procedure load has been inadequate at the facility or acceptable alternative facilities for rendering a judgment as to the acceptability of performance, and additional provisional time is required. The bylaws should specify a time limit (e.g., 12 months) beyond which the provisional period may not be extended. At that point, a decision will have to be rendered as to staff membership and privileges. If the practitioner has failed to comply with the caseload requirement, particularly over a long period (e.g., two years), he or she should be dropped from the staff (as provided in the bylaws) and notified of this in writing. The practitioner is entitled to any procedural rights specified by the bylaws.
3. If the practitioner has adequate cases for review, yet patient care has been deemed not to meet the standards, whether in the initial or an additional provisional period, he or she should be suspended or dropped from the staff (as provided in the bylaws) and notified of this in writing. The practitioner is entitled to any procedural rights specified by the bylaws. When a practitioner is dropped for failing to meet the quality of care standards, it should be ensured that he or she has had more than one proctor, that the proctors agree on the level of care provided, and that, to the degree possible, the proctors are not in obvious competition for the same patients. When competition exists, it is preferable to arrange for a respected peer practitioner from outside the economic competitive area to review the cases.

Within the provisional period, the practitioner being proctored should also be monitored for compliance with other staff and hospital requirements (e.g., timely completion of medical records, adequacy of medical records, meeting attendance, etc.). These requirements should be essentially the same for all staff members with a provisional status and should be indicated in the bylaws. The information acquired through monitoring will be collected by the medical staff services office or department, and it should be compiled at the end of the provisional period and forwarded to the appropriate department for evaluation.

Temporary Privileges

In the absence of a rule prohibiting the use of temporary privileges, the medical staff should be quite strict in recommending or approving such privileges. In fact, they should be granted for only three reasons as indicated in the medical staff bylaws:

1. Governing body approval is pending, but *all* required information has been verified and processed and a positive response is anticipated from the hospital governing body.
2. A nontransportable patient requires the skill and expertise of a physician specialist who is not a member of the staff.
3. There are inadequate numbers of certain specialists on the medical staff or general practitioners cannot find in-house replacement. It would be wise to specify that a locum tenens must be at least as qualified as the physician he or she is temporarily replacing and will not exercise privileges other than those granted to the staff member.

Temporary privileges should not be granted to just anyone only for a limited number of visits. They should never be granted solely for patient desire or convenience (in such cases, the involved practitioner may have only recently been suspended or dropped from the hospital medical staff of another local hospital for quality or legal reasons).

When temporary privileges are granted to a medical staff applicant, all of the required verification should be complete in the applicant's file and the department chief should have reviewed it and approved the application. The chief of staff should also review the completed file and make a recommendation. The hospital chief executive officer is usually the third person who will review and add his/her approval to the granting of temporary privileges.

STAFF REAPPOINTMENT

Credentials

The credentials process also involves staff reappointment. Reappointment is necessary for many reasons, including the currentness of licenses, DEA registration, and professional liability coverage (note that these should be updated as they expire), critical information related to claims and litigation, health, and changes in outside affiliations; and additional training, education, and certification. It is also mandatory to assess the practitioner's profile since the last staff appointment to ensure that peer review activities have provided a sound basis for supporting reappointment or reprivileging (see Exhibit 8-4).

One frequently overlooked medical staff and governing body responsibility is the obligation to ensure that the practitioner has met any requirements for privileges the exercise of which requires evidence of continued proficiency. If a procedure has not been done enough to give reasonable assurance of proficiency, the privilege should be withdrawn or the practitioner proctored. Consideration should be given, of course, for documented cases done at another facility. Another check at the time of reappointment should be made to ensure that all clinical privileges are still hospital specific. A practitioner may have different privileges in each of three different hospitals based on the particular patient services offered by each. Thus professional qualifications are not the only determinant of privilege delineation.

During the period between staff appointments, a staff member's credentials are established through the medical staff quality assurance and peer review system. The medical staff committees and departments perform reviews of prescreened patient care information as well as initiate reviews on their own. An ongoing practitioner profile is maintained and includes the findings of the quality assurance activities (see Chapter 9). Findings should be included from the procedure evaluation, drug therapy evaluation, blood therapy evaluation, medical record documentation review, utilization review, hospital risk management program, and other monitoring and evaluation programs. These numerator findings should be included on a profile that also notes denominator information (i.e., the number of admissions, procedures performed, and consultations). The denominator information is important as it helps to put into perspective any negative data generated. A practitioner who has admitted only three patients and had quality problems with the treatment of all three is in a different category from a practitioner who has admitted dozens of patients but experienced quality problems with only three.

It is important, especially for a large medical staff, to have a staggered system of reappointment. That is, the entire staff is not reappointed at the same time but is divided by department, by birth date, by appointment date, or alphabetically so that

---

Exhibit 8-4 Basic Checklist for Review of Medical Staff Reappointment and Reprivileging

1. Current licenses, DEA registration, and professional liability coverage.
2. Health status.
3. Use of the hospital (admissions, procedures, and consultations).
4. Specific peer review performance data, with numerators and denominators.
5. Professional liability history of pending and resolved claims and lawsuits.
6. Information from the National Practitioner Data Bank.
7. Medical record completion (adequacy and timeliness).
8. Medical staff support (offices held and committee support).
9. Backup information for a requested increase in privileges.

large numbers are not reappointed at the same time. This permits a more in-depth evaluation of each candidate for reappointment and of the concomitant clinical privilege delineation.

The Reappointment Form

A reappointment form should be sent to each staff member for completion along with a copy of his or her current privilege delineation form. The reappointment form should require the following:

1. Confirmation of all required demographic information.
2. Confirmation of current licenses, DEA registration, and professional liability coverage (hard copies should be required). Because states vary with respect to licensure date requirements and hospital medical staffs vary with respect to reappointment dates, it may be necessary to verify each state license twice—once at the expiration date and once at the time of reappointment. This has become more important in recent years, because medical staffs have wisely shifted to staggered reappointment systems.
3. Confirmation of the attainment of specialty board certification since appointment or last reappointment.
4. An indication as to whether a privilege change is being requested and, if so, whether specific additional privileges are the issue. If additional privileges are requested, the staff member must state in terms of training and so on why he or she is qualified to exercise the additional privileges. A practitioner may also wish to drop privileges due to a change in the pattern of practice. For example, an older obstetrician/gynecologist may want to discontinue practicing obstetrics and limit his or her practice to gynecology. It is important that this change be noted on the clinical privilege form.
5. The answers to critical questions relating to status *since the previous appointment*, including these:
   - Has your membership in another health care facility been denied, revoked, or otherwise acted against or have you been subjected to disciplinary action?
   - Have any privileges been voluntarily or involuntarily withdrawn in another health care facility?
   - Are you currently under charges that, if upheld, could lead to conviction for a felony or misdemeanor (other than minor traffic offenses)?
   - Have any judgments been made against or settlements been obtained from you in professional liability cases?
   - Are any professional liability cases pending against you?

- Have you been under treatment for drug addiction or alcoholism?
- Have you been under psychiatric treatment or care?
- Are you currently under care for a continuing health problem?
(Note: If the answer to any question above is yes, please include details.)
- Do you feel that your health status is adequate enough to permit you to provide the patient care services for which you are requesting clinical privileges? (Note: If the answer is no, please include details.)
6. Description of continuing education since last appointment (optional).
7. Any other requirement of the medical staff bylaws, rules, and regulations.
8. The signature of the individual seeking reappointment.
9. The reappointment fee (if any).

The completed application must be accompanied by profile information supplied through the quality assurance program and the medical staff services office. This information includes both administrative aspects of staff membership (e.g., meeting attendance statistics, medical record delinquency status, committee appointments, and hospital practice statistics) and clinical performance data (e.g., clinical outcome statistics, committee and department citations, governing board sanctions, and peer review and quality assurance reviews and actions). All hospitals are also required to check with the National Practitioner Data Bank to determine whether any adverse information has been reported during the past period of appointment.

Reappointment of Practitioners with Low Activity

Some hospitals have large numbers of staff members whose primary practices are centered at other area facilities. It is difficult to obtain an adequate performance data base for these practitioners at reappointment time. In each such case, the facilities at which the practitioner most actively practices must be contacted to obtain the information needed for reappointment. Form letters that contain specific questions about the quality of the practitioner's work are commonly used for this purpose. As with reference letters used to obtain information for the initial appointment, these should be carefully worded to elicit the precise information needed. The value of the information obtained is also dependent on the quality and scope of the quality assurance and peer review programs at the other facilities. However, some attempt should be made to determine whether the practitioner has experienced professional problems at these facilities. Some hospitals are attempting to reduce the number of staff members who mainly practice elsewhere by requiring (as provided in the bylaws) a minimum number of admissions, procedures, or consultations for maintenance of staff membership and privileges.

Routing Reappointments through Channels

The completed reappointment form and profile information should be evaluated and signed off by the following, with an indication of approval, approval with stated exceptions (e.g., denial of certain privileges), or disapproval and the reasons therefor (Exhibit 8-5):

1. The medical staff clinical department chairperson, who should indicate that he or she (a) has reviewed the application and profile information and found it in satisfactory order, (b) has no knowledge of any health problem that would prevent the individual seeking reappointment from exercising the privileges requested, and (c) has made a recommendation (e.g., approval). (This statement may have to be made by the chief of staff in a hospital that is still not departmentalized.)

2. The credentials committee or the body performing the credentialing function.

3. The medical staff executive committee.

4. The governing body, which has final approval authority.

Exhibit 8-5 Steps in the Reappointment Process

1. Ninety days prior to the membership expiration date, the medical staff services
   * sends a reappointment application to the practitioner, including the deadline for receipt
   * notifies the quality assurance department of the need for a practitioner clinical profile and the date needed
   * submits the name of the practitioner being reappointed to the National Practitioner Data Bank and requests information
2. Sixty days prior to the expiration date, the practitioner returns the completed application form. The quality assurance department forwards the profile to medical staff services.
3. Medical staff services verifies the information on the completed application and sends the application, administrative data, National Practitioner Data Bank information, clinical profile, privilege delineation request form, and verification from other facilities (in the case of a practitioner relatively inactive at the hospital) to the department chairperson for review.
4. The department chairperson reviews the profile and all supporting information, comments on the practitioner's health status, and sends a written recommendation for privilege delineation and reappointment to the credentials committee.
5. The credentials committee reviews all information and the department chairperson's recommendation, submits its recommendation to the executive committee.
6. The executive committee reviews the previous recommendations, makes its own recommendation, and then forwards it to the governing body. (If an adverse recommendation is made, the applicant must be offered due process.)
7. The governing body takes final action.
8. The applicant is notified of the governing body's decision.

Any person required to sign the reappointment form can request further relevant information before signing. However, if the process is performed properly, this type of delay will rarely occur.

If a medical staff member voluntarily relinquishes certain privileges (e.g., because of age, a desire to cut back practice, or poor results), it is critical that the change be formalized through the medical staff and governing body system. Otherwise, the staff member may decide after several years of inactivity to exercise the same privileges again. This could be catastrophic. Before formalizing the voluntary relinquishment of privileges, check state or federal reporting requirements relating to privilege changes.

ALLIED HEALTH PROFESSIONALS

Allied health professionals appear under various other names, for example, specified professional personnel or designated professional personnel. They are of concern to the medical staff services office because they provide services to the patients of medical staff members (99 percent of whom are physicians). The medical staff thus has a responsibility to ensure the qualifications and competence of allied health professionals and determine what services they may provide.

Allied health professionals may be hospital or physician employees or may contract to provide services. They may be granted privileges or the authority to provide designated patient services. There appears to be no limit to the number of possible titles; for example, certified registered nurse anesthetists, physician assistants, nurse practitioners, perfusionists, registered nurse-midwives, speech pathologists, and so on. The hospital and medical staff determine who these individuals are, and the procedure for appointment and the scope of practice should be defined in the medical staff rules and regulations, not in the bylaws.

Factors common to allied health professionals include the following:

- The source of employment has absolutely no bearing on their need to be credentialed through the medical staff and governing board. In other words, a hospital-employed nurse anesthetist, a physician assistant employed by a medical staff member, or a speech pathologist under contract with the hospital must be credentialed through the regular medical staff channels.
- They usually provide direct care to patients, that is, "lay hands on" or are in close verbal contact with patients.
- Some may render judgments on their own.
- They require some degree of supervision, which may be direct or indirect.

Some allied health professionals must have a license, certification, or registration and are regulated or guided by state requirements. However, the hospital has the final say as to the extent of services the individual may provide within the hospital's jurisdiction. This is defined in a task list or privilege list of allowable services, which is usually included in the medical staff rules and regulations.

Allied health professionals must apply, on a designated form, to provide patient care services in the hospital. Their performance must be evaluated regularly and objectively. And they must be reappointed by application and on the basis of a satisfactory performance record.

An allied health professional application form[5] should include the following:

1. Name, home or office address, telephone numbers, citizenship, marital status, and professional affiliations.
2. Licenses, certification, and registration, with expiration dates.
3. Education and training (high school, college, nursing school, and other graduate education or training).
4. Current hospital affiliations.
5. Military service and any specialized training.
6. Membership in professional organizations.
7. Previous experience in hospitals or other health care facilities.
8. References (three individuals with personal knowledge of professional ability, and ethics, character).
9. Evidence of professional liability insurance (carrier, policy number, dates, and limits).
10. Type of practice anticipated if granted privileges:
    • Self-employed (free-lance).
    • Employed by medical staff member part time.
    • Employed by medical staff member full time.
    • Member of or affiliated with a group practicing this specialty.
    • Other (specify).
11. Distance from office or home to hospital (in miles).
12. If the answer to any of the following questions is yes, please give full details on a separate sheet of paper. All questions must be answered. (One possible answer is "not applicable.")
    • Has your license to practice in any jurisdiction ever been limited, suspended, placed on probation, or revoked?
    • Has your certification or registration status ever been revoked?
    • Have your privileges at any hospital or other health care facility ever been revoked, suspended, reduced, subject to observation (beyond what is normal), or not renewed?

- Have you ever been denied membership (or renewal of membership) or been subject to disciplinary action in any professional organization?
- Have you ever been a defendant in a professional liability or negligence case?
- Is there any professional liability claim pending against you?
- Has a settlement of any professional liability claim involving you ever been made?
- Is there any health status problem that might prevent you from performing the privileges requested?

13. Continuing education. List on a separate sheet of paper all continuing education courses for which you have received credit in the past two years.

14. Duties you desire to perform in the hospital. (Be specific. If the hospital is to employ you, and a current job description covers all areas of practice, so state.)

15. Liability coverage. If you are the employee of a member of this hospital's medical staff, have your employer answer the following two questions:

- Is this applicant covered by your liability carrier? List carrier name, amount of coverage, and expiration date.
- Is this applicant covered by his or her own liability insurance? List carrier name, amount of coverage, and expiration date.

The application should also contain a statement by the employing practitioner who is a medical staff member.

I hereby certify that _____ is in my employment in the capacity of _____ and that he or she will be under my direction and supervision at all times. I agree to assume full responsibility for his or her actions in dealing with my patients who are hospitalized in (name of facility), and I also agree to notify the hospital if this individual should leave my employment.

The employing or sponsoring practitioner should also sign the application form.

The application form should also include a statement signed by the applicant. Suggested language for this statement follows:

I fully understand that any misstatement in or omission from this application constitutes cause for denial of my application for privileges in this hospital. All information submitted by me in this application is true to the best of my knowledge and belief.

In making this application, I signify my willingness to appear for interviews and authorize the hospital, its medical staff, or their agents, employees, and representatives to consult with administrators, medical staffs of other hospitals or institutions with which I have been associated, and with other employers, individuals, or entities that may have information concerning my professional performance, competence, character, ethics, and other qualifications. I consent to the inspection by the hospital, its medical staff, and their agents, employees, and representatives of all records and documents that may be pertinent to the evaluation of my professional, moral, and ethical qualifications and my competence to exercise the clinical privileges I am requesting. By executing this application, I release the hospital, its medical staff, and their agents, employees, and representatives from any and all liability for any and all causes of action and damages, including consequential damages, in any way growing out of or in any way connected with the evaluation of this application; and I further release all individuals, organizations, and their agents, employees, and representatives who provide information to the hospital or its medical staff in good faith and without malice concerning my professional qualifications, competence, character, and ethics, including otherwise privileged or confidential information.

I understand and agree that I have the burden of producing adequate information for proper evaluation of my professional competence, character, ethics, and other qualifications and for resolving any doubts about such qualifications.

I further authorize and consent to the release of information concerning me by (name of facility) and its medical staff to other hospitals and medical or professional organizations requesting such information so long as the release of such information is done in good faith and without malice. I release the hospital and its medical staff from any and all liability for any and all causes of action and damages arising from, or in any way growing out of the release of such information.

If approved by the hospital and the medical staff to see and/or treat patients in (name of facility), I agree to:

1. never engage in the practice of medicine as defined by the state medical practice act, the state board of medical examiners, and relevant statutory or regulatory provisions;
2. adhere to the medical staff bylaws, medical staff rules and regulations, and hospital policies as they apply to my actions or duties;

3. comply with all relevant requirements of the Joint Commission on Accreditation of Healthcare Organizations as interpreted by the hospital;

4. wear proper identification indicating my name and title whenever I am in the hospital; and

5. maintain adequate liability insurance coverage at all times.

The applicant should sign and date the application.

Reappointment of Allied Health Professionals

Allied health professionals should also be reappointed at least every two years in the same manner as medical staff members. The reappointment form should include the following:[6]

- A copy of current licenses, registration, or certification, with expiration dates.
- The current liability carrier, and the address, policy number, and amount of coverage (a hard copy of the face sheet or letter from the carrier should be provided).
- A list of any liability litigation, claims, or settlements since the previous appraisal or now pending.
- Any change in employment status.
- Any desired change in privileges or patient services allowed in the hospital. If additional privileges are requested, supporting information on education and training should be included.
- Any health status problems that would keep the allied health professional from exercising the privileges requested.
- Relevant continuing education programs completed since the previous appraisal.

The applicant for reappointment should sign a statement that, at a minimum, declares his or her commitment to

1. never engage in the practice of medicine as defined by the state medical practice act, the state board of medical examiners, and relevant statutory or regulatory provisions

2. adhere to the medical staff bylaws, medical staff rules and regulations, and hospital policies as they apply to the applicant's actions or duties

3. comply with all relevant requirements of the Joint Commission on Accreditation of Healthcare Organizations as interpreted by the hospital

4. wear proper identification indicating name and title whenever in the hospital

5. maintain adequate liability insurance coverage at all times

If the allied health professional is employed by a physician member of the medical staff, the member should sign a statement to that effect.

The reappointment should be routed through the department and credentials and executive committees for recommendations, and it should be sent to the governing body for final action. Quality assurance findings that involve the applicant must be included.

ROLE OF THE MEDICAL STAFF SERVICES PROFESSIONAL IN THE CREDENTIALS PROCESS

Whereas it is the responsibility of the medical staff organization to evaluate information on applicants for medical staff membership and privileges, it is the responsibility of the medical staff services professional (MSSP) to gather the information (see Exhibit 8-6 for steps in processing an application). Credentialing policies and procedures in place in the hospital must be applied objectively and equitably by the MSSP, who should be alert to potential problems and initiate further investigation whenever there is questionable, equivocal, or negative information on any applicant.

The vast majority of applicants for medical staff privileges will be well-trained and well-qualified practitioners. It is the unqualified or substandard few whom the MSSP needs to keep a watch for. When verifying information returned to the hospital is incomplete, vague, or negative, the MSSP must take the initiative to start the process of further checking. Medical staff leaders are frequently inexperienced in these matters and will look to the MSSP for guidance.

As mentioned earlier, medical staff leaders and administration should be asked by the MSSP in these cases to make telephone calls to peer references, training program directors, or past hospital affiliations in an effort to clarify vague or incomplete information or confirm (or disconfirm) negative information. Respondents will frequently be willing to discuss physician to physician or administrator to administrator sensitive information they would not want to put in writing. An effort should be made to obtain names of additional references for the purpose of checking reports of professional problems. All persons contacted should be encouraged to put the information in writing, but if someone is unwilling, the person making the call should prepare a memo to the file that contains a summary of the conversation.

For each applicant, the information gathered should be sufficient to dispel any discomfort in recommending the appointment and the clinical privileges or be sufficient to demonstrate the unreasonableness of so doing (in which case the appointment should be denied).[7]

Exhibit 8-6 Steps in Processing an Application

Preapplication Process

1. Upon request, send the preapplication form and the standard cover letter to the applicant. Record the name and address of the applicant and the date sent.
2. Upon receipt of the completed preapplication form, check for completeness and determine whether the applicant meets the eligibility criteria. Check for copies of current license, narcotics registration, and liability insurance (coverage must at least meet the required minimum). If applicant does not meet the criteria, check with the supervisor.
3. If applicant meets the criteria, send the application packet, the cover letter, and the appropriate privilege request form. Record the date sent.
4. If the applicant does not meet the criteria, send the form letter.

Processing a New Application

1. Check the application form for completeness. All blanks should be filled in and all questions answered. The entire period from the time of graduation from medical school to the time of application must be accounted for. The application form and the privilege request form should be signed. Check for receipt of the required fee. If any document is incomplete, obtain the missing information. Pull the preapplication file containing the copies of the license, narcotics registration, and liability insurance and place with the application form.
2. Within three days of receipt, verify the following, using a standard form letter for each (enclose a copy of the applicant's statement releasing information and a copy of the privilege request form [except in the letter to medical school, state licensing boards, and certifying board] and a return envelope):
   - *Medical, dental, or podiatric school*. Address the letter to the registrar and include the year of degree and date of birth of applicant.
   - *Licenses*. Include the license number of the practitioner.
   - *Internship and residency*. Address the letter to the chairperson of the training program. Include the dates of training. Send separate letters if the training was completed at different facilities.
   - *Fellowship*. Address the letter to the chairperson of the program. Include the dates of training.
   - *Peer references*. Peers who have not directly observed the applicant's clinical work, as well as relatives and professional partners, are not acceptable.
   - *Board certification*. If applicable.
   - *Hospital affiliations*. Address the letter to the chairperson of the credentials committee c/o the medical staff services department of the hospital.
   - *Other positions or affiliations*. Use the peer reference letter and state the applicant's position and dates of association.
   - *Insurance coverage and claims history*. Also check with the National Practitioner Data Bank for information on the applicant.
3. Prepare a checklist to note the dates of receipt of letters.
4. Set up a credentials file.
5. Monitor the return of letters and note their receipt on the checklist. Discuss bad or questionable references with the supervisor and department chairperson. Initiate any necessary follow-up in response to negative references.
6. Send second requests if answers are not received within three weeks. If there is no response within three weeks of a second request, notify the applicant and ask him or her to assist with the return of references. (The burden of proof is on the applicant.)
7. When the documentation is complete, prepare a summary of references and notify department chairperson to review the application.
8. Set up required interviews.
9. Submit the application to the department, credentials committee, executive committee, and governing body.

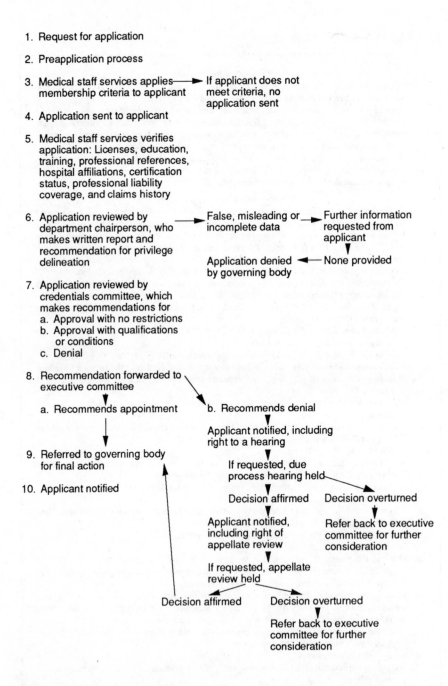

1. Request for application

2. Preapplication process

3. Medical staff services applies⟶ If applicant does not
   membership criteria to applicant   meet criteria, no
                                       application sent

4. Application sent to applicant

5. Medical staff services verifies
   application: Licenses, education,
   training, professional references,
   hospital affiliations, certification
   status, professional liability
   coverage, and claims history

6. Application reviewed by   False, misleading or⟶ Further information
   department chairperson, who ⟶ incomplete data   requested from
   makes written report and   applicant
   recommendation for privilege
   delineation   Application denied ◀— None provided
                                    by governing body

7. Application reviewed by
   credentials committee, which
   makes recommendations for
   a. Approval with no restrictions
   b. Approval with qualifications
      or conditions
   c. Denial

8. Recommendation forwarded to
   executive committee

   a. Recommends appointment   b. Recommends denial

                                    Applicant notified, including
                                    right to a hearing

9. Referred to governing body   If requested, due
   for final action   process hearing held

10. Applicant notified   Decision affirmed   Decision overturned

                                    Applicant notified,   Refer back to executive
                                    including right of   committee for further
                                    appellate review   consideration

                                    If requested, appellate
                                    review held

                    Decision affirmed   Decision overturned

                                           Refer back to executive
                                           committee for further
                                           consideration

Figure 8-1 Steps in Routing an Application

When the credentials file is completed, the MSSP is responsible for routing it through the appropriate medical staff channels to the governing body (see Figure 8-1). Supporting the credentials process is one of the most critical responsibilities of the MSSP. In providing support, medical staff bylaws and credentialing policies should be followed to the letter. Accurate, thorough, and complete documentation should be obtained on each applicant. Legal counsel should be consulted when a question arises as to whether the hospital is carrying out the process appropriately. Medical staff and hospital leaders will look to the MSSP to guide the process skillfully and diligently.

NOTES

1. F. C. Dimond, Jr., "A Legal Basis for a QA/RM Program," *Medical Director's Letter* (National Medical Enterprises) May–June 1984, 1–2, 4–5.
2. Joint Commission on Accreditation of Healthcare Organizations, *1990 Accreditation Manual for Hospitals* (Chicago: Joint Commission on Accreditation of Healthcare Organizations, 1989), 106.
3. F. C. Dimond, Jr., *Model Medical Staff Bylaws*, National Medical Enterprises, 1985; F. C. Dimond, Jr., *Model Medical Staff Application Form*, National Medical Enterprises, 1985.
4. Dimond, *Model Medical Staff Bylaws*.
5. F. C. Dimond, Jr., "Application for Privileges Form, Allied Health Professional (Name Optional)," *Medical Director's Letter* (National Medical Enterprises), January 1983, 6–11.
6. Ibid., 13–15.
7. Cindy A. Orsund and Donald P. Wilcox, "Credentialing the New Applicant—Practical Advice," *Texas Medicine* 84 (April 1988): 79.

Chapter 9

Medical Staff Monitoring and Evaluation of Quality and Appropriateness of Care

F. C. Dimond, Jr., MD

INTRODUCTION

The medical staff has the delegated responsibility of ensuring that the same level of appropriate, high-quality patient care is provided throughout the hospital and in any patient care facility or service under the aegis of the hospital, even if remote. Recently, knowledgeable professionals in the acute care hospital field have been gradually coming to accept the long-known fact that effective quality assurance (QA) is preventive in nature and that, if performed efficiently, all care can be objectively reviewed for both quality and appropriateness.

Care must be taken to differentiate between the real-world definition of medical staff peer review (when peers review any staff member objectively and fairly for any care rendered) and the usual legal definition (which implies a fair hearing and possible appellate review by the medical staff through the process established in the medical staff bylaws, rules, and regulations for alleged inadequate or improper care). In fact, most peer review is of acceptable care and rarely leads to invoking a formal fair hearing and appellate review.

COMPONENTS OF MEDICAL STAFF QUALITY ASSURANCE

Regardless of how the medical staff structures itself and organizes its peer review functions, the medical staff QA system has traditionally consisted of these components:[1]

1. the proper initial credentialing, with matching of clinical privileges to documented credentials

2. an initial provisional period for new staff members during which there is appropriate supervision involving the direct evaluation of performance and care provided and the review of associated medical records

3. any functions that monitor patient care provided by medical staff members as required by the medical staff bylaws, rules, and regulations (these functions are commonly determined by traditional rote requirements by the Joint Commission on Accreditation of Healthcare Organizations (Joint Commission), such as blood use evaluation, drug therapy evaluation, surgical case evaluation, medical record evaluation, etc.)

4. the ongoing objective evaluation by clinical departments (or by the full medical staff if nondepartmentalized) of the care rendered and of clinical performance

5. the periodic appraisal, at least at the time of reappointment, of each individual staff member as to clinical performance and competence and any other parameters deemed important to the reappointment process

6. consistent and uniform enforcement of sound medical staff bylaws, rules, and regulations

WHAT'S WRONG WITH MOST QUALITY ASSURANCE SYSTEMS?

There is nothing wrong with the medical staff QA system outlined above except that it has not evolved in most hospitals to be preventive in effect. It is fractionated rather than integrated and does not function efficiently. Today, for any hospitalization or patient intervention, the QA system requires evidence of medical necessity, appropriateness of clinical management, and evaluation of outcome. This brings into close relationship the three major components of medical staff QA efforts; QA itself, utilization review (UR), and risk management (RM).

In Figure 9-1, the overlapping shaded areas of UR and RM with QA are clinical and hence are the medical staff's concern. The UR-QA overlap represents medical

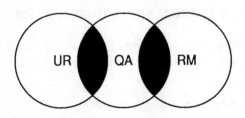

Figure 9-1 The Overlapping Relationship of Medical Staff QA Efforts

necessity; the QA nonshaded area represents primarily clinical management, and the QA-RM overlap represents adverse outcome relating to clinical care and practitioner performance. Depending only on outcome evaluation for quality assurance guarantees failure for at least three reasons. First, there will almost never be any resultant practice change. Second, the system is not preventive. Third, short of a catastrophic inadequate-practice case, the medical staff will show little interest in past events that can't be reversed or affected, and for which there is no protection for subjective review of any care with an adverse outcome.

WHAT'S NEEDED

Each medical staff must adopt a full concurrent review program and recognize that prospective review, now related primarily to cost containment, is quality related as well and required implementation is just around the corner. Each staff must also continue to seek hard data about its members' practices. It can make such data easier to gather by setting or adopting suitable measurement criteria or standards. A number of professional organizations have been and will continue to be developing such benchmarks of care for both medical necessity and clinical management purposes. Setting such standards, however, can be a two-edged sword for the following reasons: (1) if the professions don't set clinical standards, then nonprofessionals will; (2) professional groups can have serious disagreements over certain standards; (3) once the professionals have set the standards, trial lawyers and courts will attempt to hold them to these standards when it benefits a plaintiff or client; and (4) the standards will become reimbursement targets.

QUALITY ASSURANCE SYSTEMS

The patient care review system best accepted by medical staffs involves three tiers of review (see Figure 9-2). The initial review (first tier) is the comprehensive concurrent review done by one or more clinical nonphysician screeners, preferably registered nurses with a strong clinical background. Using preestablished, approved criteria, the screeners review medical records concurrently for all aspects of care (e.g., need for hospitalization, procedure necessity, drug therapy, blood therapy, etc.) as well as significant unanticipated untoward events that may not have been reported from the site of origin (as is normally required through a hospitalwide occurrence (incident) reporting system). Note that requiring the nonphysician screeners to review records against a long list of unanticipated adverse events is (1) an outrageous waste of time and money, (2) a dilution of the nonphysician review system, and (3) a subversion of the hospital occurrence-reporting system. The nonphysician screeners report the information obtained without rendering any

FIRST TIER

100% Concurrent review by nonphysician screeners for:
Need for hospitalization
Need for level of service (special care unit)
Procedure evaluation (necessity, management)
Drug therapy evaluation
Blood and blood product therapy evaluation
Infections
Significant unanticipated adverse outcome
    (complications and selected death cases)
Other _____

SECOND TIER

Review by peer group representative screener(s). Findings handled pre-department or by department chairperson
Record documentation problem
Counseling needed
Letter for repeat minor problems
Other _____
Important findings with any trending go to full department (third tier) via department chairperson
Resource use
Clinical management
Outcome
Other _____

THIRD TIER

Departmental Review

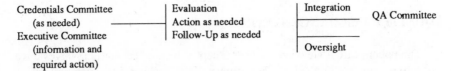

Credentials Committee
    (as needed)
Executive Committee
    (information and
    required action)

Evaluation
Action as needed
Follow-Up as needed

Integration

Oversight

QA Committee

Figure 9-2 A Three-Tiered Quality Assurance System

judgment on the findings. The findings are analyzed, trended, and referred to a subcommittee or to one or more designated physicians of the appropriate medical staff peer department.

The second-tier review, done by one or more designated medical staff department physician members or a departmental subcommittee, separates the wheat from the chaff and determines through the department chairperson what information is important enough for review by the department. The second tier usually handles problems that would not need departmental input, such as record documentation problems, isolated events that did not result in harm or significant costs to patients, and so on.

The third-tier review level is the peer medical department itself, which, usually without patient or practitioner identifiers, evaluates unnecessary or inadequately managed patient care services (particularly those associated with a trend or pattern) and recommends appropriate action or institutes action within the limits prescribed in the medical staff bylaws (Figure 9-2).

The advantages of this tiered review system are many:

1. Unnecessary physician review time is reduced.

2. Unnecessary committee meetings are reduced in number as certain traditional medical staff committees (e.g., surgical case review, blood use evaluation, drug therapy review, medical record review, critical care review, etc.) can be eliminated unless mandated by other than the medical staff.

3. Evaluation then occurs in a peer group that can make the necessary decisions: the medical staff department.

4. Because of the concurrent review system, medical records are more readily available after patient discharge for practitioner completion and signature and for any other specific evaluation needed. A spinoff bonus is fewer delinquent or deficient medical records.

5. The long-antiquated system of random individual chart review is dispensed with, a system that allows only a token review of patient care and is unlikely to (a) find any instances of inadequate care or (b) improve practice to any great extent.

6. With the elimination of many medical staff committees, there are fewer groups among which an issue can be ping-ponged, thus delaying decision making.

7. Subjective review is eliminated.

8. The fractionation of patient care review is eliminated. The old system had one committee looking at blood therapy, another at drug therapy, another at the surgery, and so on.

9. The medical staff retains control of the system by (a) establishing or approving the review criteria used by nonphysician screeners, and (b) controlling the final evaluation and decision making.

10. The data and the data trending are suitable for computerization.

In the absence of an established concurrent review system (in which review occurs while the patient is in the hospital), the department review is limited to a retrospective (postdischarge) review of outcome data, which is evaluated only subjectively. As a general rule, little practice change ever results solely from medical staff outcome review, because postoutcome subjective evaluation of cases is too challengeable by practitioners being reviewed.

In the absence of medical staff departmentalization—but with a concurrent review system in place—the findings must be submitted to the full medical staff at its monthly meetings. In this setup, the main missing ingredient is realistic peer review grouping, which is impossible to attain because of the mix of staff members.

If the medical staff is nondepartmentalized for any reason other than small size (15 or fewer active staff members without identifiable surgical and nonsurgical components) and there is no concurrent review system in place, then there is little chance for any meaningful peer review and resultant practice change.

In the absence of medical staff departmentalization, medical staff review of care traditionally has been carried out through committees. The problem with this is that committees are almost never peer groups and lack authority to take significant action to correct a practice problem. Even today, most departmentalized medical staffs have retained the committee structure as well, and often the committees delay the movement of information to the department, which is the true decision point. In departmentalized hospitals, the system is further inadvertently compromised because the Joint Commission still only requires committee reports (findings) to go to the medical staff executive committee, not to the appropriate medical staff departments and the quality assurance committee (not a specific Joint Commission requirement), where they should go before or at the same time they are sent to the executive committee.

QUALITY ASSURANCE DEPARTMENTS

The development of managed QA departments in hospitals is a healthy trend in this country. In a given case, development of such a department may be related to hospital size, sophistication, and budget; to the need to coordinate and integrate the interaction between and reporting system for generically related QA activities; to the need to improve efficiency and effectiveness; to local preference; or to the need for management assistance.

The varieties of QA department components are myriad. In varying combinations, the following functions, activities, and individuals have been found as part of some QA departments: QA coordinator, UR coordinator, risk manager (RM), safety officer, infection control practitioner, clinical nurse reviewers, discharge planning, preadmission screening, diagnosis-related group (DRG) coordinator, social worker, and patient representative. A standard department includes at least QA, UR, RM, discharge planning, and infection control functions and, depending on census and budget, one or more clinical nurse reviewers. A close relationship must exist between any QA department and the medical staff services professional, although that individual ordinarily should not be a member of the QA department.

The role of the QA coordinator is a vital one in every hospital. A clinical background is advantageous and probably required. When a QA department is formed, it is desirable for the department director to have some managerial expertise.

The advantages of having such a department[2] include the obvious managerial and informational benefits; increased communication among all the quality-related efforts; prevention of duplication of effort but with all the bases being covered; better coverage (especially when some department personnel are absent) through cross-training in related activities; multiple screening of information components as opposed to screening through one individual (the QA coordinator); and increased visibility of the quality aspect of care yet with all aspects focused on, including cost.

Information is routinely collected and analyzed and unsatisfactory findings and trends are fed into the medical staff preevaluation system and, as appropriate, into the reappointment and privilege delineation system. The QA process is basically very simple in principle and very comprehensive in scope, involving the use of findings from medical necessity evaluation, clinical management evaluation, and occurrence screening analysis, with each of the elements of this triad being performed objectively.[3]

A Quality Assurance Model (Medical Staff Department Evaluation)

Figure 9-3[4] graphically illustrates an efficient, comprehensive, and ideal medical staff QA process that encourages realistic peer evaluation. In the example shown, there is 100 percent concurrent evaluation, with all information coordinated through the QA department and only relevant findings transmitted to the appropriate medical staff department through a tiered review system. The following points should be noted:

1. Figure 9-3 indicates that certain consistent timely information should feed into any medical staff department.
2. Medical staff committees other than the QA, credentials, and executive committees are not always required. In the case of a small hospital or medical staff, the credentials function may be performed by the executive committee.
3. Physician use and control of the information is ensured through a tiered review system.
4. The department is the peer decision point for patient care evaluation and, in this role, is responsible to the executive committee.
5. The system ensures overall integrated evaluation of the care of any patient.
6. The system enhances communication between related review disciplines and the integration of information.

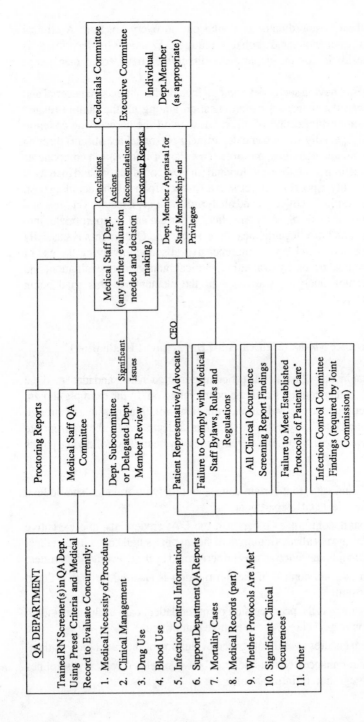

Figure 9-3 Example of the Comprehensiveness of the Medical Staff Department Role in Quality Assurance. *Source:* Dimond, F.C., Jr., M.D. Adapted from *Medical Director's Newsletter*, p. 3, No. 3-85, May–June 1985.

* May be identified by concurrent screening or reported by nursing service, pharmacy, respiratory care department, and so on.

** This includes significant discrepancies between the performing physician's and pathologist's diagnoses in specimen cases and between the performing physician's preprocedure and postprocedure diagnoses in nonspecimen cases. Reporting of the specimen case diagnostic discrepancies may originate in the pathology department.

In addition to the above, Figure 9-3 indicates types of information appropriate for inclusion in medical staff department meeting minutes.

When a 100 percent concurrent evaluation is performed, the worksheets used by the trained nurse screeners are always available but, because of their volume, are usually filed separately from the department minutes (yet they still are under any protection afforded medical staff quality-related activities). Only the relevant findings from the QA department integrated report and the second-tier review go to the medical staff department. A proper QA department report serves to expedite a medical staff department evaluation because the department physicians can then focus on very specific patient care or clinical practice issues. In-depth chart review by the department should be required only rarely, and the need for the department itself to select a small number of charts for subjective review will have been eliminated.[5]

By use of the review system or sequence shown in Figure 9-3, valuable physician time will be saved, with the physicians making peer decisions based on organized, pertinent hard data.

QUALITY-RELATED MEDICAL STAFF FUNCTIONS

The two most pervasive medical staff patient care review functions are procedure evaluation and drug therapy evaluation. More limited clinical functions usually in place are blood and blood-product therapy evaluation and mortality and morbidity review. The most common nonclinical function is medical record review, which documents to varying degrees the quality and pertinence of the medical records. The ultimate quality-related functions (the credentials and privileging process functions) are discussed elsewhere in this book. Other functions and committees are the prerogative of the individual medical staff. All quality-related functions should focus primarily on prevention rather than on evaluation of untoward outcomes.

Procedure Evaluation[6]

The number of procedures performed by medical staff members under the aegis of the hospital has increased greatly in the past ten years, as has the number of staff members performing these procedures. Most procedures are invasive and are related in no small way to equipment development and increased clinical skill. Laser use has expanded. Noninvasive procedures such as electroconvulsive therapy (ECT) and some lithotripsy procedures require close review. On the invasive side of the coin, it is not uncommon to find some types of endoscopy performed by gastroenterologists, internists, surgeons, and family practitioners. Both medical and surgical specialists are performing endovascular diagnostic studies and therapeutic procedures. Hence there is a need for a strong "procedure evaluation" function, with the findings transmitted to each medical staff department that has members performing the procedures. This ensures peer review of the procedures by department members. Provision of the same level of care is ensured, to the greatest degree possible, by (1) using the same necessity criteria as well as any available management criteria, (2) meeting all monitoring requirements, and (3) evaluating adverse outcomes for patterns of unacceptable care. Privileges are granted based on the three categories above, and evaluation.

The integrated review system described above does not permit only "surgical cases" to be reviewed. The 100 percent review system eliminates the risk involved in trying to determine what may not need to be reviewed as well as the risk that medical staffs will review only the appropriateness of procedures related to the third-party payer bureaucratic process. Cost is important, but so is quality.

Procedure evaluation includes procedures performed in endoscopy units or labs, catheterization labs, radiology special procedure rooms, special care units (intensive care units, coronary care units, neonatal intensive care units, renal dialysis units, burn units, etc.), as well as all inpatient and outpatient surgical procedures. Included are elective, emergency, diagnostic, therapeutic, specimen, nonspecimen, invasive, and noninvasive procedures.

Procedure necessity criteria have long been available from commercial, governmental, and professional sources. Clinical practice (management) criteria have lagged in availability except for limited professional review organization (PRO) criteria, but they are now being developed by professional medical specialty organizations. Occurrence-screening (RM) criteria have been used by many hospitals for at least 15 years. The clinical aspect of RM is a part of QA and must be managed separately from the nonclinical aspects.

When procedure evaluation fails or is essentially nonproductive, the medical staff can often pinpoint the problems by checking each tier of the system. Consider the following issues (among others):

- Have criteria for the procedure been established and used?
- Were the criteria set to meet actual practice or a nationally accepted practice?
- Were the findings understandable and relevant or were only meaningless statistics provided to the reviewing physicians?
- Did subjective review enter into the evaluation process at any point?
- Was the information or problem allowed to ping-pong among multiple review groups without ever being resolved at the proper decision point?
- Were all the findings generated by the QA review system considered adequate by the reviewing physician groups?
- Was nothing considered serious enough to reach the appropriate department?

- Were complications reviewed only for the appropriateness of their management rather than to determine why they occurred and what should be done to prevent them in the future?
- Was random review permitted for anything?
- Was review stymied by blind acceptance of a threshold percentage? If thresholds other than zero and 100 percent are set, the medical staff should have an enforced rule that review of all cases will be carried out. For instance, one cannot set an acceptable death percentage when it is not known if the right patients died. Possibly, different care would have saved some of these patients. Thus unqualified thresholds can subvert quality care review and may be legally dangerous if full review is not done. To find any undesirable patterns early, a medical staff should stick with trending and be suspicious when any finding surfaces more than once.
- Is there staff reluctance to review the procedures of a single specialist (e.g., neurosurgeon) on the staff? If so, one solution is to provide a comparable specialist who practices outside the "competition for patients" geographic area to do an evaluation.

Drug Therapy Evaluation

The most important reason for evaluating drug therapy in acute care hospitals is that essentially 100 percent of inpatients (and probably 100 percent of outpatients undergoing procedures) receive one or more prescribed drugs as part of their primary treatment. Given this percentage, drug therapy cannot be used as the sole basis for reviewing nonsurgical care, as indicated by some Joint Commission surveyors. There are also some surgical cases that do not require procedures but may be treated with antibiotics, fluids, analgesics, or chemotherapeutic agents. Other reasons for the medical staff to get a handle on drug therapy include the multitude of potent new drugs continually being introduced, the increasing need for hospitalization and treatment for untoward drug reactions (both drug-drug and drug-food reactions), the related claims and lawsuits, the ever-increasing cost of drugs, and the interest of the Joint Commission.[7] The Joint Commission, incidentally, insists that there be a distinction between "Drug Usage Evaluation" and the "Pharmacy and Therapeutics Function," a distinction not evident in the hospital field, probably because of the medical staff's natural penchant for establishing a pharmacy and therapeutics committee and because of the normal close relationship between artificially separated functions.

In evaluating drug therapy, both clinical and administrative aspects of the process must be included. Ordering practices must be measured against established indications and contraindications, dosages and serum levels must be monitored, drug administration requirements must be spelled out in adequate detail and followed, drug use protocols must be established, formulary control must be effective, significant untoward reactions to drugs and medication errors must be evaluated, and the role of therapeutic substitution must be determined.[8] Further, certain principles must be followed, including these:[9]

- The emphasis should be *prevention* rather than outcome evaluation, stressing prospective and timely concurrent intervention whenever possible.
- Evaluation should focus on drug use indications and contraindications, drug administration, therapeutic management, and unanticipated occurrences.
- All categories of drugs must be evaluated in an ongoing manner, particularly high-risk and problem-prone medications.
- Protocols should be developed for as many drugs as possible, beginning with the most potent (high-risk drugs) and those that require the most controls for administration and frequency of testing.
- Categories of drugs for which protocols have not been developed and implemented should be monitored in the interim to a reasonable degree through ongoing indicators or screens that will trigger a review automatically.
- All information obtained in the drug therapy evaluation process relating to medical necessity, clinical management, or adverse outcomes must be trended to identify problem areas and individuals. This information may be broken down as needed by specific drug, criterion, prescribing physician, patient diagnosis, medical staff department, specialty, and so on.
- Unless there is a reason to do otherwise, drug therapy should be evaluated hospitalwide, including inpatient, outpatient, emergency department, and hospital-sponsored home care.
- Orally, parenterally (intravenous, intramuscular, intraarterial, subcutaneous, intrathecal), and topically administered drugs should be included in the overall drug therapy evaluation process.

The use of drug therapy protocols is the ultimate example of prospective prevention-oriented QA. Protocols help to ensure the same high-quality level of drug care for all patients receiving a particular drug regardless of who prescribes it.[10] They also provide a pharmacist-nurse-physician team approach to drug administration. Protocols should be used prospectively to determine whether clinical indications for a drug's use are met (including any required predetermined testing), and to avoid errors during drug preparation and administration. Protocol drugs should be monitored concurrently by unit nursing personnel to prevent or identify quickly any adverse events or untoward effects, to determine the degree of clinical effectiveness, and to ensure that required blood serum or urine sample testing is performed and required monitoring (e.g., vital signs) is provided. In this way mistakes can easily be prevented or caught at the time of commission and thus be corrected prior to actual patient harm. On the other hand, QA department nurse reviewers may need only one or two high-impact criteria to monitor individual drugs from the review perspective. Review of complete drug protocols retrospectively by nurse reviewers is a waste of time and essentially negates the value of the protocols.[11] There should be a medical staff requirement that if a physician deviates from an established protocol, then (1) he or she must explain the deviation in the medical record and (2) an automatic review will be triggered.[12]

Three other points related to drug therapy evaluation need reinforcement:[13]

1. It is helpful to have a requirement that drug therapy criteria and protocols be submitted for any drugs being considered for addition to the formulary. Thus, when a new drug is approved, the criteria and protocols can be simultaneously adopted. This system prevents the drug therapy evaluation process from continually falling behind.

2. An antibiotic order sheet or form (Exhibit 9-1) is essential to data collection for the comprehensive evaluation of antibiotic usage. It takes only a few seconds of time to complete the form, and the physician is not required to write the order a second time. The most important aspect of antibiotic evaluation is related to empiric therapy. Empiric therapy information cannot be established without the physician indicating it either on an antibiotic order sheet or the regular medical record order sheet. For example, on the regular order sheet the physician might mark the antibiotic with an *E*, for empiric use. If the medical staff balks at using an antibiotic order sheet, other approaches may work. The staff could be requested to try the system for a four- to six-month period; at the end of this period, the order sheet will almost certainly have proven to be both harmless and helpful. The medical staff is more apt to respond positively when the change is not locked in forever. Another approach is to use the antibiotic order sheet in one or more medical staff departments whose members do not feel threatened by its use. Once it is known to work without difficulty, other departments will sign on.

3. There are many good reasons for selecting a drug for review or establishing a protocol; "high volume" is not productive. It might be used as a criterion (a) for cost-evaluation purposes; (b) if most of the physicians on staff prescribe a given drug, in which case reviewing use of the drug provides a mechanism for indicating that all physicians are included in the evaluation, and (c) if the drug in question is misused by one or more physicians and it is politically desirable to check all physicians' use in order to avoid any semblance of a witch hunt.

Exhibit 9-1 Sample Antibiotic Order Sheet

Antibiotics must be ordered on this sheet and include an indication for use.

THIS FORM FOR ONE-TIME USE ONLY

Select One:

Automatic Stop Order
(per Medical Staff Rules
and Regulations) after

☐ Surgical Prophylaxis
Operation: _____   _____ hours

☐ Empiric Therapy-Site or Pathogen Unknown
Suspected Site: _____   _____ days
Suspected Pathogen: _____   _____ days

Culture ordered: ☐ yes   ☐ no

☐ Documented Infection
Site: _____   _____ days
Pathogen: _____   _____ days

☐ Nonsurgical Prophylaxis
For: _____   _____ days

☐ Other (specify): _____   _____ days

Check One: ☐ New Order   ☐ Renewed Order

Date Ordered	Time Ordered	Antibiotic Ordered

ALLERGIES:

Patient Identification Plate

Source: Dimond, F.C., Jr., M.D. "Antibiotic Order Sheet" in National Medical Enterprises *Medical Director's Letter*, p. 6, No. 10-81, October 1981. Reprinted by permission.

Using Drug Indicators[14]

Because of the ongoing proliferation of new drugs (many of which have powerful actions and require increased attention to administration) and because it is not feasible to develop and implement protocols rapidly, a system of screening criteria or indicators may be used "to hold the fort" in the interim. There is potentially an endless number of indicators that could be used to trigger a review of possible breach in proper medical necessity of drug therapy, a management problem (either in the clinical or the drug administration process), or an unanticipated untoward event. Screening criteria or indicators may be developed for any category of drugs, for any individual drug, for quality, risk, or cost purposes, for drug interaction potential (food, tests, other drugs), and so on. The system must ensure that the review of the drug field is as broad as possible, that the minimum safe number of indicators for any drug category or individual drug is used, and that all problem-prone or high-risk drug areas are covered. Limiting the number of screens through careful selection is clearly essential when one considers all the other clinical reviews being done and the large amount of information that will have to be gathered, analyzed, and trended.

Probably the most obvious screening criterion or indicator is incorrect prescription or administration of a drug. Other examples of indicators include the following:

- The medication prescribed does not meet established use indications.
- Culture and sensitivity testing was not done (assuming it was possible) before initiating antibiotic therapy.
- The patient is receiving more than two antibiotics at a time.
- The patient is receiving more than one aminoglycoside at one time.
- The baseline theophylline level is not determined prior to initiating therapy in a patient who has been on theophylline products.
- The t-PA (or other) protocol was not followed.
- Digoxin is administered at the same time as antacid therapy.
- Full-dose (infusion) heparin is administered without establishing baseline coagulation levels.

Evaluation of Untoward Drug Reactions[15]

An important function and component of drug therapy evaluation that is often not performed or performed poorly is the evaluation of all *significant* untoward drug reactions, either confirmed or suspected. This requires that the medical staff define what a "significant" reaction is. Its importance is enhanced by its also being a long-time Joint Commission requirement. With a soundly functioning reporting system, a considerable number of significant reactions may be identified, with most of them being mild, transient, and not seriously harmful. However, because untoward drug reactions are usually underreported, a system for identification of reactions must be in place, and periodic nursing in-service education may be necessary. All nursing staff members should be required to report any suspected drug reaction as part of the hospitalwide incident or occurrence reporting system. Medical staff members should support this reporting, since the final determination of whether a drug reaction occurred is still theirs to make.

Because the physicians who perform this review function are busy, a system must be set up that makes them aware of all untoward reactions yet ensures the available time for drug reaction evaluation is focused only on those significant reactions that merit attention. Thus, the list should be screened prior to going to the physicians to be sure that specific cases are tagged for evaluation and discussion. In this way, the medical staff can be informed of all untoward drug reactions but will focus on only a select few. The medical staff should determine how these cases will be screened out for evaluation. However, a good selection guide is offered in the Food and Drug Administration's *Adverse Drug Reaction Reporting System,* and the supported criteria can be adopted or modified for use by the medical staff.

The FDA recommends reporting all suspected or confirmed significant reactions, including:

- new and unexpected reactions not indicated in the labeling
- serious, life-threatening, or fatal reactions.

In addition, the FDA recommends reporting unusual increases in the number and severity of reactions as well as drug use associated with congenital anomalies.

The FDA suggests that the following information is particularly helpful in evaluating adverse drug reaction reports: the temporal relationship of the drug administration to the reaction as well as to the duration of treatment; whether the reaction improved when treatment with the suspected drug was ended; whether the reaction recurred when the drug was reintroduced; whether there were concomitant diseases that may have caused the effect; and whether other drugs were used concomitantly. Such information should be considered by the medical staff member or group that evaluates untoward drug reactions.

The medical staff may want to add reactions that require reversal or treatment by another drug as a major category of untoward events. Many hospitals have expanded the FDA list. The following are also recommended:

- reactions that prolong hospital stay beyond the anticipated discharge date
- reactions associated with improper use of a drug
- reactions that result in permanent or prolonged disability.

Blood Therapy Evaluation

Because blood is a precious, sometimes lifesaving, but not always harmless commodity, blood use evaluation is an important medical staff responsibility. For a long time, changes in blood-ordering practices were related only to medical staff education and blood availability. Initially, these two factors helped to decrease the unnecessary use of whole blood in this country. But now there is little reason to use whole blood or any blood product improperly. Criteria are readily available to determine whether a patient needs blood in some form and whether the proper form (whole or component blood) is being administered. Criteria selected should be recognized nationally and not based on a "community" standard unless the latter equals or exceeds the national standard. The medical staff must evaluate its members' blood-ordering practices against these criteria to determine how blood and blood products are being used in the facility, and it must then make appropriate changes if the criteria are not met. Criteria supported by the American Association of Blood Banks through it publications or through articles[16] are acceptable. The Joint Commission, in 1987, as part of its Medical Staff Monitoring Functions Series, offered sample blood usage review criteria, use of which has been recommended by Joint Commission surveyors during accreditation survey visits.[17]

Albumin is the most common blood component omitted from medical staff review. This occurs because it is dispensed from the pharmacy rather than from the blood bank.

In addition to the criteria specific to the use of whole blood or any component, other screens or indicators may automatically trigger a review, including:

- nontraumatic cases requiring more than 2500 cc of blood (whole or red blood cells)
- actual or suspected reactions to transfusion rate of less than 2 percent
- a transfusion without determination of the hemoglobin or hematocrit within 48 hours pre- and posttransfusion (whole blood or red blood cells)
- a platelet transfusion without determination of the platelet count pretransfusion (usually within 24 hours) or posttransfusion
- a platelet transfusion of less than ___ units of platelet concentrate
- excessive or unnecessary wastage of blood
- hepatitis (type ___) patients who received a blood transfusion within the preceding ___ months.[18]

Ordinarily, blood use is evaluated for all patients receiving whole blood or a blood product. This means that not all units require review, for one patient may receive multiple units. When a patient receives more than one blood-related product, each must be evaluated for appropriateness. Initial 100 percent concurrent review is anticipated through the pre-physician screening system, with the trended fallout going to the second and third departmental tiers, as appropriate. In facilities where, for some reason, 100 percent review is not done, the blood use cases reviewed must not be selected based on the largest volume of use. Low volume is probably a better guideline when volume is used at all as a screening criterion.

In the handful of facilities that have an extraordinarily large volume of blood use internally (usually a large tertiary center providing all patient care services and perhaps even blood bank services to other facilities), it may be expedient to develop a system for evaluating a representative sample. Any system that has even a hint of random review should be avoided. It must be ensured that the whole blood and the blood components used in the facility are evaluated and that all physicians who order blood for their patients are included in the review process. Particular care should be taken to look for any trends that might signify an unacceptable pattern of blood use (e.g., examining the status of patients for whom blood has been ordered).

As with any screening fallout in patient care review, all cases of possible improper use of blood or blood components should be referred to the appropriate medical staff departments for physician peer evaluation.

In addition to blood-ordering practices, blood transfusion–related functions that require medical staff evaluation include but are not limited to the following:

- the appropriate use of the type and screen procedure based on individual procedure and practitioner profiles
- monitoring of the crossmatch to transfusion ratio to at least ensure that it does not exceed recognized national guidelines including procedure and practitioner profiles
- monitoring of blood wastage, taking into consideration physician ordering practices, storage, handling, and administration
- monitoring of in-house blood donor services, including screening of donors and donated blood for infectious agents and use of autologous and directed blood transfusions
- approval of all blood sources from outside the facility

Medical Record Review

Medical record review can be easily combined with review of records for other reasons. The primary medical staff (physician) review effort is to determine if records are clinically pertinent, thus providing a peer review of the quality of the records rather than of the actual care provided. Much of each medical record can be reviewed objectively by registered nurse reviewers and medical record specialists.

The review information can be readily made part of a worksheet and thus be available to the physician reviewer who bases his or her opinion of clinical pertinence on the nonphysician review findings and on his or her own review. Following are the sort of questions to keep in mind during the review: Does the medical record reflect all changes in the patient's status for this admission? Were needed laboratory, X-ray, or other tests ordered and the results received in time for use in care of the patient? Were consultations required prior to surgery requested and the findings reported prior to surgery?

The record review process must ensure that certain basic requirements are met, such as these:

- Over a reasonable period of time, the records of all staff members are to be evaluated for quality and clinical pertinence.
- The records are to be evaluated for their soundness as medicolegal documents.
- Nursing entries in the records are to be evaluated for their quality, and the findings are to be fed into the overall medical record review process (this is a responsibility of the nursing service).
- Any significant discrepancy between nursing and physician record entries (or those of any other medical staff practitioner) is to be reported and reviewed.
- Medical record delinquency and significant deficiencies (especially deficiencies in histories, physical exams, and operative notes) are to be routinely monitored and reported to the appropriate medical staff departments.
- All findings from the record review process, with trending, are to be referred to the appropriate department's second and third tiers for a final peer decision.

A record review worksheet (or a worksheet with a record review component) should maximize the pertinent information sought and minimize the amount of writing. Usually a checksheet format can be used for most of the review items. However, there must be evidence of physician review for clinical pertinence, not just a physician signature under a list of items reviewed by a nonphysician.

Other Medical Staff Functions

Medical staffs vary in their handling of other quality-related functions, which may include UR, RM, safety, infection control, mortality review, and disaster planning. Some medical staffs appoint medical staff committees, some appoint medical staff members to hospitalwide committees, some receive and review the findings from the initial nonphysician reviews, and some use a combination of the above methods. A staff's role and responsibilities should be defined in the medical staff bylaws. The medical staff services professional must be aware of these review findings either through reading the meeting minutes or through QA in order to ensure that any positive or negative fallout gets into the practitioner profile for use at the time of reappointment and reprivileging. Also the staff should be made aware that *hospital* committee meeting minutes do not usually enjoy the confidentiality protection afforded medical staff QA or peer review meetings.

Some comments on these functions are worth considering, and the medical staff services professional can help tremendously by ensuring that the critical elements are included in the meeting agendas and minutes and that nothing falls through the cracks. Function-specific comments include but are not limited to the following:

- From a quality standpoint, UR focuses on the medical necessity for hospitalization and intervention. UR can be preventive when used prospectively or concurrently. From a cost viewpoint, the UR functions also include both length of stay and cost outliers, and these can have quality ramifications as well. Usually, severity-of-illness comparative analyses result from the outlier cases, but these analyses should be limited to specific physicians and disease status patients. For instance, if two comparably trained and experienced physicians in the same specialty treat comparable chronic obstructive pulmonary disease patients and the outlier lengths of stay and costs for one are four times greater than for the other, a medical staff objective severity-of-illness study is indicated. Again, however, elimination up front of unnecessary admissions, care, and procedures holds more potential for quality and cost improvement. The medical staff services professional can also encourage the medical staff to define in the bylaws, rules, and regulations (under UR) its responsibility for discharge planning.

- The main medical staff RM responsibility is to report and review the reported unanticipated adverse clinical events. These events are usually reported through the protected hospital occurrence or incident reporting system, then trended and referred to the appropriate medical staff department review system. Unfortunately, this important function is outcome-oriented, hence not a preventive aspect of QA. When the function is hospitalwide or is performed in combination with a safety committee, medical staff participation is greatly reduced. In such cases, the medical staff services professional and QA coordinator working together can ensure that only clinical patient care events are reported to the medical staff departments and that physicians are not loaded down with nonpatient care RM responsibilities (e.g., liability for visitor personal losses and injuries and hospital losses). Also, an essentially lay committee should not deal with clinical issues.

- Infection control activities are hospitalwide by definition, hence they are often monitored by a hospital infection control committee. This undoubtedly offers no protection for confidentiality under federal or state QA or peer review statutes. It is better for the infection control committee to be a medical staff committee so as to control the accessibility of information (see Chapter 14). The Joint Commission mandates an infection control committee but does not designate whether it is to be a hospital or medical staff committee. However, the Joint Commission seems to favor making it a hospital committee, since the Joint Commission requires the committee minutes to be sent to the medical staff executive committee, thus allowing the medical staff departments to be bypassed. This may be a concession to those few staffs that are so small they meet as a staff-of-the-whole or to staffs that have refused to departmentalize and are let off the hook by the Joint Commission for whatever reason. The most important role of the findings of the infection control program is to ensure that each medical staff department receives information (with any trends) that is specific to its members and patients. Again, coordination between the medical staff services professional and the infection control practitioner or QA coordinator will be necessary in order to ensure that the medical staff department meeting agendas and minutes reflect the information presented, the peer review findings, and the resultant recommendations and actions.

- Mortality review is a medical staff option usually triggered by an occurrence or incident report, and such reviews are always performed subjectively by the medical staff. Thus their worth is highly questionable, particularly as any review is readily challengeable by the practitioner whose patient care is in question. Also it may otherwise waste physician review time in that many patient deaths are predictable and fully anticipated; thus reviewing them is neither practical nor enlightening. This suggests that criteria should be developed to determine which deaths actually require medical staff review. One of the problems with subjective evaluation is that deceased patients are almost always felt to have received proper care. Other than in cases of obvious and visible mismanagement, no death is ever stated to have been avoidable or preventable. This will always be the finding until medical necessity and clinical management criteria and standards can be applied. By definition, an outcome review of a death is too late for the patient and, as a result of its subjectivity, is unlikely to improve subsequent care or practice. The medical staff services professional can at least help ensure that death case discussions are reasonably reported in the departmental meeting minutes. Other sources of mortality-related information of interest to the medical staff include autopsy findings and "code blue" evaluation reports.

- The medical staff's role in internal and external disaster plans should be defined. Normally, patient care from triage to treatment to transfer is strictly a medical staff function, with administrative support in all areas outside of direct care. The medical staff's role appears to have been watered down to one of several "other review functions" in the evolving Joint Commission *Accreditation Manual for Hospitals*.[19]

WHAT MUST BE DOCUMENTED?

Minutes of medical staff department meetings must include (1) the identification of the QA information sources used to ensure that a comprehensive scope of care was screened objectively and evaluated and (2) the relevant findings of each activity and the action taken or recommended. *Each evaluation activity (e.g. blood and drug use evaluation, medical necessity, adverse occurrences, etc.) should be individually listed in the minutes, with the specific findings and the action taken or recommended.* The minutes will thus demonstrate that a comprehensive objective review of medical and surgical care has been performed, that there is adequate monitoring through a multiscreen system, and that action has resulted. For completeness and evidence of review, the minutes should indicate when there are no substantial findings for any aspect of practice rather than just omit the subject.

Care should be taken to ensure the medical staff does not fall into the trap of reporting QA activities inadequately, particularly at the department level. At the same time, identifying patients and practitioners by name should be avoided in committee, department, and medical staff meeting minutes.

Unacceptable Evidence of Quality Assurance Activity Reporting[20]

Just as there will always be room for flexible and innovative approaches to performing QA activities in hospitals, so also will there be a need to document adequately their performance and findings. However, to try to indicate every acceptable method would be impossible because new methods are still evolving. On the other hand, much needless and costly effort can be saved by indicating at least some of the *unacceptable* ways of demonstrating compliance with QA requirements. These include but are certainly not limited to the following:

- Seemingly sterile staff evaluation of patient care and clinical performance through departmental or committee meetings, with only findings of "good case management" documented month after month. This situation indicates a failure to use criteria, inadequate criteria, an inadequate screening system and poor case selection, a reluctance to acknowledge and/or resolve existing problems, or a combination of these.
- A list of medical chart numbers as the total evidence of evaluation done.
- Subjective rather than objective review.
- Random review.
- Evaluating only catastrophic events (mortality and morbidity), which, if infections are not included in the morbidity review, probably account for a very small percentage of total patient care. An objective look should be given to the

appropriateness of noncatastrophic patient care.
- Failure to act when the meeting minutes indicate the need for action based on the QA findings.
- Focusing on only surgical aspects of care rather than including nonsurgical care.

RESISTANCE TO QUALITY ASSURANCE ACTIVITIES

The Myth of Cookbook Medicine[21]

Physicians often defend their practice with references to licensure and the long-established tradition of "the art of medicine." A license is simply a piece of paper or plastic that permits the owner (who has the appropriate medical degree plus at least a year of training) to minister to patients in a nonhospital setting. The status of licensure has not improved much over the years, and licenses have never become the hoped-for warranty against inadequate patient care. Licensure may even have become diluted in states that have attempted to bolster its image by requiring many hours of continuing education, as the education credits are usually accepted regardless of their relevance to the type of care provided by the physician. The concept of medicine as an art is no longer a defense. Although medicine cannot be touted as strictly a "science," it has progressed a long way in this direction compared with early state-of-the-art practice, in which common sense and astute observation at the bedside guided the diagnosis and therapy.

Dependence on licensure and medicine as an art helps to foster the concept of cookbook medicine, hence they have no place as the sole basis for hospital practice. The loudest voice in support of the actual existence of cookbook medicine is that of the practitioner who is depending on licensure to back every decision and to support his or her medical practice. In the hospital, this practitioner might be heard rejecting proffered help from another physician nurse by asking rudely, "Are you trying to tell me how to practice medicine?" The same practitioner might reject help from a knowledgeable nurse by asking, "What medical school did you graduate from?" Such behavior is not conducive to establishing a smooth working relationship among all patient care team members, an essential ingredient of any QA and RM program.

The need to practice at an acceptable level is anathema to the substandard or marginal practitioner. The qualified practitioner is not threatened by a high standard of care, and indeed he or she often practices above the established level.

Setting and enforcing standards of care is anything but cookbook medicine. If the medical staff's manual of rules and regulations is a properly constituted document, then the staff has already set for itself a large number of patient care and clinical practice standards. The staff must do this to protect its patients and itself. Fortunately, staffs are increasingly willing to accept and use practice protocols, particularly for drug therapy, or continuous ventilation, and so on. Protocols (1) support team efforts by involving physicians, nurses, and other team members, such as pharmacists and therapists; (2) eliminate the need to establish and use clinically valid criteria; and (3) eliminate the need for physicians to remember to write every order at a specific time, to establish every dosage accurately (the specific levels of which may vary frequently, especially when dependent on a laboratory result), and so on. The mandatory use of consultation (e.g., in a CCU or for continuous ventilation) is sometimes labeled a form of cookbook medicine, even though physicians well recognize that it is professionally indefensible (and in some cases legally indefensible) not to offer a patient the best care available in the hospital.

The most ridiculous allegations of cookbook medicine emanate from practitioners who challenge the use of objective clinically valid criteria to measure their patient care and clinical performance, a long-recognized valid process. To condone not using an objective evaluation process suggests that the medical staff tolerates the existence of multiple levels of care for patients with the same health care problems. This idea itself is intolerable. The anti-criteria challenges are basically supported by statements such as these: "I practice good medicine, so I don't need a paper review" or "That's why I went to medical school and got my license to practice." An individual so apparently threatened can be continuously practicing "luck through" medicine and keeping it a secret even from him- or herself. An entire medical staff with this attitude is indeed a throwback to the dark ages. The use of objective clinically valid (e.g., national) criteria also serves to eliminate the myth of a geographic "community level of care."

The concept of the art of medicine will always play a significant, but increasingly controlled, role in the practice of medicine. For example, this concept is consistent with the recognition that there often are several acceptable ways to treat a patient, but it does not support using a therapy that is inadequate. It does not suggest that patients on continuous ventilation for a long period do not need to be monitored by timely blood gas determinations and be treated appropriately. Medicine merely at the level of licensure must never be tolerated in a hospital, particularly when the defense is a charge of cookbook medicine. Today, cookbook medicine exists only in the eye of the beholder.

Although care cookbooks will probably always exist for reimbursement purposes, the best approach is to use some form of decision tree. This approach essentially points the way, leaving the specifics of care to the physician. In so doing, it becomes less of a target for lawyers and reimbursers.

Resistance to objective QA and peer review is frequently attributed to the fear of legal action. What is more protective of physicians and patients and medical staffs than practicing medicine at a recognized national level?

Some resistance is also related to turf issues and to the income protection that is perceived to result from QA findings that restrict the right of some physicians to provide certain types of patient care. Even though when appropriately restricted, the physicians may raise anticompetition claims.

Some physicians claim that there is no time for QA, that time is money, and that all physicians should be paid for any QA activity in which they are involved. This is a bad door to open, for the medical staff has a collective responsibility to ensure that its members' patient care practices are objectively assessed in accordance with its own bylaws, rules, and regulations.

Rarely publicized is the biggest reason for a physician not to participate actively in the QA process: the fear of patient referral loss. It is often difficult for one physician to criticize or counsel another physician who is a good source of referrals.

Overcoming Resistance[22]

Motivating anyone to do anything depends on multiple factors. The suggestion of change raises both objection and suspicion, each to an unrealistic degree and usually based on unrealistic tenets when concepts like QA and RM are introduced. Resistance is particularly notable from practitioners who by definition and nature are individualists separated from one another by specialty, clinical privileges, and private patients. These barriers have to be overcome through the system (i.e., the medical staff) and through the pressures brought to bear on the system by governmental, legal, regulatory, and accrediting agencies; third party payers; liability, and so on.

In trying to motivate the entire staff, it is helpful to begin by identifying key individuals interested in and knowledgeable about QA and RM activities. Because physicians prefer to discuss patient care in terms of "quality" rather than "risk," look to those individuals who have served as strong leaders of the medical staff, particularly as chairpersons of key clinical committees and departments. These individuals should form the nucleus of the QA and RM effort. The chairperson of the QA committee must not be appointed solely for political reasons or based on popularity. In addition to having an interest in and knowledge about QA and the clinical aspects of RM, the chairperson should enjoy the respect of the majority of the active medical staff. Strong support from the governing board and administration is crucial to program success.

Once you have cleared this first hurdle, work to interest others by opening up channels of communication. Let it be known up front that a QA and RM program is necessary and must be implemented. Assure all professional and administrative staff members that the program is a hospitalwide team effort and that although it will focus on the clinical aspects of patient care, it will also include hospital-controlled aspects and facility and equipment factors. Assure all personnel that there will be feedback from QA and RM activities. Try to make this feedback positive and constructive. When negative feedback must be given, it should be as straightforward, nonaccusatory, nonjudgmental, and confidential as possible. All of the staffs should be informed how QA and RM information will be gathered and processed.

It should also be recognized that not everyone will accept the importance of QA and RM, which may appear as unnecessarily intrusive. The bona fide resisters (i.e., those individuals who will not come into camp after a reasonable education effort) should be identified. Problems of interest to the least motivated can be selected, and efforts can be made to win them over in this way. Peers who command the respect of resisters can be involved. The need for peer participation in all aspects of a QA and RM program should be stressed.

One last thought: QA and RM are certainly more palatable than the other two inevitabilities on this earth: death and taxes.

ROLE OF THE MEDICAL STAFF SERVICES PROFESSIONAL IN QUALITY ASSURANCE AND RISK MANAGEMENT

Because the hospital medical staff, which is made up primarily of physicians, admits, treats, and discharges all patients and plays a major role in relation to patient claims, it is responsible for about 90 percent of the QA function as well as a large component of the RM function in the hospital. As a result of his or her relationship to the medical staff, the medical staff services professional (MSSP) is automatically tied into the same functions.

How the MSSP participates in QA and RM functions will depend on the administrative organization dictated by the hospital leadership's knowledge and support of these functions. The MSSP's role will vary somewhat and require varying degrees of support (1) when these and other functions are not centrally performed, (2) when there is an integrated QA department in the hospital, or (3) when the MSSP manages or otherwise integrates the program (which is rare).

In the noncentralized QA and RM program, the MSSP has to be in frequent communication with each clinical department providing patient care services and attend each medical staff committee and department meeting. This unreasonable drain on the MSSP's time and energy is more apt to occur in a small hospital (under 15 active staff members representing both surgical and nonsurgical specialties) or in a larger hospital in which the medical staff has not departmentalized and the QA function is hospital-oriented and poorly performed. In this situation, much time is needed to gather all the required patient care information and organize it for the various committee and medical staff meetings. Little time is left for ensuring its proper presentation and documentation. Poor documentation may lead to loss of required follow-up.

The information-gathering responsibility is highly simplified when there is an organized integrated QA program into which both support departments and the medical staff QA findings feed for analysis and trending. The major MSSP function then is to ensure proper presentation and documentation and any follow-up that is required.

Rarely, the MSSP assumes the position of manager or director of an organized department with control of all components and personnel that perform quality and resource management functions. This situation requires the MSSP to become a manager and to delegate some medical staff functions to less qualified individuals. Problems may arise if the MSSP lacks a clinical background and inherits unqualified individuals to perform the various quality and resource management functions or fails to hire competent clinical members (e.g., QA coordinator, clinical nurse reviewers, etc.) for the department.

It is not recommended that the MSSP manage the whole patient care department unless a qualified medical staff coordinator is hired as well. It is also not recommended that the MSSP be placed in the QA department or under the supervision of the QA coordinator or director. The functions are best kept separate for the following reasons:

1. The MSSP is usually viewed by the medical staff as a strong medical staff supporter; the QA coordinator or department is often considered a critic or harasser of the medical staff by medical staff members and sometimes even the hospital administrator, who does not want the physicians ruffled.

2. If, for example, the QA coordinator or department is out of favor with a physician or a medical staff department or committee, the MSSP may be able to accomplish what is required, such as negotiating a difficult peer review issue. This is an important point because of the large number of medical staff responsibilities to be monitored, and the availability and usually larger number of QA department individuals monitoring them.

3. A MSSP and a QA representative usually attend meetings for different reasons. The QA representative is usually concerned with one or more aspects of the presentation and discussion of information; the MSSP with accurate, clear, and complete documentation and with getting through the agenda items.

4. The MSSP is essentially always administratively oriented in task and background and cannot be a substitute in clinical reviews even if time permits; the QA coordinator or department is essentially clinically oriented, can always take meeting minutes if required, but has not the time or the necessary information to set up the meetings.

5. Having a separate medical staff services office or department provides clear evidence of the importance that the administration places on the medical staff image in the hospital.

6. A separate medical staff services office or department is better able to provide security and confidentiality regarding credentials files, a chronic medical staff concern.

7. The MSSP and the QA coordinator or department have different computer or word processing needs. Although some software might be used in common, there still would be a need for two computers or at least two software packages.

8. Separate functions (medical staff services versus quality assurance) provide double coverage in ensuring that all required information is discussed at medical staff committee and department meetings and that nothing that requires follow-up information or action drops through the cracks, either by omission or indefinite ping-ponging among medical staff committees and departments.

The established MSSP is in a unique position to move the medical staff QA (peer review) program ahead by helping to select (through recommendation) the medical staff committee and department chairpersons when these are appointed. Staff officers are usually controlled through elections. The MSSP is aware of physicians who support QA, drug therapy evaluation, infection control, and so on, as well as physicians whose leadership is respected by other staff members. Thus, MSSP input in the selection process is usually valued.

The medical staff relies heavily on the MSSP to ensure that the bylaws, rules and regulations are up to date. The MSSP can help strengthen medical staff QA by encouraging the medical staff to include meaningful requirements for credentialing and privileging and for medical staff departments and committees in the bylaws and to include standards of care in the medical staff and department rules and regulations.

A third way that the MSSP can strengthen the medical staff QA program is to guide the documentation of the QA (peer review) functions. The MSSP, by working closely with the QA staff member who has the objective findings from the review of medical staff member patient care, can help set committee or department meeting agendas to ensure that (1) the material is properly organized and discussed, (2) any follow-up from previous meetings is addressed, and (3) the bylaws requirements of the committee or department functions have been followed.

Fourth, MSSP must assure that peer review findings related to specific practitioners get into the appropriate credentials files for use at time of reappointment and repriviléging.

NOTES

1. F. C. Dimond, Jr., "The Medical Staff Quality Assurance (QA) System," *Medical Director's Letter* (National Medical Enterprises), May 1982, 1–2.

2. F. C. Dimond, Jr., "Still More on the Quality Assurance (QA) Process," *Medical Director's Letter* (National Medical Enterprises), May-June 1985, 6.

3. Ibid., 1.

4. Ibid., 1.

5. Ibid., 1.

6. F. C. Dimond, Jr., "Procedure Evaluation." Written in August 1989 for dissemination to NME Hospitals, it has not been published and the author is unsure of its final form.

7. F. C. Dimond, Jr., "More on Drug Therapy Evaluation," *Medical Director's Letter* (National Medical Enterprises), August 1987, 1.

8. Ibid., 2.

9. Ibid., 1–2.

10. F. C. Dimond, Jr., "More Drug Practice Protocols," *Medical Director's Letter* (National Medical Enterprises), July-August 1985, 2.

11. Dimond, "More on Drug Therapy Evaluation."

12. Dimond, "More Drug Practice Protocols."

13. Dimond, "More on Drug Therapy Evaluation."

14. Ibid.

15. F. C. Dimond, Jr., "Untoward Reactions to Drugs (Diagnostic/Therapeutic)," *Medical Director's Letter* (National Medical Enterprises), March-April 1984, 6–7.

16. For example, A. J. Grindon et al., "The Hospital Transfusion Committee," *JAMA* 253 (1985): 540–43.

17. Joint Commission on Accreditation of Healthcare Organizations, *Medical Staff Monitoring Functions: Blood Usage Review.* Oak Brook, IL: JCAHO, 1987: 19–25.

18. F. C. Dimond, Jr., "Evaluation of Blood Use," *Medical Director's Letter* (National Medical Enterprises), November 1982, 5–6.

19. Joint Commission on Accreditation of Healthcare Organizations, *1990 Accreditation Manual for Hospitals* (Chicago: Joint Commission on Accreditation of Healthcare Organizations, 1989), 115.

20. F. C. Dimond, Jr., "Unacceptable Evidence of Quality Assurance Activity Reporting," *Medical Director's Letter* (National Medical Enterprises), June 1982, 3–4.

21. F. C. Dimond, Jr., "The Super Myth of Cookbook Medicine," *Medical Director's Letter* (National Medical Enterprises), May-June 1985, 10–11.

22. F. C. Dimond, Jr., "Motivating Individual Acceptance of the QA/RM Program," *Medical Director's Letter* (National Medical Enterprises), July 1983, 3–5.

Chapter 10

Other Medical Staff Organization Functions

Cindy Orsund-Gassiot, CMSC

The major functions of a medical staff organization, credentialing and quality assurance, have been discussed in earlier chapters. This chapter will focus on other medical staff organization functions, specifically, the functions performed by institutional review boards, cancer committees, and continuing medical education programs.

INSTITUTIONAL REVIEW BOARDS

Hospital institutional review boards (IRBs) are required to oversee protection of the rights and welfare of human subjects involved in clinical investigation of drugs and medical devices regulated by the Food and Drug Administration (FDA). These boards were formed in many community hospitals for the first time in the 1970s, when intraocular lenses were invented but not yet approved by the FDA and ophthalmologists began implanting them in conjunction with surgery to remove cataracts.

The FDA has regulations that hospitals must follow governing the protection of human subjects involved in research on products regulated by the agency. Additionally, other federal agencies and departments, and some states, have regulations that govern human subject protection. The medical staff services professional (MSSP) should be familiar with those regulations that apply to research being done at his or her institution.

Products under investigation include drugs that are being evaluated by the FDA and medical devices (e.g., intraocular lenses and other surgical implants) not yet fully approved by the agency. (The research must be based on adequately performed laboratory and animal experimentation and on thorough knowledge of the scientific literature.) When physicians use investigational products in the hospital (and sometimes on an outpatient basis), they must do so under carefully controlled conditions and using scientific principles. The IRB's functions are to review, approve, disapprove, or modify the protocol for any study; weigh the risks against the foreseeable benefits for the patients involved; determine whether the consent document adequately informs the patients of the aims, methods, anticipated benefits and potential hazards of the study; monitor the progress of the investigation; and discontinue approval of a study when the hazards are found to outweigh the potential benefits.[1]

Briefly, FDA regulations[2] require an IRB to

1. be established at any institution engaging in any investigation, study, or research involving human subjects

2. be composed of not less than five members with voting authority (members must be qualified by experience, expertise, and diversity of background to give advice for safeguarding human subjects; the IRB may not be composed of all men or all women and must have one member whose only affiliation with the institution is IRB membership; there must be one member whose primary activities are nonscientific, for example, a lawyer, ethicist, or clergy; at least one licensed physician must be appointed and no member should have a conflicting interest)

3. perform two primary functions:
   - *review* and approve or disapprove of any proposed investigational study
   - *monitor* any ongoing study (the IRB has a responsibility to ensure each study is carried out as stated in the protocol; any investigation must be followed until it is completed, discontinued, or suspended)

4. follow written procedures and conduct business only if there is a quorum, which cannot be less than a majority of the members of the committee

5. maintain records sufficient to clearly describe the results of any study

6. ensure that investigators obtain legal informed consent (the elements of which are specified by the FDA)

7. receive, investigate, and act on complaints relating to any study under review regardless of their source (e.g., subjects, the sponsor of the study, members of the medical staff, etc.)

8. make records available for inspection by authorized agents of the FDA

To assist these committees in operating according to regulations, the FDA has developed a self-evaluation guide. The following guidelines, reproduced in part from that document,[3] should be used by the institution to determine what written policies and procedures are needed.

Policies and procedures are required describing the functions of the IRB with respect to

1. conducting initial and continuing review
2. reporting findings and actions to the investigator and institution
3. determining which projects require review more often than annually
4. determining which projects need verification from sources other than the investigators that no material changes have occurred since previous IRB review
5. ensuring prompt reporting to the IRB of changes in research activities
6. ensuring that changes in approved research are not initiated without IRB review and approval
7. ensuring prompt reporting to the IRB of unanticipated problems or scientific misconduct involving risks to subjects or others

Additional policies and procedures should describe the operations of the IRB with respect to

1. The review process:
   - All members should review the entire protocol.
   - One or more "primary reviewers" should review the entire protocol, report to the IRB, and lead discussion on the protocol.
   - All members should have access to the entire protocol.
   - The role of subcommittees of the IRB should be delineated.
   - Emergency studies must be reviewed.
   - Procedures for expedited review should be followed.
2. Criteria for approval of investigation:
   - The risks to subjects must be minimized.
   - The risks to subjects must be reasonable in relation to anticipated benefits.
   - The selection of subjects must be equitable.
   - Informed consent must be adequate.
   - Where appropriate, there should be adequate provisions to protect the privacy of subjects and maintain the confidentiality of data.
   - Appropriate safeguards must be included in the study to protect the rights and welfare of vulnerable subjects.
3. Voting requirements:
   - A quorum must be required to transact business.
   - There must be quorum diversity requirements.
   - Approval or disapproval of a study should require a certain percentage of the vote.

- All members must have full voting rights.
- Proxy votes should not be allowed.
- Investigators should not vote on their own studies.

IRB records that the institution must maintain include

1. a list of IRB members and qualifications
2. written procedures and guidelines
3. minutes of meetings:
   - members present
   - record of discussion of controversial issues
   - record of IRB decisions
   - record of voting
4. protocols and consent documents as submitted and as finally approved
5. communications to and from the IRB
6. adverse reaction reports
7. IRB consideration of adverse reaction reports
8. periodic continuing reviews
9. budget and accounting records regarding acquisition and expenditure of resources
10. emergency use reports
11. statements of significant new findings provided to subjects

Each investigator must provide information to the IRB. This information must include

1. professional qualifications to do the research (including a description of necessary support services and facilities)
2. the title of the study
3. the purpose of the study (including the benefit to be obtained by doing the study)
4. the sponsor of the study
5. results of previous related research
6. subject selection criteria
7. subject exclusion criteria
8. the justification for use of special subject populations (e.g., the mentally retarded, children, etc.)
9. the study design (including a discussion of the appropriateness of research methods)

10. a description of procedures to be performed
11. provisions for managing adverse reactions

FDA INSTITUTIONAL REVIEW BOARD INSPECTIONS[4]

In response to a Congressional mandate to expand its monitoring of biomedical research conducted under its regulations, the FDA developed the Bioresearch Monitoring Program and, as part of that effort, began an expanded review of IRBs in April 1977. The aim of the program is to ensure the protection of human subjects by ensuring the existence of well-organized and properly functioning local IRBs. The Bioresearch Monitoring Program, which encompasses IRB, clinical investigators, sponsors, monitors, and nonclinical laboratories, is also intended to ensure the quality and integrity of data submitted to the FDA for regulatory decision making. For this reason, the IRB regulations note that the FDA may inspect IRBs and review and copy IRB records.

Institutional Review Board Program

Under the Bioresearch Monitoring Program, the FDA conducts on-site procedural reviews of IRBs. These reviews are conducted to determine whether an IRB is operating in accordance with its own written procedures as well as current FDA regulations.

When an institution is selected for a procedural review, an investigator from one of the FDA's field offices contacts a responsible individual at the institution, usually the IRB chairperson, and arranges a mutually acceptable time for the visit. When the field investigator arrives at the institution, he or she will show FDA credentials and present a Notice of Inspection to the chairperson of the IRB or another responsible official. This is done simply to let the staff at the institution know that the investigator is a duly authorized representative of FDA.

The investigator will first interview appropriate staff members and obtain information about the IRB's policies and procedures. Then the investigator will examine the IRB's performance by following one or more studies through the review process in use at the institution. IRB procedures and membership will be examined to see whether they conform to current FDA regulations. The investigator may request copies of records of IRB membership, IRB procedures and guidelines, minutes of the meetings at which the studies were reviewed and discussed, materials on the studies submitted to the IRB by the clinical investigators, and any other materials pertaining to these studies. These materials become part of the field investigator's report to FDA headquarters.

After the inspection has been completed, the investigator will conduct an exit interview with the responsible institutional representative, usually the IRB chairperson. At this interview, the investigator will review the findings, describe any deviations from the current regulations, and suggest corrective actions. If appropriate, a List of Observations (Form 483) may be left with the institution.

After the investigator returns to the district office, a written report with recommendations for action, if necessary, will be prepared. This report will be forwarded to FDA headquarters for evaluation. When this evaluation is completed, a letter will be sent to the IRB chairperson or other responsible institutional officials. The letter may state that no deficiencies were found or, if the applicable regulations have not been followed, ask for correction. Where major corrections are needed, a written response may be required. At times, a follow-up inspection may be conducted.

A copy of the FDA's *Compliance Program Guidance Manual for IRB Inspections* (Program 7348.809) is available to the public by writing to Freedom of Information Staff, HFW-30, Food and Drug Administration, 5600 Fishers Lane, Rockville, MD 20857.

APPROVED CANCER PROGRAMS

The Commission on Cancer of the American College of Surgeons (ACS) sponsors a voluntary approval program for hospital cancer programs.[5] Although the medical record department's tumor registry is the locus of a cancer program, the MSSP may provide administrative support to the hospital cancer committee that is seeking approval for its cancer program. An understanding of the components of a hospital cancer program is helpful for performing these tasks.

The goal of the ACS cancer program is to decrease the morbidity and mortality of cancer patients. This goal is pursued by encouraging hospitals to improve cancer control efforts through prevention, early detection, staging, treatment, rehabilitation, and surveillance for recurrence of cancer. These efforts are overseen by a hospital cancer committee.

In order to seek ACS approval, the hospital must be Joint Commission accredited and have specific resources for state-of-the-art diagnosis and treatment of cancer. An approved cancer program consists of four components:

1. a cancer committee
2. cancer conferences
3. patient care evaluation studies
4. cancer registry

The Cancer Committee

The cancer committee must be a standing, multidisciplinary committee, and it must be included in the bylaws. It must meet at least quarterly and maintain documentation of its proceedings. The committee's functions are to provide consultative services to patients; provide education programs, including discussion of major cancer sites, for hospital staff; evaluate the quality of care of cancer patients in the hospital; and supervise the cancer data systems in the hospital.

Cancer Conferences

An approved cancer program includes conferences to educate the medical and ancillary staffs and provide consultative services to patients. The conferences must be patient-oriented and consultative, not didactic, and they must include participation by disciplines other than physicians. All major cancer sites treated in the facility must be addressed in the conferences, the frequency of which are determined by hospital category.

Patient Care Evaluation Studies

Two patient care evaluation studies must be conducted annually for ACS cancer program approval. These studies must review the quality of care, identify problems and opportunities to improve care, measure the effectiveness of treatment, and compare the facility's performance with national patterns of care and survival rates.

Cancer Registry

A system to monitor all types of cancer diagnosed or treated in an institution is of paramount importance to an approved cancer program.

A facility must collect and maintain cancer patient data for two years prior to seeking approval by the ACS. The registry must include a patient index file with a card for each patient entered and an abstract of pertinent information about each patient, the cancer, and its management. Patients must be tracked annually for follow-up.

To meet the reporting requirement, hospital cancer programs must publish and distribute an annual report to the hospital medical and administrative staffs. The report includes a summary of the goals, achievements, and activities of the cancer program for the reporting period; a statistical summary of registry data for the year; and a detailed analysis of one or more major sites of cancer, including survival data.

The ACS survey includes a site visit and is similar to a survey by the Joint Commission (although it includes review of only the items noted above). Three-year approval is awarded to programs in full compliance.

CONTINUING MEDICAL EDUCATION PROGRAMS

A large number of states have mandatory continuing medical education (CME) requirements for relicensing or for membership in the state medical association. Some malpractice insurance plans require participation in CME.

Since there is a significant cost to practitioners, not only in tuition but in time away from practice, many hospitals offer CME programs for their medical staffs. Such programs are frequently supported by medical staff services departments.

CME should play a role in a practitioner's delineation of clinical privileges, and CME programs offered should be based in part on the results of the medical staff's quality assurance findings, as required by the Joint Commission.

Depending upon the sophistication of the CME program, medical staff services personnel can spend a significant amount of time assisting the CME committee with curriculum development, contacting speakers for conferences, notifying medical staff members, compiling and analyzing program evaluations, and recording CME credits for reporting to medical staff members.

To provide additional motivation to pursue CME, the American Medical Association (AMA) offers the Physician's Recognition Award. Applications are based on one, two, or three years of CME, and the certificates issued are valid for one, two, or three years from the date of application. Criteria for the award are as follows:[6]

1. Categories
   - Category I: CME activities with accredited sponsorship or cosponsorship
   - Category II: CME activities with nonaccredited sponsorship, medical teaching, papers, publications, books and exhibits, and nonsupervised CME, such as self-instruction, consultation, patient care review, and self-assessment. (former Categories II through VI)
2. Credit Hour Limits
   - three-year total must equal 150 hours (Category I minimum is 60 hours, no maximum limit)
   - two-year total must equal 100 hours (Category I minimum is 40 hours, no maximum limit)
   - one-year total must equal 50 hours (Category I minimum is 20 hours, no maximum limit)

Category I credit refers to programs accredited by the AMA. The AMA has delegated to the state medical associations authority to survey, evaluate, and accredit CME programs at community hospitals whose programs meet the essentials of approved programs. Guidelines for meeting the AMA's requirements can be obtained from its Office of Physician Credentials and Qualifications.

NOTES

1. *Federal Register* (January 27, 1981) Vol. 46, p. 8953.
2. *Federal Register* (January 27, 1981) Vol. 46, pp. 8942–79.
3. U.S. Department of Health and Human Services, Public Health Service, Food and Drug Administration, *A Suggested Self-Evaluation Guide: Human Subject Protection Institutional Review Boards* (Washington, D.C.: Government Printing Office, 1989).
4. U.S. Department of Health and Human Services, Public Health Service, Food and Drug Administration, *FDA IRB Information Sheets* (Washington, D.C.: Government Printing Office, 1989).
5. American College of Surgeons, Commission on Cancer, *Cancer Program Manual 1986* (Chicago: American College of Surgeons, 1986).
6. American Medical Association, *Continuing Medical Education Fact Sheet* (Chicago: American Medical Association, 1989).

Part IV

Medical Staff Problems

Jealous in honor, sudden, and quick in quarrels,
Seeking the bubble reputation
Even in the cannon's mouth.
Shakespeare, *As You Like It*

Chapter 11

Problems in Credentialing and Peer Review

Cindy Orsund-Gassiot, CMSC

APPROACHES TO IMPROVING HEALTH CARE: DEALING WITH THE "PROBLEM" PHYSICIAN*

Improving the quality of patient care in hospitals requires change. In most instances, health care professionals respond to change initiatives that appeal to their professionalism. Occasionally, however, an individual either will be unwilling or unable to respond to well-directed efforts to change his or her behavior. When this individual is a physician, a particularly difficult problem is created because of physicians' legal relationships to hospitals.

Physicians employed by the hospital act as its agents, and the institution is responsible for their actions under the legal doctrine of *respondeat superior*. Physicians who are not employed by a hospital are granted privileges by a hospital's governing board to practice in that institution. As specified in most hospitals' corporate bylaws and medical staff bylaws, the initial grant of hospital privileges has a time limitation and is subject to renewal. Renewal of privileges should be based on "demonstrated competence" or "acceptable quality of professional performance" as specified in the bylaws.

As a general rule, hospital credentials and privileges committees and governing boards assume that physicians are competent and professional unless evidence is presented to the contrary. Thus, continuation of privileges usually is a *pro forma* exercise. If a physician's behavior or performance is questioned, however, the privileges may need to be reexamined. Should such a situation arise, a clear understanding of the process of modifying or revoking privileges becomes essential for the medical staff leadership and members of the hospital's governing board.

---

*The section, "Approaches to Improving Health Care: Dealing with the Problem Physician," is reprinted from *Quality Review Bulletin* 8 (January 1982): 11–13 by William F. Jessee, MD, and Lawrence H. Brenner, JD. Copyright 1982 by the Joint Commission on Accreditation of Healthcare Organizations, Chicago. Reprinted with permission.

Performance Problems

Accurate data are not available on the numbers of physicians who become professionally disabled each year. It is generally agreed, however, that the incidence of suicide, emotional illness, and chemical dependency (including alcoholism) is substantially higher among physicians than among the general population. One author has estimated that as many as 10 percent of all physicians become professionally impaired by emotional illness or chemical dependency at some point in their careers.[1] In addition to the "impaired" physician, a small number of "recalcitrants" simply refuse to conform to the requirements of medical staff membership despite repeated efforts by the hospital to stimulate changes in their behavior.

When problems of impairment, incompetence, or recalcitrance arise, they usually become known to a hospital's quality assurance program through either formal or informal mechanisms. A means of identifying these problems and ensuring that they are followed up is an essential component of an effective quality control program.

Careful verification of the nature and extent of a physician's problem is critical. In-depth assessment through review of patient records, incident reports, malpractice claims, or other sources of documentary evidence may be necessary. In any event, the extent and severity of the problem must be documented carefully prior to initiation of disciplinary action. The presence of a pattern of poor performance should be the critical prerequisite to any plan to modify or reduce privileges.

Consequences of Privilege Reduction: Myth and Reality

The apprehensions most physicians experience when confronting a problem colleague frequently are exacerbated by uncertainty over the legal consequences of any disciplinary action. Unnecessary and misplaced fears or retaliatory action by the colleague who has lost privileges often impede effective action. Fear of a lawsuit is a powerful force that may cloud the real issue: does a particular physician pose unacceptable health risks to his or her hospitalized patients?

In almost all instances, the fear of retaliation is based on a misunderstanding of the consequence. The potential for legal repercussions should not prevent dealing with a problem physician for two reasons. First, when properly understood, the body of law that regulates approaches to matters such as privileges revocation is logical, sensible, and fair. Second, the "legal requirements" are concise, easy to follow, and should facilitate a just and appropriate result.

Although the law itself is straight-forward, the legal and moral dilemmas posed by the alleged problem physicians still are substantial. The stakes involved in such issues are high, and the stress and emotional burden of resolving such problems are considerable. From the viewpoint of the physician against whom action is directed, loss of privileges can be the practical equivalent of losing the right to practice in a community and may lead to devastating consequences including loss of livelihood and public disgrace. Conversely, a problem physician may be responsible for serious patient injury or death; in addition, a severe economic and professional risk to the hospital may be posed by such an individual through malpractice suits. The problem that must be addressed is simple: how, on the one hand, can hospitals protect patients from professionally disabled or incompetent physicians while assuring, on the other, that physicians are protected from the devastating consequences of privilege revocation based on unfounded, arbitrary, and capricious actions?

Legal Approaches to Fairness

Two legal principles govern procedures for ensuring fairness when reviewing, modifying, or revoking hospital privileges.

Medical Staff Bylaws Procedures

Hospital medical staff bylaws usually contain specific provisions for dealing with matters of staff privileges. In fact, the procedures contained in the medical staff bylaws may be considered a contract between the hospital and the physician. By accepting privileges to practice at the hospital, each physician becomes a party to this contract. The provisions of these bylaws set the legal standard (assuming that they are at least equal to constitutional requirements) for the procedures that must be followed before staff privileges may be revoked or substantially modified. When these procedures are violated during the revocation process, the affected physician may seek legal redress for breach of contract.

Constitutional Due Process

The Fourteenth Amendment to the United States Constitution states in part "nor shall any state deprive any person of life, liberty, or property, without due process of law." This sweeping, somewhat vague, yet powerful amendment to the Constitution raises important questions concerning appropriate procedures for revoking physician privileges. To properly understand what the Fourteenth Amendment requires, three questions must be addressed:

- Because the amendment uses the words "any state," are the requirements of this amendment limited to state-operated hospitals?
- Does revocation of privileges constitute a loss of liberty or property under the meaning of the Fourteenth Amendment?
- If due process is required, what does it entail?

In the nineteenth century when the Fourteenth Amendment was promulgated and ratified, what constituted state action was relatively simple and easy to resolve. More recent developments, however, have obscured the definition of state action. In addition, it often is difficult to determine whether a hospital's activities are so closely related to the government as to constitute state action. Certainly, with the influx of state and federal funds for patient care, construction, and utilization review, the modern hospital cannot escape close ties to government.

Whether or not an otherwise private hospital that accepts federal aid and is subject to federal regulation becomes public for purposes of the Fourteenth Amendment is a question that has produced an array of differing court decisions. When one examines the tapestry of cases that attempt to determine when a private hospital becomes sufficiently public to warrant Fourteenth Amendment protection for privileges revocation proceedings, a confusing and often inconsistent picture begins to emerge.

For example, hospitals have not been automatically found to be public when they receive compensation for care of the indigent, Medicare funds, or other governmental assistance.[2] At least one jurisdiction, however, is adamant that mere receipt of Hill-Burton funds makes an otherwise private hospital public and necessitates Fourteenth Amendment protection.[3]

Given the absence of any meaningful test that produces consistent results, the applicability of the Fourteenth Amendment for physician privileges on grounds of state action remains questionable for physicians in private hospitals. However, the courts are moving away from a strict interpretation of due process in privileges revocation cases to one that would promote a universal right to fair treatment, regardless of the public/private distinction.[4]

If the "public" and "private" hurdles can be overcome, the next Fourteenth Amendment question that must be answered is whether or not privilege revocation constitutes a loss of liberty or property and is, therefore, protected by Fourteenth Amendment requirements for due process. It is a well-established constitutional principle that infringement of liberty requires that an individual be the victim of an action that seriously damages associations or standing in the community or imposes a stigma limiting possibilities for future employment. In this regard, the law appears to distinguish between initial denial of privileges and the act of reducing or revoking privileges. With regard to denial of an application for initial privileges, the courts are split on the question of whether or not these actions are protected under the Fourteenth Amendment. In *Holderman v Lockhaven Hospital,* the court held that a physician with conduct "incompatible with good medical care and acceptable professional behavior" was not entitled to Fourteenth Amendment protection.[5]

Further, in *Schlein v Milford Hospital,* a mere rejection of an application for privileges where no direct charges were made was not considered denial of Fourteenth Amendment rights.[6] More recently, in *Miller v Eisenhower Medical Center,* the California Supreme Court held that in order to deny Miller's application for privileges, the hospital must show that granting privileges would pose a "realistic and specific threat" to the quality of medical care.[7]

When involved in a privileges revocation action, a physician is subject to accusations that may seriously damage his or her standing in the community; thus, the potential to deny liberty or property interests protected under the Fourteenth Amendment is clearly present. Therefore, in any public hospital or private facility that receives state monies a physician facing possible revocation of privileges should be provided with due process of law.

Elements of Due Process

The Fourteenth Amendment does not prevent a hospital from revoking medical staff privileges; rather, it simply prevents the facility from taking actions that unfairly deprive a physician of the right to practice in the institution. Therefore, the only mandatory test imposed by the Fourteenth Amendment can be stated succinctly: the physician must be treated fairly.

Like many other aspects of the Fourteenth Amendment, the concept of "fair treatment" does not lend itself to precise definition. However, a number of procedural safeguards have been recognized as a *sine qua non* of fairness. These requirements provide guidelines for the constitutionally required fair procedure. The guidelines, which should be followed regardless of whether they are stated in the medical staff bylaws, include:

- A hearing;
- An impartial determination of privilege revocation;
- A written statement of specific charges or reasons for revocation;
- The physician's discretionary right to counsel;
- A decision based on substantive evidence; and
- A written decision.

Hearing

One of the basic requirements of due process is the physician's right to a hearing. Although the hearing requirement is not to be construed as the equivalent of a trial, it is an adjudication and should include the opportunity to present evidence for and against revocation of the physician's privileges. Moreover, the procedure should be orderly and should preserve the basic integrity of an adjudicatory proceeding by requiring that all claims be supported by evidence.

Impartial Determination

The ultimate determination concerning privilege revocation should be made by a hearing body consisting of individuals who are capable of making an impartial decision. None of the members should have any vested interest in the outcome of the procedures, nor should any of them have any preconceived biases concerning the outcome. Depending upon the hospital's bylaws, this committee may be the board of directors; however, if members of the board do not think that they can be objective a committee may be chosen from other physicians either within the hospital or unassociated with it. In any case, it is the hospital attorney's responsibility to make certain that members of the hearing body, like a jury, are impartial and that the above guidelines are followed properly. The board must then abide by the committee's decision.

Traditionally, the hearing follows an investigation or ad hoc committee recommendation. While the investigators or committee members may appear at the hearing to present evidence or testimony, allowing them to participate in the discussion or to vote on the ultimate disposition of the case is improper. Perhaps the single most important component of a fair hearing is the impartiality of the decision-making group.

Bill of Particulars

The individual physician should receive a written statement of specific charges or reasons revocation of privileges has been recommended. The charges must be specific enough so that the physician can understand the accusations against him or her and prepare a meaningful defense. Vague charges such as "incompetence" or "unprofessional conduct" are too imprecise to allow the preparation of a proper defense. Further, specific charges must be given to the physician well enough in advance of the hearing so that he or she will have sufficient time to prepare a defense. Simply handing the physician a list of charges immediately before the hearing, for example, does not give the physician an adequate opportunity to prepare evidence in his or her defense.

Discretionary Right to Counsel

Although representation by an attorney is not a physician's absolute right, granting the physician the right to counsel is the preferred practice in such cases. Obviously most physicians are unschooled in matters of legal procedure and substance and are not trained in the presentation of evidence.

Allowing a physician the right to be represented by counsel helps to ensure a fair hearing, especially if the hospital's attorney is present.

Decision Based on Substantive Evidence

Because the process of privilege revocation is an adjudication, the decision of the tribunal must be based on substantive evidence produced at the hearing. Although this evidence may include hearsay (which should be given less weight than documentary evidence), the hearing body must make a decision based only on the record before it.

Written Decision

The final disposition of the case should include a written decision that specifies the basis and reasons for the decision. This document is essential if the physician's right to judicial review is to be preserved. Without a written decision, a court could only guess at the basis for a decision to revoke a physician's privileges.

Hospital compliance with these six simple requirements ensures that a physician is treated fairly and diminishes the likelihood that a revocation decision will be overturned by the courts. Prudence, as well as fairness, dictates that these procedures be followed whenever privilege reduction or revocation appears necessary.

Comment

In taking action to protect the hospital and its patients from poor practice by an impaired or incompetent physician, the guiding principle must be fairness. Care should be taken to follow any procedures specified in the medical staff bylaws and to fully document both the process and the substance of the proceedings. Above all, action to resolve a physician problem must not be avoided or deferred because of concern for or fear of legal consequences. The courts, and public opinion, are very intolerant of failure to act on a known physician performance problem.[8] Although the political and emotional barriers to dealing with physician performance problems may be high, the consequences of inaction are almost always higher.

HOW TO AVOID PEER REVIEW PITFALLS*

Physicians who receive adverse peer review results are frequently frightened, angry, and prone to sue those who participated in the decision. A variety of legal theories may be used to bring such a lawsuit. Key to the defense is the presentation of evidence that a fair, orderly, objective and unbiased process was followed in arriving at the adverse result.

The plaintiff's lawyer will look for flaws in the process that may be evidence of unfairness or bias. Those flaws will be used to generate a sense of injustice and to support arguments that poor quality was not the real reason for the adverse result.

---

* The section, "How To Avoid Peer Review Pitfalls," is reprinted from *QA Review* 1 (August 1989): 4–5 by Edward B. Hirshfeld. Copyright 1989 by the American Medical Association, Chicago. Reprinted with permission.

Common flaws that the plaintiff's lawyer will look for, and which should be avoided in the peer review process, are as follows:

Conflict of Interest

Ideally, physicians who participate in peer review should not be in a position to benefit economically, or in some other way, if the physician being reviewed loses hospital privileges. Physicians who may benefit economically include direct competitors in the specialty involved and partners of competitors. Physicians who may benefit in some other way include, for example, those with a long history of enmity toward the physician who is being reviewed.

In smaller communities, it may be difficult to find peer reviewers who have no conflicts of interest. In those situations, the medical staff should seek reviewers from outside the community who have no conflicts. Ideally, the medical staff and the physician being reviewed should agree on who from outside of the community should be asked to participate. The presence of agreed on outside reviewers provides assurances that the review process will be fair and objective.

Poorly Documented History

Sometimes a medical staff will gradually lose confidence in a physician. Then an incident occurs which is seized upon as a reason to engage the peer review process. The incident may then become the primary, documented reason why the physician loses privileges. Sometimes the incident is the "straw that breaks the camel's back"; meaning that it appears minor or trivial in nature, but comes at the end of a long sequence of transgressions. If the transgressions are not documented and expressly made part of the decision to withdraw privileges, the withdrawal may appear to be unreasonable or arbitrary.

An appearance of unreasonableness lends credibility to arguments that the process was biased. Therefore, it is important to carry out peer review on a regular and orderly basis, and to document the process so that a proper foundation for future decisions is in place.

Taking the Proper Steps

When key members of a medical staff have lost confidence in a physician, they may decide that it is time to terminate his or her privileges, and the only remaining question is how to do it. A period of consensus building may follow, during which the medical staff seeks support from other physicians "to get rid" of the transgressor.

Evidence that a decision was made to terminate a physician's privileges before the peer review hearings took place is convincing evidence that the review process itself was not fair and objective.

Such evidence also lends credibility to charges that anticompetitive or Machiavellian motives tainted the process. Therefore, it is very important to let the peer review process work. When physicians become concerned about a colleague, the information that caused the concern should be put into the peer review process, and the process should then be left alone.

Uneven Standards

Physicians with abrasive personalities sometimes fare more poorly in peer review than those who are well liked. There is a tendency to judge more harshly those individuals who have generated a lot of ill will. If such a physician sues, his or her record will be compared with others who may have committed similar transgressions without subsequent loss of privileges. Therefore, it is important for peer reviewers to be consistent in their application of standards.

The Importance of Fairness

Peer reviewers should use fair procedures and not take short cuts in arriving at a decision. There are an infinite number of ways to structure a fair process. Key elements are: (a) reasonable notice to the physician being reviewed of charges and times and places of hearing; (b) access by the physician to information necessary to defend against the charges; (c) an opportunity to respond to the charges; (d) an opportunity to have the benefit of a skilled advocate; and (e) a chance to have an adverse decision reviewed by a different set of reviewers. Lack of any of these elements may be evidence that the physician was not treated fairly.

REPORTING PRACTITIONER PROBLEMS

The Health Care Quality Improvement Act

For some time, many states have had mandatory requirements for reporting actions against physicians to state licensing boards to identify potentially serious instances of unprofessional conduct. The reporting requirements vary significantly from state to state, and until passage of the Health Care Quality Improvement Act of 1986, there was no national clearinghouse for reporting by hospitals and other health care related organizations.[9]

In November 1986, the Act (Public Law 99-660) became law. Congress stated in the "Findings" section of the Act that there is a national need to restrict the ability of incompetent physicians to move from state to state without disclosure or discovery of their prior damaging or incompetent performances, that this national need can be met through effective professional peer review, and that there is an additional national need to provide incentives and protection for physicians who engage in effective professional peer review.

Title IV of the Act mandated the establishment of the National Practitioner Data Bank (Data Bank). A five-year, $15.9 million contract to establish and operate the Data Bank was awarded effective January 1, 1989, to the Unisys Corporation. The following reporting requirements were established by the Act.

Reporting Requirements

The Act requires all entities, including insurance companies, that make payments under an insurance or self-insurance program in settlement or judgment of malpractice claims to report information regarding such payments to the Data Bank.

The Act requires health care entities, including hospitals, to report to the state licensing board all professional review actions taken that adversely affect a physician's clinical privileges for a period longer than 30 days. "Adversely affecting" is defined under Section 431(1) of the Act as including "reducing, restricting, suspending, revoking, denying, or failing to renew clinical privileges or membership in a health care entity." The Act also requires reporting of any acceptance of a physician's surrender of clinical privileges while the physician is under investigation by the entity for incompetence or improper professional conduct or when the surrender is accepted in return for not conducting such an investigation. Additionally, Section 423(a)(2) of the Act provides for permissive reporting by health care entities of an adverse professional review action taken against a licensed practitioner if such action would require reporting if the practitioner were a physician.

Information to be reported includes the name of the physician or practitioner, a description of the acts or omissions made the basis of the action, and any other information which the Secretary of Health and Human Services (HHS) may deem appropriate. Any health care entity that reports information pursuant to the Act is immune from civil liability for making such report unless it had knowledge of the falsity of any information contained in the report.

In final regulations relating to the Data Bank issued by the Public Health Service in October 1989, HHS clarified that reports would not be required in situations where the action taken did not concern professional competence or conduct that could adversely affect the health or welfare of a patient. Revocation or suspension of privileges for such matters as failure to attend staff meetings or complete medical records or billing forms would generally not need to be reported. Further, HHS stated that a physician's voluntary reduction in clinical privileges for reasons of personal preference would not need to be reported. But a voluntary reduction in privileges in response to an investigation or threat of investigation by the hospital should be reported. Failure to report an adverse professional review action may result in the health care entity's loss of immunity from claims brought under federal antitrust laws.

Duty of Hospitals To Obtain Information

The Data Bank will serve as a central source for the information concerning physicians or other licensed practitioners that is reported pursuant to the Act. Hospitals will have a duty to request such information in connection with medical staff appointment and reappointment and the granting of clinical privileges. If a hospital fails to request such information, it will be presumed to have knowledge of any information that has been reported. Hospitals must begin requesting this information on and after the date the Data Bank becomes operational.

Information concerning a given practitioner that is reported pursuant to the Act is confidential and may only be disclosed to that practitioner and to health care entities and state licensing boards that request the information. However, an attorney who has filed a medical malpractice action or claim against a hospital *may* query the Data Bank for information regarding a specific physician, dentist, or other health care practitioner who is also named in the action. However, this information will only be disclosed if the attorney submits evidence that the hospital failed to request information from the Data Bank, as required by law. The information may be used solely with respect to the medical malpractice action against the hospital.

State medical and dental boards must report to the Data Bank disciplinary actions taken against the license of a physician or dentist. Additionally, state licensing boards may query the Data Bank regarding a physician, dentist, or other health care practitioner.

Individual physicians, dentists, and other health care practitioners may query the Data Bank concerning themselves. An individual may obtain his or her record at no cost, whereas others who are authorized to obtain information from the Data Bank will be charged a fee.

Immunity Provisions

Section 411 of the Act provides that if a professional review body conducts an action in accord with the standards of the Act, its members and staff, as well as any person who participates in the action or provides assistance, shall not be liable with respect to the action in damages under any federal or state law. (See Chapter 14 for a description of the standards relating to due process.) Additionally, any person who provides information to a professional review body also enjoys immunity from claims unless the information provided was false and the person knew it was false.

NOTES

1. J. E. Collier, "The Maryland Physician Rehabilitation Program," *Maryland State Medical Journal* 10 (1980): 36–39.

2. *Mulvilhil v. Julia L. Butterfield Memorial Hospital*, 329 F. Supp. 1020 (D.C. NY 1971).

3. *Duffield v. Charleston Area Medical Center, Inc.*, 503 F.2d 512 (4th Cir. W. Va. 1974).

4. *Ascherman v. San Francisco Medical Society*, 39 Cal. App. 3rd 623. 114 Cal. Rptr. 681 (1974).

5. *Holderman v. Lockhaven Hospital*, 377 F. Supp. 1178 (D.C. Penn. 1974).

6. *Schlein v. Millford Hospital*, 383 F. Supp. 1263 (D.C. Conn., affd. 561 F.2d 427. 2nd Cir. 1974).

7. W. J. Curran, "Medical-Staff Privileges in Private Hospitals: Can Modern Hospitals Exclude Uncooperative Applicants," *New England Journal of Medicine* 304 (1981): 589–91.

8. *Gonzales v. Nork and Mercy Hospital*, unpublished order, Superior Court of Sacramento County, Calif., Docket No. 228566, 1973; "Surgical Trauma in California," *Time*, July 20, 1981, 72.

9. 42 U.S.C.A., sec. 11101–11152 (Supp. 1988).

Chapter 12

Dealing with the Impaired Physician

Cindy Orsund-Gassiot, CMSC

The exact numbers of physicians impaired by alcohol or drug abuse and mental disorders are unknown. Adding to the problem, aging physicians may be impaired by senile dementia or another illness that is progressively debilitating. It has been estimated that 10–14 percent of practicing physicians are impaired.[1] Medical staff services professionals (MSSPs) will more than likely encounter the problem of dealing with physician impairment sooner or later in their careers. Every hospital should have in place (1) guidelines and procedures to follow in motivating impaired physicians to seek treatment and (2) a monitoring program that will allow rehabilitated practitioners to return to practice. "Ignoring the value of documented recovery or correction of prior problems only causes attempts to hide disabilities, thus delaying treatment and recovery. The risk of harm to patients treated by a disabled practitioner increases unless the credentialing process recognizes rehabilitation."[2] In the case of an aging physician who no longer has the skills necessary to practice, privileges should be curtailed.

HOSPITAL-BASED PROGRAMS[1]*

A hospital has certain legal responsibilities to take action against an incompetent physician. With respect to an impaired physician, however, responsibility and liability are not as clearly defined. Administrators and colleagues often ignore or overlook signs of developing impairment in the hope that it will disappear. Only in cases of blatant impairment do they tend to intervene, and then usually in a punitive manner.

Preferable is a non-punitive approach in which the hospital works as an advocate for the physician, rather than against him, while still safeguarding patients from harm. This type of program can detect emerging impairment, offer support to the

---

*The section, "Hospital-Based Programs," is reprinted from *Proceedings of the 4th AMA Conference on the Impaired Physician*, pp. 27–31, with permission of the American Medical Association, © 1980.

physician and his family and encourage early treatment. Helping the impaired physician is in the best interest of the hospital as well as the impaired physician himself and the hospital's patients.

Is a Hospital Program Necessary?

Whether a program at the hospital level is necessary or even feasible depends on several variables, including:

a. state mandatory reporting laws
b. geographic location
c. size of state
d. activities and strengths of county medical society programs
e. activities and strengths of state medical society programs
f. size of the hospital
g. hospital constitution and bylaws
h. interest and level of awareness of the medical staff and administration

Generally speaking, impairment is more likely to be detected at the hospital level much earlier than it is at the county or state medical society level. This is particularly true in a large state or in a densely populated area.

Small hospitals, however, may be especially resistant to initiating programs because of their size, the intimacy among staff or time constraints. This may necessitate the involvement of the county or state medical society program.

Ideally, a hospital, county, and state medical society program will complement one another. For example, if a hospital working in concert with a state program is unsuccessful in encouraging an impaired physician to seek treatment, the state society may become involved and thereby assure that the physician does not evade the issue even if he changes his hospital affiliation or practice mode.

Organization

No single model is applicable to all hospitals because of the many variables in hospital bylaws, size and state laws. These differences, however, give each hospital the capability of establishing a program that is tailored to its individual needs. The local hospital association, county medical society or state medical society may be able to identify programs operating in other hospitals in the area which can be used as a model.

A formal policy on physician impairment should be incorporated into the bylaws and should include a provision for immediate suspension of privileges if a physician is a threat to himself or his patients. Legal input will assure that due process elements, informed consent, confidentiality aspects and the legal rights of both the hospital and an impaired physician are adequately addressed. Additionally, the bylaws should include a provision of immunity for those acting on behalf of the hospital program.

A program to aid impaired physicians should be organizationally separate from . . . credential review and peer review, although it is desirable that input from committees charged with carrying out these functions be utilized where feasible in case-finding activities.

The hospital should continually promote its advocacy program to assure visibility and use. In this regard, an ongoing education component encourages reporting from staff and other hospital personnel, and is beneficial in increasing levels of awareness, changing negative attitudes and stereotypical perceptions, and providing cognitive information on the nature and treatability of impairment. Where possible, educational programs for spouses should be initiated. The spouse is often aware, far earlier than hospital personnel, of a physician's impairment.

In addition to education and promotion, other components of a hospital-based program include case-findings, intervention, rehabilitation and re-entry. It is generally recommended that treatment be arranged on an outpatient basis or in another hospital.

Case-Finding

A hospital is responsible for implementing policies to assure that its staff members are capable of providing quality medical care, as well as procedures to assess their mental and physical health. These existing mechanisms can be the foundation for early case-finding and prevention.

Medical staff reappointments (usually made on an annual or biennial basis) offer an avenue to reviewing a physician's performance and discussing potential or existing problems.

While credentialing, peer review and medical staff [quality assurance] functions should be outside the purview of activities relating to helping impaired physicians, members of these committees can help identify physicians who are impaired or potentially impaired.

Reports about a physician who is having problems should be encouraged and accepted from nurses, colleagues, other hospital personnel and family members. For this reason, a visible contact person or contact mechanism (e.g., special "hotline") is imperative. Whether reports, in addition, are accepted from patients, and whether reports may be made on an anonymous basis, is up to the discretion of the hospital. Anonymous reports can be valuable as well as detrimental. In any event, the identity of the person who reports a physician who may possibly be impaired should be kept confidential, and provision for such confidentiality should be stressed to encourage reporting.

Several suggestions have been made with respect to the structure and composition of the specific committee to receive and act on reports of impairment and requests of help. Potential members might include:

1. well-liked, respected senior staff members
2. staff members or administrators recovering from impairment
3. resident and student representatives
4. hospital administrators
5. department heads
6. chiefs of staff
7. president, past-president and president-elect of the medical staff (to allow for ongoing knowledge and interest)

Four basic types of committees have been identified: 1) structured, with administrative and physician members; 2) non-structured, with physician members only; 3) structured, with physician members only; and 4) non-structured, with basic members plus others added depending on the individual case. Those programs that are defined as structured have standing committee status with ongoing functions, whereas non-structured committees are constituted on an ad hoc, as needed, basis.

Some people feel strongly that staff officers with disciplinary authority should not be included because their presence might deter reporting from those who fear punitive action. Others feel equally strongly that these people with "power" should be included because their responsibility for quality care cannot be abdicated or delegated.

The question of whether the committee should be a standing committee or be convened on an ad hoc basis is equally debatable. Both forms have merit.

Regardless of how the committee is composed, it should focus exclusively on problems relating to impairment, as opposed to incompetence or illegal activities.

A mechanism for verifying allegations of impairment should be incorporated into any program. Options include verification by a solo physician member or by a subgroup of the committee.

Intervention

Intervention at the hospital level can emphasize the human factors that have been shown to be positive elements for encouraging a physician to seek treatment. If the committee finds its efforts are hampered by loyalty, embarrassment or overprotectiveness, it may then be necessary to involve the county or state medical society in the intervention process.

If intervention is carried out within the confines of a hospital program, a special group or subcommittee should receive training in intervention techniques. The county or state medical society may be willing to provide training courses. The intervention team may also well include a colleague of the impaired physician whom the "informer" has identified as the person most likely to induce the physician to get treatment.

Basically, the intervention process should be an organized attempt to persuade the physician to get help, while conveying the hope that treatment can be effective. Sources of help should be identified, a definite treatment plan presented and a program for rehabilitation outlined. If the bylaws include a formal policy on physician impairment, this can be used as leverage to encourage the physician to seek help promptly.

If the physician refuses help, it may be necessary to refer him to the usual hospital disciplinary channels. The hospital has the "stick" of being able to restrict or suspend hospital privileges. Even then, discipline should be applied in conjunction with a plan of rehabilitation wherever possible.

Re-Entry

The hospital committee should monitor the physician's treatment and recovery, and should continue its advocacy role through the re-entry phase. Once the formerly impaired physician has returned to the hospital, the committee should recommend reinstatement of his privileges based on his current ability to practice. If monitoring of his activities is thought to be necessary for hospital, patient or physician protection, the hospital committee can delineate structured re-entry points that allow for such monitoring (e.g., proctoring of surgical privileges, review of charts, supervised patient care, urine screening).

A CONTRACT WITH AN IMPAIRED PHYSICIAN

Once intervention has occurred and the practitioner has agreed to seek treatment, the hospital or medical society committee should enter into a contract with the affected practitioner. The contract (Exhibit 12-1) should specify the terms under which the hospital or medical society committee will act in an advocacy role vis-à-vis the state licensing board, hospital boards, medical societies, and the Drug Enforcement Agency. The purpose of the contract is to prevent any misunderstanding as to the terms specified. The contract should be specifically designed to meet the needs of each individual and be uniquely suited to the particular circumstances.

MONITORING PHYSICIANS*

Monitoring a Physician at the Level of the Hospital Medical Staff after Treatment for Chemical Dependence

The purpose of monitoring is to assure the medical staff that a physician resuming patient care responsibilities after treatment for chemical dependence can practice medicine safely.

---

*Reprinted from *Guidelines for Physician Aid Committees of Hospital Medical Staffs* by the California Medical Association, pp. 6–11, with permission of the California Medical Association, © 1988.

Exhibit 12-1 Sample Contract[3]

Name: _____ Date: _____

1. I, _____, agree to the terms of this contract for a period of two (2) years from the date of this contract.
2. I understand that all expenses connected with my treatment are to be rendered at my own expense and are my own responsibility.
3. I agree to cease the practice of medicine until clearance is received from the Committee.
4. I agree to enter an approved treatment center for evaluation and detoxification on _____ (date).
5. I agree to Phase I of treatment, which will consist of 28 days or longer of treatment in an in-house rehabilitation center.
6. I agree to Phase II of treatment, which will consist of an outpatient program, including attendance at regular AA meetings and at the weekly Physicians' Recovery Group.
7. I agree to Phase III of treatment, which may consist of staff training and, if necessary, a gradual phasing into medical practice under the Committee's supervision.
8. I agree to completely abstain from any mood-changing chemicals (alcohol, sedatives, stimulants, narcotics, soporifics, over-the-counter drugs, etc.) except on prescription from my primary care physician and after consultation with the Committee. I will not prescribe any medication for myself.
9. I agree to provide random urine or blood samples in the presence of another physician or designee at the discretion of the Committee.
10. I agree to identify a primary care physician before completion of Phase I. All aspects of my case history will be made known to this physician. He or she will receive a copy of this contract and agree to meet and consult with the Committee on Physician Health and Rehabilitation.
11. I agree to the following special terms as they apply to my illness (if any are stipulated).
12. I agree that should I leave treatment, the Committee will cease to act as my advocate vis-à-vis the Board of Medical Examiners.

_____
Signature of Impaired Physician

Witness:

_____

Approved:

_____
Chairman, Committee Monitoring the Physician

The medical staff must be satisfied that the physician's current health and mental health meet the medical staff's standards for appointment, reappointment or resumption of patient care.

The medical staff must acknowledge that ongoing, consistent monitoring is required for a specified period of time (a minimum of two years), and sufficient resources of physician time and attention must be allocated for it.

A monitoring plan should be drawn up and it should serve as the basis of a monitoring agreement between the designated medical staff committee and the physician. The following elements should be addressed as the plan is designed:

- **Treatment.** The medical staff committee should satisfy itself that the physician received the kind of treatment appropriate to the problem and sufficient to assure that the problem is being addressed effectively. The medical staff committee should satisfy itself that the physician's current health and mental health are sufficient to allow him/her to practice safely.

  An initial course of treatment appropriate to the situation should be instituted and completed. The monitoring plan should incorporate the elements of an aftercare plan and recovery plan which have been recommended by those responsible for the initial treatment.

- **Release of Information.** The medical staff committee should require that the physician authorize the therapist(s) to communicate information to the medical staff committee. Information should come from those responsible for primary care (initial treatment) as well as aftercare and/or on-going care.

- **Recovery Plan.** The physician should have a specific, on-going recovery plan sufficient to the situation and to the physician's status in recovery. The monitoring plan should be designed to accumulate the information which will, over time, document the physician's participation in this recovery program.

  Regular participation in a self-help group of persons recovering from chemical dependence (where appropriate, a group of recovering physicians or health professionals) should be required.

- **Information To Be Gathered and Reviewed.** Information about the health status of the physician in recovery and about his/her performance should be gathered and reviewed. The process of gathering and evaluating such information is called monitoring. Information should come from several sources appropriate to the physician's situation, such as from:

  —the hospital work place

  —body fluid test results

  —an aftercare coordinator

  —on-going therapist

  —family

  —office colleagues

  The medical staff committee should designate those who are in a position to gather and submit to the coordinator of monitoring the different kinds of information appropriate to the case. These monitors should be appointed as members of the medical staff committee for the purpose of carrying out this activity so that the peer review protections will be applicable.

- **Regular Contact with a Knowledgeable Observer.** There should be regular, face-to-face contact between the physician and a monitor knowledgeable about chemical dependence and about what to look for in a physician with the condition being monitored. The time and place of the contact should vary. The frequency and length of contact should be determined for each case. For some, daily or even more than once-a-day contact may be indicated, especially in the first days/weeks of the monitoring process. Most usually, three times a week would be considered a minimum. The frequency would vary with the physician's status in recovery. The length of contact must be sufficient to make an observation of the physician's behavior. The record should include periodic notes based on this observation.

The monitors should be able to create a relationship of mutual trust, support, helpfulness and respect. Monitors, however, should maintain objectivity and diligence throughout the monitoring process.

- **Coordinator of Monitoring.** All who serve as sources of information should report to one coordinator of monitoring for the case, and that person should be a member of the medical staff committee. The function of the coordinator is to assemble all the information and to review, interpret, evaluate and respond to the comprehensive picture.

- **Body Fluid Testing.** Body fluid testing is desirable as one element of a monitoring plan. Body fluids (most commonly urine) should be collected on a random schedule and under direct observation. NOTE: Body fluid testing alone does not comprise a sufficient monitoring plan and is not the highest priority element of the plan. Greater weight is given to regular observation of behavior by a knowledgeable monitor.

  The monitoring agreement should specify what role body fluid testing will have in the overall monitoring plan. Where body fluid testing is required, the test done must be able to detect the drug(s) which the physician might use. The agreement should describe how positive results will be interpreted and what will be the response of the medical staff committee to positive results. The monitoring agreement should specify the costs of testing and who pays the costs. The results should be sent to the coordinator of monitoring.

- **Regular Conferences.** There should be a mechanism for face-to-face conferences, at the request of any of these parties, between the monitors, the physician being monitored, the coordinator of monitoring and the medical staff committee responsible for the monitoring.

- **Re-Evaluation of the Recovery and Monitoring Plans.** There should be regular re-evaluation at some interval, perhaps every six months, by the medical staff committee to assure that it is sufficient to meet the need but does not require elements no longer necessary to the situation. Changes to the plan should be made so that it fits the current situation of the physician and his/her status in recovery.

  It may or may not be appropriate to have this evaluation made by an acknowledged expert outside of the medical staff who will provide a written report. The monitoring agreement should specify the costs of this evaluation and who pays the costs.

- **Record Keeping.** For each case where there is monitoring, there must be a record. The record should include a copy of the signed monitoring agreement between the physician and the committee. The medical staff committee must have adequate information to assess the physician's status in recovery and compliance with the elements in the agreement. This information must be accumulated in the record and must be kept in strict confidence, preferably in a locked file or other secure storage which may be accessed only by committee members. This information should be retained indefinitely, preferably as long as the physician practices in the hospital plus five years. Disclosure of this information outside of the committee should be made only at the written request of the individual involved or with the advice of legal counsel.

- **Response to "Slips."** The monitoring plan should take into consideration the fact that a relapse or resumption of use of alcohol or drugs (or "slip") is not an uncommon phenomenon for those recovering from chemical dependence, especially in the early phases of recovery. Statistics show that slips occur in a significant percent of cases, usually within the first year of sobriety. The response to a slip should be the same as a response to the initial diagnosis; that is, it should be evaluated by a knowledgeable, experienced evaluator and the response should be tailored to the situation. A slip alone should not be considered cause for termination of privileges or loss of employment or position. The customary response to a slip is to intensify the treatment plan, of which monitoring is a part, for a period of time appropriate to the case. It may or may not be appropriate to require that the physician take a leave from patient care for a period of time appropriate to the situation. Consideration should be given to the physician's health and to patient safety in reaching a decision about whether a leave is appropriate.

The purpose of monitoring described here is to assure the medical staff that the physician is in recovery, continues in recovery and is participating in an appropriate recovery program. Monitoring is designed to allow the medical staff to evaluate the status of the physician's recovery.

Monitoring is a service to the physician as well as to the medical staff. For the physician, a comprehensive monitoring program establishes a history of performance, with documentation, which can be invaluable in vouching for a physician's current status in recovery. For the hospital medical staff, a record is established over time, showing that the medical staff is acting in a knowledgeable, timely, thorough and responsible way to assure that the physician continues to deliver safe care.

Monitoring for Conditions Other Than Chemical Dependence

When monitoring for a situation or condition other than chemical dependence is required, all principles of monitoring described here should be adapted and applied.

Proctoring

The medical staff must also satisfy itself that the physician's clinical skills are intact. To that end, the monitoring plan should contain provisions for proctoring, appropriate to each case.

There should be concurrent peer review and regular record review for all monitored physicians, for a period of time to be determined in each case. For those with surgical privileges, or those who perform other procedures in the hospital, there should be a proctor for a period of time to be determined in each case.

When the Physician Has Privileges at More Than One Hospital

The monitoring agreement should provide for notifying the appropriate medical staff committee(s) of the other hospital(s) where the physician has privileges. In an optimal situation, monitoring activities will be integrated in a way which meets the responsibilities of each medical staff without unnecessary duplication. At a minimum, each medical staff should have a monitoring agreement (or each medical staff should be a party to one monitoring agreement) and there should be regular contact with a knowledgeable observer at each hospital whose reports are submitted to one coordinator of monitoring.

Protection of the Physician's Identity

It is possible to carry out every element of monitoring described here and still protect the identity of the physician. The physician's identity and information about the situation need to be known only to the signers of the monitoring agreement, the monitors and the medical staff committee responsible for the monitoring. Disclosure of this information may be required if it becomes relevant in a staff privilege dispute.

NOTES

1. E.M. Steindler, *The Impaired Physician, American Medical Association Department of Mental Health Bulletin,* Chicago: AMA, 1975.

2. Cindy A. Orsund and Donald P. Wilcox, "Credentialing the New Applicant—Practical Advice," *Texas Medicine* 84 (April 1988): 79.

3. Texas Medical Association Committee on Physician Health and Rehabilitation, *Committee on Physician Health and Rehabilitation Contract* (Austin: Texas Medical Association, 1987).

Part V

Medical Staff Law

And then the justice, ...
Full of wise saws and modern instances
Shakespeare, *As You Like It*

Chapter 13

Introduction to the Law

Carla D. Thompson, Esq.

THE LEGAL SYSTEM

The legal system impacts all aspects of personal and professional life. When a check is written, a car driven, or a street crossed, laws and regulations apply. There are laws, rules, and regulations concerning the manufacture, distribution, and labeling of almost everything bought, used, or consumed. Labor laws cover most workers, most buildings must conform to building codes, and fair credit laws govern every credit card purchase made. Laws govern and regulate almost every phase of life. The legal system also provides a forum for people to use to resolve their disputes.

Criminal Law and Civil Law

Law is often defined as social control. But whereas laws prohibiting murder, arson, and theft are obviously examples of social control through government legislation, there is more to the law than the administration of criminal justice.

The law of torts, the law of contracts, and the rest of the body of law known as "civil law" constitute a complex system of rules that attach legal rights, responsibilities, and duties to various actions.

The criminal law segment of our legal system prohibits conduct that is contrary to the public order. Each state has its own laws defining what is a crime in that state. In the United States, there are laws dealing with the crimes of abduction, abortion, adultery, arson, bigamy, bribery, burglary, counterfeiting, disorderly conduct, dueling, embezzlement, escape, extortion, false impersonation, forgery, homicide, incest, kidnapping, larceny, malicious mischief, mayhem, murder, obscenity, obstructing justice, perjury, prostitution, rape, riot, robbery, suicide, treason and vagrancy. This, of course, is not a complete list of all crimes prohibited by law in this country.

205

Crimes are divided into two major categories: misdemeanors and felonies. A misdemeanor is a crime that carries a maximum penalty of less than one year in jail and/or a fine. A felony is a more serious offense that carries a term of imprisonment of more than one year. The civil actions that health care professionals are generally most concerned about are tort actions and contract actions.

In a criminal case, the plaintiff is always the state (sometimes called "the People").[1]

A general understanding of the law that applies to health care administration is important so that health care personnel can protect themselves, their employers, and even their patients. Health care professionals need to be aware of the laws and regulations that define what they may or may not do.

The Courts

The courts are probably the most familiar part of the American legal system. Although few people have taken part in an actual trial, most people have seen a trial on television.

The court system is a complex structure consisting of federal and state courts. In every state there is at least one federal court and an entire state court system.

Federal Courts

At the federal level, the trial courts are called U.S. district courts. Each state has at least one federal district court.

The intermediate level in the federal system is called the United States court of appeals. There are 13 federal courts of appeal, and each, except for the District of Columbia Circuit, encompasses several states.

The United States Supreme Court

The final appellate court in the federal system is the U.S. Supreme Court. The U.S. Supreme Court hears appeals from the U.S. district courts and from the highest appellate court of each state. The United States Supreme Court also has jurisdiction to hear appeals involving the interpretation of a federal constitutional provision or a federal law or regulation. In very rare instances, the high court can hear appeals directly from the U.S. District Courts.

In some cases, the U.S. Supreme Court also has "original jurisdiction," for example, when one state is bringing action against another state. In these rare cases, the U.S. Supreme Court is a trial court.

There are other federal courts, such as the Court of Claims and U.S. Custom Courts. Figure 13-1 shows the federal court system structure.

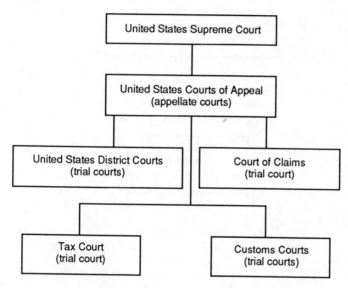

Figure 13-1 Federal Court System

State Courts

Within each state court system, there are several levels. Like the federal courts, most state court systems have three levels: the trial level, the intermediate appellate level, and the final appellate level. See Figure 13-2 for an illustration of a state court system.

In the state systems, the courts perform the same functions as their federal counterparts. Trial courts decide questions of fact, judge a defendant's guilt or innocence in criminal cases, and determine liability in civil cases. Trial courts decide if a penalty should be imposed and whether it should be a fine or a jail term. In civil cases, they determine the amount of damages to be awarded.

Appellate courts in the state system, as in the federal system, review trial court decisions to determine if the trial court correctly applied the law to the facts. Only rarely do appellate courts review factual determinations made at the trial level. When the facts are reviewed, this is called a de novo review.

In a state system, *local courts* are usually specialized and are located all around the state. Municipal courts, traffic courts, police courts, and small claim courts are all examples of local courts. Their jurisdiction is very limited.

The *courts of general jurisdiction* are the basic trial courts for the community. In some states these courts are called circuit courts or district courts. In California these courts are called superior courts. In New York State the basic trial courts are oddly called supreme courts.[2]

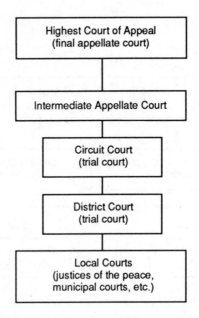

Figure 13-2 State Court System

WHAT HAPPENS IN A CIVIL LAW SUIT?

How Does a Lawsuit Begin?

As previously mentioned, court actions fall into two categories: civil actions and criminal actions. *Civil cases* are those in which an individual, an organization, or a government agency sues for damages or injunctive relief from another party. *Criminal actions* are cases brought by the state or federal government against an individual who has been charged with committing a crime.

Civil actions are usually actions that concern a breach of contract (ex contractu) or a wrong, also known as a tort (ex delicto).

Sometimes a suit is brought for "equitable relief" rather than money damages. Equity can prohibit certain wrongful conduct with an injunction or can compel the performance of certain action with an order for specific performance. Usually money damages cannot be obtained in an equitable proceeding.

When one person has been injured by another person, the injured party may consult an attorney to determine if the injury will give rise to a legal cause of action. The attorney will take the client's statement and may interview possible witnesses. The attorney will probably do some legal research to find the applicable laws and court decisions and will then determine if the client has a viable case.

If there is a cause of action, and the client wishes to proceed, the attorney will then prepare a *complaint* or a *petition* and file it in the appropriate court. The attorney's client is called the *plaintiff,* and the person or organization against whom the case is filed is called the *defendant.*

The complaint states the facts of the plaintiff's action against the defendant and sets forth the judgment or money damages sought. The filing of the complaint does not prove that the plaintiff does indeed have a cause of action—that will be decided by the court.

The plaintiff's attorney also files a document called a *summons* with the court. The summons directs the county sheriff to serve a copy of the legal papers on the defendant. In some states, the summons is served as a matter of course; in others, it must be served in advance of filing the complaint; in still others, only qualified process servers may serve the summons.[3]

After the summons is served, the original document is returned to the court and it is noted whether the defendant was actually served. The serving of the summons is the defendant's official notification that a suit has been filed and that he or she has been named as a defendant. Filing the complaint and serving the summons officially commences a law suit.

The defendant is then given a certain time period in which to file an *answer* to the plaintiff's complaint.

Venue and Jurisdiction

The attorney must file the case in the proper court. A court has no authority to hear a case unless it has jurisdiction over the persons or property involved.

Some actions are called *local actions* and can be brought only in the county where the subject matter of the jurisdiction is located. For example, a mortgage foreclosure can only be brought in the county where the property is located. Other actions are called *transitory actions* and can be brought in any county in any state where the defendant may be found and served with the summons. An action for personal injury is a transitory action.

Venue is the location, the county, or the district where the action will be tried. Venue may be changed (1) if there has been widespread pretrial publicity, (2) in an effort to find jurors who have not been exposed to that publicity, or (3) simply to provide a more neutral setting when there is a great deal of local sentiment about a certain case.

A *change of venue* is requested by motion and is granted or denied by the judge.

Trial Preparation

Before the trial begins, both parties can file documents with the court. Sometimes a defendant may file a pleading called a *Motion to Quash Service of Summons,* which asserts that the defendant should not have been served or was improperly served. A defendant may also file a *Motion to Make More Definite and Certain*, which asks the court to order the plaintiff to describe the injury more fully or to set out the facts more specifically so that the defendant can answer more accurately.

Sometimes a defendant asks the court to rule against the plaintiff with a *Motion to Dismiss* the case.

Before the actual trial, *depositions* are often taken. Depositions are out-of-court statements taken under oath, and they are used for trial preparation and may be used in court. A deposition is not a public record.

Discovery is another legal term which refers to a party's attempt to get more information about the case. Sometimes a party is required to produce books or financial or medical records or submit to a physical examination.

After the pleadings have been filed, a pretrial conference is often held. Sometimes a case is settled at this conference. If not, a trial date is set.

The Trial

Sometimes the lawyers involved decide that a judge trial rather than a jury trial would be better for the case, and the right to a jury trial is waived.

When a jury is requested, the lawyers and the judge engage in a process called *voir dire* to pick the jury. In this process, the jurors are questioned to determine if they possess any prejudice or bias regarding the case. Each side has a certain number of challenges that can be made for any reason at all. These are called peremptory challenges. Each side also has an unlimited number of challenges that can be made for cause, that is, on the grounds that the juror cannot be termed impartial and is obviously prejudiced in some way.

Once the jury has been selected, each party makes an opening statement. Then witnesses are called to present evidence. The party calling a witness questions the witness first; this is called *direct examination*. The opposing party then questions the witness in what is called *cross-examination*.

When all the witnesses have been called and examined, the parties are allowed to make summations or *closing arguments*.

The judge then *instructs* the jury, and they begin their *deliberations*. Sometimes the jurors are *sequestered*, or isolated, from the public when they are deciding a very controversial case.

After a decision is reached, the jury returns to the courtroom and the *verdict* is read in open court.

STATUTES, LAWS, AND REGULATIONS

Hierarchy of Laws
1. United States Constitution
2. Federal Statutes and Regulations

3. State Constitution
4. State Statutes and Regulations
5. County and City Ordinances
6. Common Law

Statutory Law

Statutory law is the body of law created by legislative acts (in contrast to the law generated by judicial opinion and administrative bodies).

Of course, the "supreme law of the land" is the U.S. Constitution.[4]

The structure of American government is probably familiar to all. It includes the U.S. Constitution, the national government and the individual state governments, and the three branches of government—the executive branch, the legislative branch, and the judicial branch. Administrative agencies that create administrative law are also important parts of the structure of government.

Common Law

Common law is the body of law derived from the ancient unwritten law of England. Common law consists of the principles, uses, and rules that do not rest on any express declaration of a legislature.[5]

Courts attempt to decide cases based on principles established in prior cases. Prior cases that are similar to the case being considered are called *precedents*.

Decisions found to be unreasonable may be overturned.

Stare decisis is a legal principle that mandates adherence to decided cases. It is the policy of courts to stand by precedent and not to disturb a settled point.[6]

Lawsuits are resolved by applying decisions of previous cases. Sometimes a very slight factual difference will be used by the court to distinguish the present case from previous cases.

Regulations

Federal Agencies

At the federal level, an administrative agency is created by a congressional act. The president, with the advice and consent of Congress, appoints the agency's director or highest official. The agency makes rules (called *regulations*), that have the force of law.

Federal agency regulations can be found in the Code of Federal Regulations (C.F.R.). The agency can interpret and enforce the regulations through administrative hearings and decisions. Federal courts can review the decisions made at an administrative hearing and can also be asked to review the regulations.

State Agencies

At the state level, some agencies are created by statute and some are created by provisions in the state constitution. The directors of these state agencies may be appointed by the governor, although the statute or the constitution might direct that the director or top agency official be elected. For example, in many states the attorney general is elected rather than appointed. In state agencies, as in federal agencies, government policies are implemented through rules and decisions. Agency rules and decisions are subject to review by the courts.

Separation of Powers

No one branch of the government is dominant over another branch. Each affects and limits the functions and powers of the others. Thus, the American government is sometimes called a "system of checks and balances." When Congress passes a bill, the president must sign it before it becomes law. And, if the president vetoes the bill, a vote of two-thirds of the Congress can override that veto. A law that has been passed by Congress and signed by the president can be declared invalid (overturned) by the U.S. Supreme Court.

The three branches of government (the executive, legislative, and judicial branches) work together to make, execute, review, and enforce the laws.

Statute of Limitations

Every civil and criminal case is subject to a specific statute of limitation, which is a time limit as to when a lawsuit may be filed. There is one exception: There is no statute of limitation for the crime of murder.

If a lawsuit is not filed within the limits of the statute, the right to sue is lost. The time to file a lawsuit will vary from state to state, and there are different times prescribed for various types of cases.

TORT LAW

A tort is a civil wrong. It is not considered a crime. The wrongdoer is called a *tort-feasor*. The purpose of tort law is to provide a method for peacefully determining liability and assessing damages to be paid to victims of wrongdoing.

There are many different torts, and not all torts are recognized in all jurisdictions. In the United States, the most common torts are assault and battery, conspiracy, false imprisonment, forcible entry and detainer, fraud, libel and slander, malicious prosecution, negligence, product liability, trespass, trover and conversion, and waste.

When a person is injured or property is damaged, the rights and responsibilities of the parties involved are determined by the law of torts. Many torts involve negligence. When a judge, jury, or arbitrator determines one party was negligent and that the negligent conduct caused injury or property damage, the negligent party is usually required to pay for the harm done.

Simply determining that someone caused injury to someone else is not sufficient. It must be proven that a defendant was at fault. Sometimes no one was at fault, as some accidents are unavoidable.

Usually a tort victim is compensated, with money, for the injury suffered. The sum most often includes medical expenses incurred or reimbursement for lost wages. If the damage was to property, the victim is usually awarded the amount of money needed to repair or replace the damaged property. Sometimes people are compensated for their pain and suffering. Although it is very difficult to assign a dollar value to the loss of a leg or an eye, in our society it has been decided that monetary compensation is the best alternative.

Categories of Torts

There are three categories of torts: intentional torts, negligence, and strict liability torts.

Most torts involve some sort of negligence, but in some cases there may be intentional wrongdoing. Intentional torts include assault, battery, false imprisonment, invasion of privacy, and the intentional infliction of emotional distress. There are also certain situations where the activity is so dangerous that it is public policy to demand absolute responsibility of the tort-feasor. These are known as strict liability torts.

Negligence

The most common tort is the tort of negligence. When a person or property is injured or damaged as a result of the actions of another person, an allegation of negligence is often made. Negligence is often divided into two degrees: ordinary negligence (which is the failure to perform as a reasonably prudent person would perform under similar circumstances) and gross negligence (which is the intentional or wanton disregard of care).

Forms of Negligence

There are several forms of negligence. *Malfeasance* is an unlawful or improper act. *Misfeasance* is the incorrect performance of a permitted act. *Nonfeasance* is the failure to act when an act is required by law or when there is a duty to act. *Malpractice* is the negligent or careless action of a person who is held to a professional standard of care. *Criminal negligence* is the willful indifference to the potential for injury or the reckless disregard for the safety of another.

Standards of Care

Professionals are held to a higher standard of care than nonprofessionals. A nonprofessional is judged by a "reasonable person" standard: What would a reasonable person do in this situation? A professional is held to a higher standard: What would a reasonably prudent person with this type of specialized training do in this type of situation?

How Is Negligence Proven in a Court of Law?

Usually a jury will decide, based on facts presented at trial, if a person acted reasonably or negligently. Custom and common sense often determine what standard of care the jury will apply.

Sometimes the standard of care is defined by statute. If someone acted in violation of law, he or she is usually presumed to have acted negligently and is held liable for any damages that result.

Res ipsa loquitur means "the thing speaks for itself." The doctrine of res ipsa loquitur applies when the defendant had exclusive control of the item or instrument or "thing" that caused the harm, when the plaintiff did not in any way contribute to the accident, and when the accident would not have occurred unless someone was negligent. For example, if an X-ray clearly shows that a surgical instrument was left in the chest cavity of a man who had undergone heart surgery, the plaintiff could allege that the doctrine of res ipsa loquitur applies. In this case, the mere fact that the accident happened is enough to infer that the someone (the doctor, nurse, or hospital) was negligent and will be held liable for damages.

Standards of care applicable to medical professional activities can also be found in government regulations and in accreditation manuals for hospitals and other institutions.

Sometimes a standard of care changes based on changes in statutes, rules, and court cases.

In the case of *Darling v. Charleston Community Memorial Hospital,* 33 Ill. 2d 326, 211 N.E. 2d 253 (1965), the Illinois Supreme Court held that a hospital is liable for the improper review of the credentials of its staff, that a hospital cannot limit its liability as a charitable corporation to the amount of its liability insurance, and that since the evidence supported the verdict for the plaintiff, the hospital was liable.

In the *Darling* case, a college football player was injured while playing. He was taken to the emergency room and was treated by a general practitioner who had not treated a leg fracture in recent years. X-rays were taken and the doctor set the fracture and applied a cast. The patient complained of pain. The doctor did not call in a specialist. After two weeks the plaintiff was transferred to a larger hospital under the care of an orthopedic surgeon. The surgeon found a considerable amount of dead tissue that, in his opinion, was caused by swelling of the leg against the cast. The surgeon attempted several operations to save the leg, but ultimately it was amputated eight inches below the knee.

The Illinois court held that the hospital was liable based on the evidence that the nurses at the hospital did not test the leg for circulation as often as necessary, that skilled nurses would have promptly recognized conditions that signalled impaired circulation, and that the nurses knew that the situation would become irreversible. In that situation, it became the "nurses duty to inform the attending physician and if he failed to act, to advise the hospital authorities so that appropriate action might be taken."[7]

The court also held that the hospital negligently failed to review the doctor's work and negligently failed to require a consultation with a specialist.

In the *Darling* case the court also held that the doctrine of charitable immunity did not apply and that the defendant was liable for the full judgment, even that part of the amount in excess of its insurance coverage.

Defenses against Negligence

A defendant may be relieved from having to pay damages even if he or she is found to be negligent. The possible defenses are contributory negligence, comparative negligence, assumption of the risk, and release.

Contributory Negligence. The rule of contributory negligence is still the law in some states, but most states have changed to a comparative law standard. Contributory negligence was the law in all states at one time. This doctrine provided that if a person was negligent at all, he or she could not recover against another person even if that person was far more negligent.

Comparative Negligence. Since abandoning the doctrine of contributory negligence, most states have adopted a comparative negligence rule. Under this rule, one party's negligence is "compared" with the other party's negligence. Recovery of damages will be limited to an amount reduced by the percentage of fault assessed to that party. For example, if the defendant car driver was held to be 80 percent at fault but the plaintiff was held to be 20 percent at fault, the most the plaintiff could recover would be 80 percent of his or her claim.

Releases. Many times businesses will try to limit their liability by printing a release on the back of a ticket claiming they cannot be sued if there is an injury. Sometimes this will preclude a person from suing them and sometimes it will not. If the release is written in very fine print and was not noticed, the person signing will not be held to it. If it is written in a complicated way and was not understood, the person signing will not be held to it. Also, that person's right to sue will not be waived if the injuries were caused by an act of gross negligence or if the act was intentional.

Equitable Relief

In some cases involving nuisance or trespass, a plaintiff may ask the court to issue an injunction to order the defendant to stop doing something tortious.

Money Damages

As mentioned above, a tort is not considered a crime. In a tort action, the plaintiff has somehow been injured. The plaintiff seeks damages (monetary compensation) for these injuries in his or her own name in a civil, not criminal, court. By contrast, in criminal law it is "the people" as a whole who seek justice. It is the state in a criminal case that brings the case, not the wronged individual. A victim of theft or rape cannot bring a criminal action against a person. The complaint is filed in the name of the state.

Tort law compensates a person with money. The person responsible for the injury is required to pay to make the harmed person whole again. Criminal law punishes the criminal who violated a law. The penalty can be a fine or imprisonment, or both.

Sometimes a Tort Is Also a Crime

Some crimes are also torts. This can be confusing. Battery is both a crime and a tort. If one person strikes another person, the victim can sue to recover damages. This suit would be brought in a civil court, and if the plaintiff (the person who was hit) could prove that he or she was injured and those injuries were caused by the defendant (the person who did the hitting), the plaintiff could be compensated for the injuries. The state could also prosecute the defendant for the crime of battery, in which case the defendant might go to jail.

RESTRAINT OF TRADE

Antitrust litigation is an important legal issue for health care providers. The competition in the health care industry creates an arena for many kinds of possibly illegal actions involving the restraint of trade.

In 1890, the U.S. Congress passed the Sherman Antitrust Act (15 U.S.C. §1). Section 1 provides that "every contract, combination in form of trust or otherwise, or conspiracy, in restraint of trade or commerce among the several States, or with foreign nations, is hereby declared to be illegal."

Any time there is an action to reduce market competition, fix prices, bar or limit members, or provide a "preferred provider" system or when there is an exclusive contract, there is the possibility of restraint of trade.

There can be a potential antitrust problem when a hospital limits its medical staff. The process a hospital uses to determine who may have staff privileges and who may not must be based on objective criteria and not on the financial advantages that may be realized by granting or denying the right to practice at the hospital.

Of course, a hospital may deny privileges to certain individuals, but the decision must be made for cause (for instance, the doctor involved has been cited for improper actions or does not possess the qualifications required for all doctors) and not merely to limit competition.

Sometimes a hospital will enter an exclusive contract with ancillary groups to provide services to the hospital. Often a hospital will contract with a pathology, radiology, or anesthesiology group or with emergency technicians. If these contracts are reasonable and are not made to limit competition, they are usually permitted. In several cases in which hospitals were sued, the courts held that the contracts were not against public policy.[8]

Hospitals and other health care facilities must be sure that any action or proposed action to limit access or to close its medical staff is based on objective criteria. In many states, government agencies review hospital actions regarding the granting or the denying of hospital privileges. Individual physicians and medical groups will continue to challenge hospital actions, and if objective standards are not the basis for an action, the challengers will prevail. See the following chapter for details.

NOTES

1. In any case, the title of the case is always written *Plaintiff v. Defendant*. The plaintiff (or plaintiffs), the party bringing the action, will always be listed first. Also, each case will have a citation. With the citation the case can be looked up and the complete decision read. For example, in "220 F. 2d 118," "F. 2d" refers to the Federal Reporter, Second Series, "220" refers to the volume, and "118" refers to the page number of that volume. The citation also can be used to learn if the case has been upheld or overturned by a higher court and to determine if there are other cases with similar results.

2. The highest court in New York State is called the Court of Appeals.

3. In some states, a summons may only be served by a person who is over 21 years of age and who is not a party to the action.

4. U.S. Constitution, Art. VI.

5. *Bishop v. United States*, 334 F. Supp. 415 (S.D. Tx. 1971), *cert. denied* 414 U.S. 911 (1973).

6. *Neff v. George*, 364 Ill. 306, 4 N.E. 2d 388 (1986).

7. 211 N.E. 2d at 258.

8. *Jefferson Parish Hospital v. Hyde*, 446 U.S. 2 (1984). See also *Belmar v. Cipolla*, 96 N.J. 199, 475 A. 2d 533 (1984).

Chapter 14

Medical Staff Legal Issues

Steven V. Schnier, Esq.

Medical staff law is not merely the concern of the legal counsel chosen to advise the medical staff and the hospital concerning credentialing, quality assurance, and peer review issues. The law governing medical staff activities is also the direct concern of the medical staff services professional. Medical staff law defines the relationships among the hospital, the medical staff, the members of the medical staff, and the practitioners who seek membership and privileges. And, more than anyone else, it is the medical staff services professional who stands at the center of the cross-currents. The medical staff services professional may be among the few who sense the larger picture and are thus able to balance the competing pressures. The purpose of the general description of medical staff legal issues presented in this chapter is to acquaint the medical staff services professional with the legal considerations that always underlie, frequently affect, and occasionally thwart the credentialing, quality assurance, and peer review activities of the medical staff and the hospital.

THE MEDICAL STAFF AND ITS RELATIONSHIP TO THE HOSPITAL

Legal Status

A hospital medical staff is ordinarily viewed as a somewhat diffuse unincorporated association, and the ability to distinguish it as an entity from the hospital corporation depends upon the factual and legal setting. Most observers do not view the current medical staff organization as a separate and independent legal entity. However, physician leaders who are concerned about lay infringement on credentialing and peer review decisions often advocate "self-governance" for the medical staff in these areas. This, in turn, frequently leads them to assert that the medical staff is a separate legal entity.

Medical Staff Membership

The essence of medical staff membership is a cluster of complementary hospital and physician rights and obligations. Achievement and maintenance of medical staff membership ordinarily allows the physician to practice medicine in the hospital on behalf of those patients who have sought his or her services. In exchange, the physician is expected to discharge the organizational responsibilities associated with membership. For its part, the hospital provides certain facilities and services for the direct benefit of the patient and for the indirect benefit of the physician. The hospital is also expected to accept, evaluate, and monitor the physician in accordance with the requirements of the medical staff bylaws and judicial and statutory law.

Admitting and Clinical Privileges

The precise scope of practice allowed the physician in the hospital is defined by the clinical privileges that, after an assessment of his or her qualifications, are recommended by the medical staff and approved by the hospital governing body. These clinical privileges define the procedures that may be performed and the conditions that may be treated by the physician within the hospital. They are subject to limitation or revocation given substandard practice or errant conduct.

Medical Staff Bylaws

The organizational relationships among physicians and the relationship between the physicians as a group and the hospital as an entity are defined by the medical staff bylaws adopted by the hospital governing body after recommendation by the hospital medical staff. The medical staff bylaws describe the purposes of the medical staff, its relationship to the governing body, the criteria for granting and maintaining medical staff membership and privileges; the means by which membership and clinical privileges may be granted, restricted, suspended, and revoked; the manner in which hospital clinical services are organized; and the medical staff officers and committees that are to discharge the responsibilities delegated by the governing body to the medical staff. The medical staff bylaws serve, at the very least, as authoritative guidelines. Courts in some jurisdictions have viewed them as an enforceable agreement between the hospital, the medical staff as an organization, and individual physicians.

The Credentialing Process

A physician desiring medical staff membership and clinical privileges must submit an application listing his or her education, training, experience, and past and

present hospital affiliations. This application, together with supplementary information provided by the physician and obtained from other sources, is then evaluated
according to the credentialing process described in the medical staff bylaws. As is
evident from the very existence of that process, a hospital may make the granting
medical staff membership and clinical privileges conditional upon demonstration
of qualifications beyond mere licensure by the state.

The burden of persuasion (or proof) in the credentialing process is on the
applicant: He or she must resolve any reasonable doubt about qualifications if
membership is to be granted. The credentialing process ordinarily includes three
steps: (1) an evaluation of the application by medical staff members sharing the
same specialty (the relevant clinical department or service), (2) an evaluation by a
medical staff credentials committee whose task is to assess the more general
qualifications of the practitioner, and (3) an evaluation by a medical staff executive
committee that serves as the chief administrative body of the medical staff. Should
the credentialing process result in favorable medical staff recommendations, the
application is then forwarded to the governing body for a decision regarding
membership and clinical privileges. Should the process result in a negative
recommendation, the physician is ordinarily afforded an opportunity to request
review by a separate committee of medical staff members (a medical staff hearing).

The Peer Review Process

The practice of a physician who has achieved medical staff membership is
evaluated, both generally and specifically, by a series of medical staff peer review
activities that assess his or her management of particular hospitalized patients and
his or her general performance and conduct as a physician and medical staff
member.

Corrective Action

The physician whose practice or conduct attracts negative attention may become
the subject of the disciplinary and corrective action processes described in the
medical staff bylaws. These processes are often activated by evidence of questionable judgment or technique, generally deficient conduct, or disruptive behavior.
The corrective action process typically involves investigation by a departmental or
special committee, further consideration by the medical staff executive committee,
and a possible recommendation of restriction or revocation of medical staff
membership and privileges. This recommendation usually affords the physician the
right to review by a special medical staff committee (a medical staff hearing) and
final or appellate consideration by the hospital governing body.

OBLIGATION FOR CREDENTIALING AND PEER REVIEW

Peer Review Responsibilities

The hospital and the medical staff are obligated by institutional requirements (e.g., directives of the Joint Commission on Accreditation of Healthcare Organizations) and by assumed responsibilities to scrutinize the claimed qualifications of applicants, monitor and supervise the practices of medical staff members, and limit and revoke the medical staff membership and privileges of errant physicians.

Potential Legal Liability

Given the manner in which litigation is currently conducted in our society, a hospital should expect that any allegation that a member of its medical staff has engaged in professional negligence will be accompanied by an allegation of hospital negligence. The attempt to obtain a financial award from the hospital will be based on theories that the physician was in fact an employee or agent of the hospital, that the physician appeared to the patient to be the agent of the hospital, that the hospital negligently failed to monitor and supervise the physician's practice during a particular hospitalization, or that the granting of clinical privileges to the physician was the result of negligence during the credentialing or peer review process.

No Liability for Independent Contractors

Absent allegations of independent hospital negligence or an ostensible or actual principal-agent relationship, the hospital is not *automatically* responsible for the professional negligence of a physician who serves as an independent contractor in the course of his or her practice of medicine on behalf of the patients who have sought his or her services.

Hospital Liability Given Ostensible Agency

Although the hospital and a medical staff member may readily agree that he or she is an independent contractor, the practitioner may reasonably be viewed by a patient as an "agent" of the hospital. For example, this perception of agency may follow from the fact (1) that the hospital and the particular practitioner are bound by an agreement allowing the practitioner the exclusive or preferred right to provide certain diagnostic or therapeutic services and (2) that the patient did not select the particular physician. Therefore, a judicial finding of "ostensible agency" can be expected should the allegedly errant physician be a radiologist or pathologist, a member of a panel of anesthesiologists, an emergency department physician, or perhaps even a consultant retained by the attending physician.

Corporate Negligence in Supervision

A court finding of hospital liability based on "ostensible agency" was an evolutionary rather than a revolutionary development. The courts began placing more significance on the perceived appearance of a hospital-physician relationship rather than on the particular label chosen by the hospital and the physician. The first truly revolutionary development in hospital liability was the increased willingness of the courts to find a hospital independently responsible for monitoring and supervising and, if warranted, controlling the care provided by a physician during the course of a particular hospitalization. This perceived basis of liability obliterated the comforting assumption that a hospital only provided the stage upon which physicians might perform through its employment of nurses, construction of facilities, and purchases of equipment.

The single judicial decision that is most often cited as the herald of this new form of liability is *Darling v Charleston Community Memorial Hospital*, 211 N.E. 2d 253 (Illinois Supreme Court 1965). This decision involved a professional liability lawsuit against a family physician that was coupled with allegations of hospital negligence for alleged failure to adequately supervise that physician (see Table 14-1). The Illinois Supreme Court affirmed the judgment against the hospital, holding that liability could be based on a finding that the hospital had failed to require that the errant physician seek consultation. The hospital was therefore deemed *independently* negligent, and its liability could not be restricted to potential responsibility for the negligent acts of employed nursing personnel.

Corporate Negligence in Credentialing and Peer Review

Many courts share the unstated belief that the general public is not capable of assessing the qualifications of physicians and making informed choices. Additionally, the courts have correctly perceived that state licensing bodies usually only bar the practice of medicine to those who are spectacularly unqualified. Moreover, the courts appreciate that only hospitals and medical staff are capable of determining who is and who is not qualified to practice medicine.

These beliefs increasingly lead courts to find that a hospital owes a duty to a patient to exercise due care in the credentialing and peer review processes. This finding provides the basis for hospital liability should a hospital be found to have been negligent in failing to scrutinize the claimed credentials of an applicant for medical staff membership and clinical privileges or in failing to monitor and, if appropriate, restrict the practice of a member of the medical staff. Therefore, a hospital may be found financially liable not only for failing to prevent a particular instance of substandard professional practice but also for granting and continuing the medical staff membership and clinical privileges that made it possible for the negligent practitioner to conduct any practice within the hospital.

Table 14-1 Case Law Chart

Case	Description	Impact
Darling v. Charleston Community Memorial Hospital (Illinois Supreme Court, 1965)	Football player seen in ER by family MD for leg fracture. During hospitalization, pt. complained of pain and no consultation obtained. MD hadn't treated a fracture in 3 yrs. Pt. transferred after 2 wks. and required leg amputation. The hospital claimed that the MD practiced medicine, not the hospital.	End of the doctrine of charitable immunity. Hospitals are independently responsible for monitoring, supervising, and controlling care where necessary to protect the patient.
Purcell and Tucson General Hospital v. Zimbleman (Arizona Court of Appeals, 1972)	MD misdiagnosed pt. and performed inappropriate surgery, which resulted in major complications. MD had done this in the past with a history of 4 malpractice suits—2 for the same procedure. In doing peer review, the Dept. of Surgery had failed to act on this information (which it had). The hospital claimed it wasn't liable because the dept. hadn't acted.	Hospitals are required to assume the duty of supervising the competence of physicians. Hospitals cannot delegate responsibility for credentialing and peer review to a dept. The dept. acts on behalf of the hospital.
Gonzalez v. Nork and Mercy Hospital (California Court of Appeals, 1976)	Unsuccessful laminectomy performed, resulting in complications leading to decreased life span. Surgery determined to be inappropriate and negligently performed. MD had history of 3 dozen unnecessary or negligent surgeries in past 9 yrs. MD was not board certified in orthopedics.	Hospital owe patients a duty of care. Hospitals required to have peer review system. Joint Commission increased standards related to MSO and peer review.
Johnson v. Misericordia Community Hospital (Wisconsin Court of Appeals, 1981)	While removing pin fragment from a pt.'s hip, the MD severed the femoral nerve and artery, resulting in permanent hip paralysis. Hospital was sued because it had failed to follow its bylaws and had failed to investigate MD's background before granting privileges. MD's application was incomplete and inaccurate.	Hospitals have a duty to exercise due care in selecting medical staff. Bylaws and complete credentialing must be adhered to. Another example of corporate negligence.
Robinson v. Magovern (Western Pennsylvania Federal District Court, 1981)	MD brought antitrust suit because he was denied privileges. Hospital based decision on shortage of OR space, unfavorable recommendations, failure to publish. MD on 7 other staffs and would not be able to contribute to hospital teaching program.	A hospital may determine proper limitations on competition within the hospital and surrounding areas. Careful and thorough adherence to bylaws that contain objective criteria required.
Elam v. College Park Hospital (California Court of Appeals, 1982)	Podiatrist performed surgery on patient that resulted in chronic pain and inability to walk normally.	Hospitals liable to patients under doctrine of corporate negligence. Hospitals have a duty to properly select and monitor physicians.
Patrick v. Burget (U.S. Supreme Court, 1988)	MD left clinic to open own practice. Following hospital peer review, MD denied privileges. After hospital hearing, MD resigned. On MD's attempt to be reinstated, hospital asked BME to write letter. Reinstatement denied and MD removed from medical staff. MD sued on restraint of trade. Supreme Court found that state wasn't involved enough in peer review action.	Negative peer review and credentialing are not immune from federal antitrust laws. A hospital cannot argue that peer review is done at the state's request. MDs can be sued for peer review if, for economic reasons, denial occurs. Resulted in passage of the Health Care Quality Improvement Act of 1986.

Therefore, the new approach to potential liability indicated by *Darling* has now evolved to the point that the credentialing and peer review processes themselves can be the basis for liability. For example, in *Johnson v. Misericordia Community Hospital*, 301 N.W. 2d 156 (Wisconsin Supreme Court 1981), the court ruled that a hospital may be found liable in a professional negligence action for failure to exercise due care in the evaluation of the claimed credentials of an applicant for medical staff membership. The court held that evidence of *negligent* credentialing would include a failure to contact listed references and other hospitals at which an applicant asserted he or she enjoyed clinical privileges. Additionally, the court indicated that a hospital has some obligation to contact a professional liability insurer to determine if the applicant has been the subject of medical malpractice litigation. Furthermore, a hospital must exercise due care in the evaluation of the qualifications of *present* members of the medical staff, and the reasonableness of hospital credentialing and peer review decisions will be determined on the basis of what information would have been revealed by an adequate inquiry. The *Johnson* decision has now been followed by a series of like decisions in other states. This succession of cases confirms that "corporate responsibility" for credentialing and peer review will be the rule nationwide, not the exception. Moreover, so to make this rule even more pointed, earlier decisions such as *Purcell v. Zimbelman*, 500 P. 2d 335 (Arizona Court of Appeals 1972) make it clear that the hospital corporation cannot persuasively argue that it had protected itself from credentialing and peer review liability by "delegating" responsibility for those activities to the medical staff.

STANDARDS AND CRITERIA FOR MEMBERSHIP AND PRIVILEGES

Membership May Be Selective

The need for standards and criteria is apparent for institutional reasons alone, for it would be the unusual hospital that elected to allow all licensed and interested practitioners to practice within the institution. Therefore, given that choices are to be made, criteria and standards are necessary.

Administrative Rejections

Certain hospital decisions regarding allowable access to its facilities will be based upon administrative considerations and physical constraints. For example, a hospital may well decide that only a select few of a larger number of qualified physicians will be allowed to perform certain diagnostic or therapeutic services. However, decisions on applications for medical staff membership and clinical privileges are generally based not on the perceived need for or ability to accommodate a particular medical specialist but rather on the apparent professional qualifications of the applicant. In this sense, the hospital only determines whether the practitioner will enjoy the theoretical right to practice at the hospital. Decisions as to whether the practitioner will *actually* practice at the hospital are made by patients and by colleagues who make referrals.

General Criteria

Hospital credentialing criteria, therefore, are generally concerned with the required education, training, experience, and expertise of the successful applicant and his or her potential for providing a particular quality of medical care.

Elevated Credentialing Criteria

Viewing the credentialing process from the perspective of the allegedly injured patient, a significant number of courts have imposed an obligation of due care on the hospital. Viewing the credentialing process from the perspective of the individual applicant, the court accepts the proposition that a hospital may demand more than mere licensure by the state and may also make the "right" to practice within the hospital conditional upon satisfaction of its own standards and criteria.

For example, in *Sosa v. Board of Managers of Val Verde Memorial Hospital*, 437 F.2d 173 (5th Cir. 1971), a public hospital denial of an application for medical staff membership was based on evidence of questionable medical care and disruptive conduct. While the applicant for medical staff membership appeared to meet the basic medical staff bylaws requirements of licensure and practice within the community, the court of appeals held that the hospital could properly enforce additional standards reasonably related to considerations of patient care and hospital operations. Furthermore, the court of appeals recognized that credentialing standards cannot be precisely articulated and that a hospital must be afforded wide latitude in prescribing necessary qualifications.

Permissible Criteria

Given the perception that the hospital and the medical staff share the common goal of quality medical care, a hospital may adopt any credentialing criterion or standard that is reasonably related to considerations of patient care and general hospital operations. For example, in *Miller v. National Medical Hospital of Monterey Park*, 124 Cal. App.3d 614 (California Supreme Court 1980), the California Supreme Court held that a private hospital may deny an application for medical staff membership given the applicant's failure to demonstrate compliance with the medical staff bylaw credentialing criterion requiring documentation that the physician can "work with others" with sufficient adequacy to ensure that any patient treated by the physician will receive "a high quality of medical care." While the court cautioned that a private hospital credentialing criterion cannot be so vague as to create a substantial danger of arbitrary or discriminatory application, this criterion was acceptable to the extent that it demanded a demonstrable connection between the personality of the applicant and either his or her ability to provide quality patient care or the level of care in the institution as a whole.

The courts recognize that descriptions of acceptable medical practice and physician performance cannot be minutely described in the form of a civil service job description. Therefore, as noted in the decision in *Sosa*, credentialing criteria that are stated in general terms or even as desired goals will ordinarily be accepted as long as they include the requisite relationship to considerations of patient care and hospital operations. Likewise, in *Miller v. National Medical Hospital of Monterey Park*, 124 Cal. App.3d 81 (California Court of Appeal 1981), the court of appeal upheld the suspension of privileges of a physician convicted of a criminal act even though his appeals regarding the criminal sentencing had not been exhausted and his state license remained intact. Similarly in *Huffaker v. Bailey*, 540 P.2d 1398 (Oregon Supreme Court 1975), the court held that a credentialing criterion calling for "a high quality of medical care" is not impermissibly vague and ambiguous. The court also held that a medical staff bylaw provision allowing for disciplinary action should the conduct of a physician be "lower than the standards or aims" of the medical staff was not impermissibly ambiguous or vague, particularly given that the bylaws offered as examples of the proscribed behavior "unprofessional conduct, immoral conduct [and] unethical practice."

Personality As a Criterion

One of the more popular bases for litigation has been credentialing criteria that focus on the "personality" of an applicant for medical staff membership. The courts will generally allow consideration of personality if it appears that the hospital has attempted, through its credentialing criteria and the credentialing process itself, to measure the personality of the applicant only to the extent that it might affect his or her practice of medicine or the general operations of the hospital. Court disapproval of criteria that focus on the personality of the applicant has ordinarily occurred in cases where the criteria were not expressly related to legitimate hospital concerns or there was evidence that an assertive personality was mistaken for an abusive or abrasive one. Rulings to this effect were announced in the California Supreme Court decision in *Miller* and in earlier decisions, such as *Rao v. Auburn General Hospital*, 573 P.2d 834 (Washington Court of Appeals 1978).

Vague Criteria

The recognition that credentialing criteria must be stated in general terms has been accompanied by occasional cautionary statements by the courts that criteria cannot be so vague or ambiguous as to serve as a cloak for irrational credentialing decisions. The latter strain of judicial thinking and statements has often been prompted by the perception that a particular applicant was denied without regard to his evident professional qualifications. For example, in *Milford v. People's Community Hospital Authority*, 155 N.W.2d 835 (Michigan Supreme Court 1968), the court disapproved of a public hospital medical staff bylaw provision allowing the clinical privileges of a physician to be reduced if the reduction would be in the "best interest of the hospital and its patients." The court found this to be vague and ambiguous, for it made no reference to the knowledge, skill, character, or conduct of the physician.

Permissible Credentialing Decisions

A rational credentialing decision is one that is based on the likely quality of the performance of the applicant should medical staff membership be granted. By definition, decisions on applications for medical staff membership most often are based on expertise obtained by the practitioner in training programs and on the quality of care rendered by the applicant at other institutions. As credentialing thus involves an effort to predict the future based on evidence of the past, the projection must appear to be reasonable. Therefore, the hospital must consider the practice of the practitioner elsewhere but may not automatically deny an application merely based upon difficulties that may have occurred in the *distant* past. For example, in *Theissen v. Watonga Municipal Hospital Board*, 550 P.2d 938 (Oklahoma Supreme Court 1976), the court considered a public hospital denial of an application for medical staff membership submitted by a physician who had earlier been expelled. The court generally agreed that mere evidence of past misconduct was not a sufficient basis for a negative credentialing decision but noted that the physician involved had not offered any evidence of rehabilitation. To the contrary, in *Bronaugh v. City of Parkersburg*, 136 S.E.2d 783 (West Virginia Supreme Court of Appeals 1964), the court made it clear that a hospital may not automatically deny medical staff membership based on the mere status of a physician's membership at another hospital.

Requirement of Specialty Training

A thorough examination of the experience of the practitioner in other settings can impose substantial burdens on medical staff services professionals and medical staff members involved in the credentialing process. Furthermore, the practice of medicine is increasingly marked by specialization, referrals, and involvement by a number of practitioners during a particular hospitalization. Therefore, hospitals are increasingly interested in basing membership and credentialing decisions on evidence of appropriate specialty training. At the same time, a hospital should avoid any appearance that credentialing criteria do not take appropriate account of the particular professional qualifications of an individual applicant. Consequently, the courts generally support criteria that require evidence of specialty training but are skeptical of criteria that make the granting of clinical privileges conditional on specialty board certification. For example, in *Hay v. Scripps Memorial Hospital*, 183 Cal. App.3d 753 (1986), one facility of a particular hospital denied an obstetrics privilege to a family practitioner even though the same privilege had been granted to him at another facility of that hospital. The applicable credentialing criterion required completion of a residency in obstetrics and gynecology. The applicant could only point to an eight months' rotation through obstetrics and gynecology during his family practice residency. The court of appeal sustained the credentialing decision by concluding that it was permissible for a hospital to decide that specialty training is a threshold credentialing requirement.

Criteria May Be Made More Restrictive

Given the recognition of potential hospital liability for deficient credentialing practices, one may be thankful that the courts ordinarily will support a hospital that has attempted to increase the stringency of its credentialing criteria. In *Kahn v. Suburban Community Hospital*, 340 N.E.2d 398 (Ohio Supreme Court 1976), the court sustained the enforcement of new credentialing criteria that required specialty board certification, "eligibility" for certification, or a minimum of ten years of experience.

Professional Liability Insurance Coverage

Due to the increasing potential for hospital liability for a number of reasons, credentialing standards that require a demonstration of adequate professional liability insurance coverage have been well received by the courts. These criteria occasionally are expressly authorized by state statutes and are justified on the basis of a number of patient care and administrative considerations. For example, financial prudence supports a requirement of physician insurance coverage in states that enforce joint and several liability and that recognize a right to look to others for financial recovery. Additionally, a hospital may reasonably believe that it is all the more likely to be a target for litigation if practitioners lack insurance coverage. Furthermore, a hospital may believe that patients who have, in fact, been the victims of professional negligence should be able to obtain a financial award from practitioners who were at fault. Additionally, some hospitals have expressed a reasonable concern that the absence of insurance coverage may affect the diagnostic and therapeutic decisions made by a treating physician.

Delegation of Responsibility

A hospital that wishes to exercise significant discretion in credentialing decisions must also be willing to assume significant responsibility for the credentialing process. Therefore, the hospital should not appear to "delegate" responsibility for credentialing to outside entities, nor should it allow members of the present medical staff to exercise a "veto" power over applications for membership. Consequently, a credentialing criterion that requires membership in a local medical society or that conditions membership upon favorable references from present medical staff members (who may have economic reasons to withhold these references) will likely be criticized by the courts.

STANDARDS FOR PEER REVIEW AND CORRECTIVE ACTION

Peer Review Criteria

A hospital and a medical staff are not only responsible for determining who will be admitted to the medical staff and granted clinical privileges but who will be allowed to retain medical staff membership and clinical privileges. The criteria that guide this continuing evaluation parallel those that define the credentialing process, although, understandably, the focus is on the actual practice and conduct of the practitioner rather than on past training or general qualifications. The practice of a practitioner within a hospital may unquestionably be restricted if the practitioner has failed to provide acceptable patient care.

Deficient Behavior

A practitioner may also be subjected to disciplinary action for disruptive conduct or inappropriate behavior that negatively affects patient care or interferes with efficient hospital operations.

Selective Enforcement of Standards

The courts also recognize that effective peer review and corrective action represent major undertakings for a hospital and its medical staff. Therefore, a practitioner ordinarily may not challenge a proposed disciplinary action on the ground that similarly deficient practitioners appear to have escaped restrictions and continue to practice. For example, in *Peterson v. Tucson General Hospital*, 559 P.2d

186 (Arizona Court of Appeal 1976), the court sustained the hospital's denial of reappointment based on a finding that the physician failed to maintain medical records, failed to seek appropriate consultations, and had committed other deficiencies in medical care and in spite of his assertion that other members of the medical staff could be charged with the same deficiencies.

DUE PROCESS

Requirement of Fair Procedure

The courts are increasingly likely to require that both private and public hospitals observe procedures that strike judges and juries as being "fundamentally fair." This requirement may be imposed on a public hospital given a finding that it is obliged to afford the "due process of law" guaranteed by the Fourteenth Amendment to the U.S. Constitution. In the private context, a hospital is increasingly likely to be directed to afford the same procedural guarantees under the label of "common law fair procedure." At the core of both due process of law and common law fair procedure is the requirement that the individual practitioner be provided (1) a general statement of the reasons for the negative recommendation or action and (2) an adequate opportunity to present a response. The opportunity to respond must include an occasion for the practitioner to relate his or her position to the body that will make the ultimate decision, and it may also require a review of the dispute by a hearing body that has not been involved earlier in the peer review process. These requirements have now been strengthened by the recent enactment of the federal Health Care Quality Improvement Act. This act holds out the prospect of certain limited immunities to liability for participants in credentialing and peer review activities if the medical staff and hospital observe certain procedures specified by the act or otherwise conduct themselves in a way that is fair under the circumstances.

The essence of due process may well be extended to the private setting. This result is achieved by a judicial requirement that even a private hospital must afford common law fair procedure to a physician as part of the credentialing or corrective action process. This dictate is generally based on the fact that a physician enjoys state licensure and that denial of access to even a private hospital will likely significantly restrict his or her ability to practice medicine.

Elements of Fair Procedure and Due Process

The elements and essence of Fourteenth Amendment procedural due process and common law fair procedure are strikingly similar. The courts have generally recognized that the peer review and corrective action processes are the responsibilities of lay administrators and medical staff members and that the formality of civil litigation neither can nor should be required. Therefore, a reasonable notice of the basis for the negative action and an adequate opportunity to respond ordinarily suffice.

The notice may be expressed in general terms, need not include a detailed and exhaustive listing of each deficiency perceived in the qualifications or practice of the practitioner, and need only meet its purpose of affording the practitioner a reasonable opportunity to prepare a response.

Common law fair procedure and due process ordinarily do not require that the practitioner be allowed to be accompanied by legal counsel during any peer review hearing. Note, however, that the Health Care Quality Improvement Act characterizes the right to legal counsel as one of the elements of an *unquestionably* fair peer review process. The act does not, however, unequivocally require that the practitioner be afforded the right to an attorney at a peer review hearing.

A significant number of judicial decisions confirm other distinctions between litigation and peer review. For example, the practitioner need not always be afforded the right to engage in cross-examination, it is recognized that a peer review body enjoys no direct power to compel the testimony of witnesses or the production of documents, the opportunity to respond can be limited to written submissions, and the burden of proof may be placed on the practitioner. However, limiting the rights available at the hearing may produce a proceeding that does not automatically satisfy the procedural specifications of the Health Care Quality Improvement Act.

Medical Staff Hearing Committee

Any required opportunity to respond is generally viewed as mandating a medical staff hearing committee whose members are free from actual bias or the manifest possibility of prejudice. Consequently, the hearing committee should not include any practitioner who actively and formally participated in the medical staff peer review process during its investigatory phase or during the formulation of any negative recommendation. Likewise, in keeping with recent judicial decisions and the standards for fairness recognized by the Health Care Quality Improvement Act, the hearing committee should not include any practitioner who is a clear and direct economic competitor of the practitioner who requests the hearing. However, a practitioner may properly serve on a hearing committee even though he or she may be generally aware of the facts that led to a negative credentialing or disciplinary recommendation or action.

Medical Staff Bylaws Requirements

Without regard to whether the medical staff bylaws represent an "agreement" between the medical staff and the hospital, the courts will require that medical staff credentialing, peer review, and hearing processes conform to the procedures described in the medical staff bylaws. However, the courts are unlikely to disapprove of a credentialing or disciplinary decision based on a violation of medical staff bylaws procedures that was minimal in nature and did not significantly affect the fundamental interests of the physician (e.g., a failure to complete the credentialing process within the number of days specified in the medical staff bylaws).

Judicial Review

In addition to observing the medical staff bylaws procedures during the credentialing and peer review processes, a hospital should anticipate that the credentialing or disciplinary decision will be subjected to some form of judicial review. At minimum, a court may scrutinize a credentialing or disciplinary decision in search for a clearly improper result, even though the court may ultimately hold that a credentialing or disciplinary decision of a hospital is not "subject to judicial review." More often, the credentialing and disciplinary decisions of both public and private hospitals are understood to be the proper subjects of substantive review by the courts. The essence of substantive judicial review is an analysis of the credentialing or disciplinary results as compared with the rationales offered by the hospital or the record generated by any peer review proceedings.

The courts will often proclaim great deference to the activities of private and public hospitals and medical staffs in disciplinary actions. Consequently, they will ordinarily reserve their displeasure for decisions that appear arbitrary or capricious or that seemingly lack substantial evidentiary support. They will thus approve credentialing and disciplinary decisions that appear reasonable, even in cases where the court reviewing the decision would have reached a different one.

SUMMARY RESTRICTION OR SUSPENSION OF PRIVILEGES

Need for Immediate Action

A hospital that is required to afford some form of peer review hearing to a physician whose practice is to be limited may perceive the need for a suspension or restriction of clinical privileges in advance of that proceeding. Even those courts that have imposed requirements of due process or fair procedure recognize that the interest of patient care may require an immediate restriction or suspension of clinical privileges. Therefore, a court generally only requires that the need for immediate action be reasonably apparent and that the summary suspension or restriction be followed by an adequate opportunity for a hearing. For example, a court is likely to approve of a summary suspension or restriction of privileges based on relatively fresh information that clearly, if not unequivocally, indicates that a practitioner has been seriously deficient in the past and, more importantly, will continue to be so in the near future unless immediate corrective action is taken.

PROTECTION FOR PARTICIPANTS IN THE CREDENTIALING AND PEER REVIEW PROCESSES

Encouragement of Exchange of Information

The courts and the states have recognized that effective credentialing and peer review depend on the free exchange of frank opinions regarding the qualifications and practices of physicians. Additionally, the fact that a disgruntled physician might commence litigation in response to a negative decision has prompted some sympathy for the physicians who might be targets of litigation.

Immunities for Participants

The courts and the states have therefore created and enforced certain immunities from damages for participants in these processes. These immunities ordinarily provide either absolute or limited protection for those who communicate information and limited protection for those who serve as members of medical staff hearing committees. For example, in *Long v. Pinto*, 126 Cal. App.3d 946 (California Court of Appeal 1981), the court liberally interpreted a statute that afforded absolute immunity for physicians who communicate information as part of a credentialing or peer review activity. Similarly, other courts in other jurisdictions have recognized "limited" immunities for physicians who participate in credentialing and peer review activities as, for example, members of hearing committees or medical staff officers. These limited immunities typically provide protection against liability for physicians who act in good faith and without malice.

PROTECTION OF RECORDS OF PEER REVIEW PROCEEDINGS

Confidentiality

Society also appreciates that peer review will not be conducted with vigor if there is an unimpeded exchange of information between the peer review setting and the civil courts. Therefore, many jurisdictions have enacted statutes providing that the records of peer review proceedings are not subject to discovery in the context of professional negligence actions. However, these statutes also often provide for discovery of the records in the course of litigation commenced by a physician challenging a negative credentialing or disciplinary decision. Given the breadth of confidentiality protections, the principal threat to confidentiality comes from inadvertent rather than compelled disclosures.

Exceptions to Confidentiality

State protection of peer review records has encountered a mixed reception in federal courts. A federal court might well enforce the peer review records protection statute of the state in which it sits if the particular lawsuit does not involve a question of federal laws. However, a protection statute may well be brushed aside should a litigant seek discovery of peer review records in the course of an action that alleges the violation of a federal statute. For example, in *Memorial Hospital for McHenry County v. Shadur*, 664 F.2d 1058 (7th Cir. 1981), the court of appeals was unwilling to enforce a state confidentiality statute given a lawsuit that included allegations of violations of federal antitrust laws. The uncertainty about whether a federal court will enforce a state confidentiality statute in such settings will take on even greater importance in the future as physician lawsuits alleging violations of federal antitrust laws become even more common.

JUDICIAL DEFERENCE TO PEER REVIEW PROCEEDINGS

Delay in Litigation

The courts are prepared to defer to the substance of hospital and medical staff peer review and credentialing decisions. Additionally, the courts will often decline to entertain challenges to peer review and credentialing recommendations and decisions until the physician has exhausted the internal review opportunities provided by the hospital and medical staff. Therefore, the courts will ordinarily require a physician to complete any medical staff hearing opportunities that are afforded him or her by the medical staff bylaws. This requirement of exhaustion of administrative remedies applies even if the physician alleges that there have been, or will likely be, procedural deficiencies in the medical staff hearing.

EXCLUSIVE AGREEMENTS AND ADMINISTRATIVE BARS TO MEDICAL PRACTICE

Denials of Access

Hospitals have long believed that certain diagnostic and therapeutic services can best be delivered if a select number of physician are given an exclusive right to provide those services within the hospital. Exclusive agreements for radiology, pathology, and like services or limited membership panels for anesthesiology and emergency medical care services constitute administrative bars to hospital access. To the extent that a select group of physicians is afforded an exclusive right to practice, other potentially qualified physicians are denied that opportunity. This clash between the interests of the excluded physicians and those of the hospital and patients in general has prompted a body of litigation that has, in turn, yielded a number of court decisions generally favoring these administrative arrangements. The courts have appreciated that an exclusive agreement or similar arrangement may facilitate the efficient scheduling of services, allow for regular coverage, appropriately limit access to sophisticated equipment, and ensure desirable uniformity in diagnostic approach. Therefore, these agreements have often been upheld in the presence of arguments by excluded practitioners that the arrangements constituted impermissible restraints upon their right to practice medicine, violations of state antitrust legislation, and unreasonable denials of the right of patients to choose their physicians.

Affect on Credentialing and Peer Review

The existence of an exclusive agreement has often prompted hospitals to deny applications for medical staff membership and clinical privileges presented by new physicians sharing the specialty controlled by the agreement. Furthermore, an administrative decision to terminate an exclusive agreement often leaves the departing physician with his or her clinical privileges intact but with no ability to practice his or her specialty. However, the courts generally recognize that medical staff peer review hearings are designed to assess the qualifications, professional practice, and conduct of an individual physician and are not designed to measure the reasonableness of an administrative decision to enter into an exclusive agreement with a particular physician. Therefore, denials or effective revocations of clinical privileges for such administrative reasons ordinarily do not invoke the medical staff hearing process. Additionally, the courts have not required that a hospital engage in a notice-and-comment proceeding before embarking on an exclusive agreement.

Federal Antitrust Proscriptions

Physicians wishing to challenge an exclusive agreement increasingly assert that the agreement not only restricts their common law right to practice medicine but also constitutes a violation of federal statutes proscribing impermissible restraints of trade. The courts recognize that the essence of an exclusive agreement may well be a "restraint of trade," but in the past they have often found that a challenged decision or a physician's allegations do not demonstrate any significant effect upon interstate commerce for the jurisdictional purposes of the federal antitrust statutes. However, in recent decisions the courts have demonstrated a willingness to find the necessary effect on interstate commerce less in the impact of the administrative decision itself and more in the impact of the general operations of the hospital, particularly its purchases of supplies and receipt of monies from other states. Nonetheless, although it is increasingly likely that federal jurisdictional tests will be met, courts still ordinarily recognize the patient care and administrative justifications for exclusive agreements and do not automatically find the agreements to constitute impermissible restraints of trade.

Extension of Antitrust Theory

The denial of an application for medical staff membership or the restriction of the practice of a practitioner does not immediately suggest restraint of trade in the same sense as does the proclaimed existence of an exclusive agreement. Nonetheless, negative credentialing and peer review decisions are increasingly challenged as violations of federal antitrust statutes. These challenges have enjoyed mixed success, largely depending on the ability of the individual physician to allege and prove that the negative decision had a significant effect on interstate commerce. Perhaps the most dramatic example of this trend in recent years is the decision in *Patrick v. Burget*, 108 S. Ct. 1658 (1988), in which the U.S. Supreme Court decided that a private hospital medical staff peer review proceeding could not escape scrutiny under the federal antitrust laws based on the argument that credentialing and peer review represents immunized action conducted at the behest of the state.

CONCLUSION

This chapter provides the briefest of introductions to the world of medical staff legal issues. However, it is hoped that the discussion gives some indication of the complexities and challenges of this ever-growing area of law. At the very least, the medical staff services professional should recognize that almost all significant credentialing, quality assurance, and peer review decisions must satisfy certain substantive and procedural standards.

Part VI

Managing Medical Staff Services

I am a true labourer; I earn that I eat, get that I
wear; owe no man hate, envy no man's happiness.
Shakespeare, *As You Like It*

Chapter 15

Managing the Medical Staff Services Department

Joyce Gardner, CMSC and Sharon Lindsey, MEd, CMSC

Within a department, many people perform varied tasks to meet the departmental and institutional objectives. The manager becomes the conductor, orchestrating the flow of work and resources. Before being able to do this, the manager must have a philosophy of management that will then direct his or her actions. The purpose of management is to provide an environment that will allow individuals to do their jobs to the best of their abilities. This philosophy hinges on the belief that everyone wants to do a good job. In addition, it requires the manager to assess each individual's abilities and motivation to do his or her job. In carrying out this purpose, the manager will use the classic tools of management: planning, organizing, staffing, influencing, and controlling.

PLANNING

Planning is the process of determining where the organization or department is going. To get in the car and start to drive with no planned itinerary would not only waste resources (time and gas) but also hinder discovering when the destination had been reached.

In planning for a department, the manager must write goals and objectives stating what the department will accomplish. A goal is a broad statement describing what is to be achieved. Objectives are the specific steps needed to reach the goal. Policies and procedures further define objectives. In developing departmental goals, the manager must keep in mind the institution's mission and goals. Each department should help to achieve institutional goals.

Objectives should use action verbs and be measurable. For example, if the department goal is to maintain a qualified and competent medical staff, one objective might be to "reappoint all medical staff every two years." "Reappoint" indicates action, and the objective is specific enough to be easily measured. To accomplish this objective, the manager may have to change the reappointment

241

process, hire new staff, purchase computer systems, or simply monitor the existing method.

Policies and procedures describe how an objective will be accomplished. Policies are broad guidelines for reaching goals or conforming to standards. Procedures are descriptions of how a policy will be carried out.

One policy for the previously stated objective might be as follows: "The reappointment file will include quality assurance (QA) information." A procedure for this policy might be this: "The medical staff services professional (MSSP) will obtain all QA data from the QA coordinator on each doctor being reappointed."

Although policies and procedures may be difficult and time consuming to write, they are necessary. A lack of policies and procedures can lead to management by crisis, repetitive decision making, and poor communication. Policies and procedures are often used as legal standards and are necessary for meeting the accreditation standards of the Joint Commission on Accreditation of Healthcare Organizations. New employees and temporary staff will find useful a policy and procedure manual explaining the complicated procedures carried out in the department. Such a manual can save having to repeat explanations over and over.

It is the manager's responsibility to develop new and review existing policies and procedures. When a new or temporary employee is hired, the manager is also responsible for explaining policies and procedures. In addition, the manager may have to enforce a policy not adhered to by an employee.

It is easy to become overburdened by policies and procedures. The manager must know when to and when not to write them. Situations requiring policies and procedures include (1) frequent violation of rules, (2) behavioral inconsistencies, (3) time management problems, (4) morale problems, and (5) jobs with many tasks (e.g., credentialing).

To formulate policies and procedures, the manager must first define a purpose or need. This need must be great enough to warrant a policy or procedure. The manager should also determine that the best solution will be a policy or procedure. After gathering data from others, the manager will write a rough draft, checking it against institutional objectives. The draft should be complete, clear, and understandable. The manager should also consider whether it will be easy to enforce the policy and how the policy will be accepted.

The specific format used is usually determined by the institution. However, some additional points need to be considered. Among other things, no personal names should be used, there should be a review or revision every year, and the policies and procedures should be available to employees.

ORGANIZING

Organizing is essentially managing the activities and departmental functions to accomplish the objectives. To do this, the manager will need to delegate, coordinate, and divide the work. This can be accomplished because the institution has given the manager the authority to do it. The source of this authority is shown in an organizational chart.

Organizational charts are developed to show the relationships between the different areas of an institution. Not only should the hospital have an organizational chart, but so should the medical staff services office or department. These charts assist in clarifying the differences in line and staff authority.

Line authority is the traditional form of authority that exists between a supervisor and an employee. Most supervisor-employee relationships are line authority relationships. The supervisor has the authority to make decisions, which are then carried out by the employee.

On the other hand, staff authority is related to expertise in a specialized area. A person in a staff authority position can give advice to the supervisor, who then has the option to use it or disregard it. Staff authority does not give the advisor the right to issue directions that will then be carried out by the employees under that supervisor.

Both types of authority are necessary for the smooth running of an organization as complex as a hospital. Because the two types are very different, however, managers must understand where they and their departments are positioned.

Organizational charts can improve communications within an organization. Charts can also be used to assist in planning career promotion. In developing a chart, an organization has to complete a critical review of its structure. New employees often find organizational charts to be helpful for orientation.

Because organizations are not static, organizational charts must be kept up to date. Charts that reflect a structure no longer in place are of no use.

STAFFING

Staffing is the process of obtaining and maintaining the human resources necessary to complete the department's functions. As mentioned in an earlier chapter, because medical staff services is often thought of as a non-revenue-generating department, it can be subject to budget cuts and is often understaffed. It is therefore incumbent upon the manager to plan carefully and select judiciously the employees of the medical staff services department.

Low turnover of office personnel is desirable, because it results in greater efficiency and cost-effectiveness. Obtaining and keeping well-qualified, competent employees requires basic knowledge of sources of supply, interview techniques, and, occasionally, testing principles.

Once several suitable candidates have been found for a position, the procedure for hiring will be as simple or complex as the organization itself. The human resources or personnel department will advise the medical staff services department director of these procedures and will require that they be followed for legal reasons. Interviewing the selected candidate will be up to the department director.

Once an employee has been selected and the organization has processed the hiring, the department director must determine that appropriate training and orientation occurs. The purpose of training and orientation is to introduce the employee to departmental rules and regulations, departmental policies and procedures, and the job description in enough depth for the employee to begin to function in a productive manner. Orientation should be accomplished within the first week to ten days of employment.

All employees should have job descriptions. A job description assists a new employee in understanding the requirements of the job. The old employee can use the job description as a tool for performance evaluations. The job description can also be used when seeking a raise.

INFLUENCING

Once the work of the department has been defined and the personnel to complete the work have been hired, the manager must now motivate the personnel and lead the action required to meet the objectives. This area of management concerns human behavior. Many managers do not feel comfortable dealing with employees. However, there are many resources to assist a manager in obtaining the necessary skills.

The following suggestions might be helpful.[1] First, build common values within the department. Formally or informally, the manager should ask the employees what values should guide the activities of the work unit. Common values will promote support for actions that the manager may have to take.

Second, involve the staff in building an image of the future for the department. By asking what the ideal medical staff services would be like, the manager can begin to develop ownership in the plan. Without staff ownership, the manager may have a hard time implementing the plan.

Third, develop a spirit of shared responsibility. As the plan is developed and implemented, the manager will need the cooperation of all the staff. The plan may mean extra hours at work or postponing vacations. Without shared responsibility, staff will resent these requirements.

Fourth, facilitate the action. A facilitator assists others in completing the job. The manager's role, according to the management philosophy stated at the beginning of the chapter, is to provide an environment, not to do the staff's jobs.

Fifth, as the plan progresses, hold regular meetings to provide and ask for feedback. Not only does this prevent rumors, bad feelings, and wandering away from the plan's objectives, but it also provides a time to review the progress being made. Good communication is a characteristic of healthy management.

In addition, the manager should recognize and reward contributions made by the staff, lead by example, support and develop staff members, and celebrate successes. These strategies will assist the manager in motivating the staff, and they are also helpful in trying to solve problems or reach goals.

The style of management being described here is called *participatory* because staff have a lot of involvement. However, since the manager may have to make a quick decision and have it carried out immediately, it is best to be familiar with many styles and use them where appropriate.

CONTROLLING

Controlling is the management function that keeps the work completed within the boundaries established by the objectives. This function requires comparing what has been done with what should have been done. It is through this process that the institution ensures that the goals and objectives are met. Quality assurance is an excellent example of a hospital's controlling function. Another example is budgeting.

The process of preparing and monitoring the annual budget for the medical staff services department may fall into two separate categories with two separate sources of income and reporting responsibility: the budget for the department itself and the budget for the medical staff organization.

Funds for the medical staff budget are generated by the medical staff itself in the form of staff dues assessed to individual members. Dues are assessed annually and are set by the medical staff, not by the hospital. The MSSP must determine the funds necessary to carry out the goals and objectives set by the medical staff for the coming year, and the amount of dues is set accordingly. Or the medical staff may assess dues at a set amount, and the MSSP will have to provide services within the limits of the funds.

Functions and services covered by medical staff funds include medical staff golf or tennis tournaments, holiday dinner dances, special journals or textbooks purchased for the library, scholarships, and research projects. Medical staff funds may be used to provide travel to special conferences or seminars for staff leaders, and they may also be used for educational programs for MSSPs when the hospital is unwilling or unable to provide support for conferences and seminars.

A well-planned budget will assist the department manager and the administration in planning operations. The department budget provides an ongoing measure of the progress being made in the department. Several principles should be followed in preparing the departmental budget:

1. Budget preparation initially should be assigned to operational-level personnel so that the budget flows upward from the department supervisors to top

management. This ensures that the budget process is understood throughout the organization and gains the acceptance of those who must live within the budget.

2. The budget should be related to the department's goals and objectives and ultimately to the organization's strategic business plan.

3. The budget should be realistic, neither unusually optimistic nor pessimistic. The budget should relate to established goals and objectives and provide sufficient funds to meet them.

4. The budget must be reviewed frequently for variances that can be corrected before the budget loses its effectiveness.

To relate the budget to the organization's strategic business plan and to departmental goals and objectives, the MSSP must examine the coming year's goals to determine whether there are items that need an unusual allocation. For example, if one of the goals for the coming year is to convert medical staff information to a computerized data base, then the budget should contain a provision for the purchase of computer hardware and software to support the goal. Budget items will usually fall into two categories:

1. **Capital equipment items.** The capital equipment budget is established to cover such items as office furniture, typewriters, computers, file cabinets, and other high-cost purchases.

2. **Operating budget items.** These are recurring items required to operate the department, such as salaries, office supplies, telephone and postage costs, maintenance of equipment, and conferences and travel. Also included in the operating budget are dues for professional organizations, professional journal subscriptions, and other miscellaneous items.

Many businesses use "variable" and "nonvariable" items to differentiate between costs that are fixed from year to year and those that vary from year to year.

Those responsible for preparing the coming year's budget should look closely at the previous year's budget. In some cases, the budgeted items will be the same year after year, with adjustments only for inflation. In some organizations, zero-based budgeting will not allow this. In zero-based budgeting, a completely new budget is begun each budget period, and each item must be rejustified. Using this concept, the budget is not based on increases and decreases in previous items (automatically carried over to the new fiscal year), but the department starts from the base line (zero) each period, justifying the first as well as the last dollar spent. This is a complex process and has been infrequently used, but it is finding its way into more and more operations.

Preparation of the overall or master budget for the institution will fall to the director of financial affairs or the comptroller, who has responsibility for gathering departmental budgets from all services and consolidating them into a master budget. The individual assigned these responsibilities possesses a global view of the organization's financial picture, will have trended income and expenses, and should have projected fluctuations in census. Final adoption of the institution's master budget will be the responsibility of the governing body.

Once the budget has been prepared and the funds allocated, the department manager must monitor compliance for the entire year. Computer reports are generated on a regular basis, either monthly or quarterly, and show the department's budgeted amount, actual amount spent, and positive or negative variances. These reports may also include a year-to-date amount that provides a continuing review of the compliance of the department. Department managers must monitor the budget very carefully and be adept at selecting alternative approaches to spending, as unexpected budget overages are not taken lightly by top administration.

THE MANAGEMENT PROCESS

The manager must put the five components of management into a process that will produce results. In beginning this process, the manager should gain employee assistance in developing a list of problems, needs, and wishes. A good way to collect this information is through brainstorming. The basic technique is to get participants to write down whatever comes to mind (even if it appears outlandish). For example, an item on the list might be, "Attend 50 percent fewer meetings." At first, this may seem impossible, but the discussion generated by this idea may lead to something that is possible. The manager can write the group's ideas down as they are stated. These can then be discussed by the group and ranked according to their importance. If the group participates in developing the prioritized list, it is more likely to assist in implementing the plan.

The manager should choose one or at most two items from the list. If more than two are selected, the chances of successful implementation are reduced. Once an item is selected, the manager can begin developing a plan. Again, group assistance in developing the plan is suggested.

When developing the plan, the manager should include guidelines for evaluation. Incorporating these performance measurements in the beginning ensures that the proper data can be collected to evaluate the success of the implementation. The suggestions mentioned in "Influencing" should be helpful in developing and implementing the plan. The manager should also be sure to include the required financial resources when establishing the year's budget.

When the plan has been completed or at the end of the year, the group should evaluate the results. In completing the evaluation, the manager should look at client satisfaction. In the case of medical staff services, the clients may include the hospital chief executive as well as the medical staff. The process used should also be reviewed. The manager should be sure to provide feedback on how the group did. And whenever possible, successes should be celebrated.

NOTE

1. D. Edward Deming.

REFERENCES

Haimann, Theo, *Supervisory Management for Health Care Organizations.* 4th ed. St. Louis: Catholic Health Association, 1989.
Keeling, B. Lewis, Norman F. Kallaus, and John J. Neuner, *Administrative Office Management.* 7th ed. Cincinnati: South-Western Publishing, 1978.

Chapter 16

A Manager's Guide to Work Management Tools

Sharon Lindsey, MEd, CMSC

In managing the medical staff services department, the manager will frequently encounter problems that will restrict the work. A work management tool may be used to eliminate the difficulties inhibiting the attainment of the departmental goals. These tools are just that—aids that the manager and the employees can use to assist in organizing jobs, improving efficiency, collecting data, or solving problems. In short, these tools help to clear muddy water.

Work management tools have been used in the workplace since the early 1900s. Frederick Taylor used his principles of scientific management to improve work output at the DuPont Company.[1] In the 1930s, Allan Mogensen used his principles of "work smarter" to improve efficiency at Eastman Kodak.[2] Other terms used by industrial engineers and efficiency experts include *work simplification, ergonomics,* and *motion economy.* The end result of all these approaches was to focus attention on how work was being performed and how it could be improved.

PREPARATION OF THE WORK ENVIRONMENT

Before a work management tool can be successfully applied, the work environment must have at least three important characteristics.[3] The first characteristic is employee curiosity or discontent with the status quo. Employees who believe things are the best they can be will not be receptive to change. Creating the desire to look constantly for a better way of doing things is in itself a management challenge. The manager must motivate the employees and provide a safe environment in which they feel comfortable taking risks.

The second characteristic is open-mindedness. Employees willing to look at problems from a different angle will be more open to change. The manager can role model this by being open to employee suggestions for work improvement.

The third characteristic is respect for oneself and others. If each employee values the opinion of the others, the safe environment necessary for change will result.

These three characteristics are easy to require but not always easy to achieve. If they are lacking in the work environment, the manager should spend time developing them before using a work management tool.

When the work environment is ready, the manager, with or without the assistance of the employees, should develop a problem list. The list should be as specific as possible, and little as well as big items should be included. When the list is completed, it should be analyzed.

When analyzing the list, the manager should ask some critical questions:[4]

- Which problem deserves the highest priority? (A problem with the credentialing process would be more critical than a problem connected with the medical staff Christmas party.)
- How quickly must a solution be found? (If the copier is continually breaking down and it is the only one in this wing of the building, the solution may need to be found at once.)
- Is the problem part of a bigger problem?
- Are there several problems on the list that relate to each other? (In doing the analysis, the manager may see a pattern develop related to a system of handling information or a specific dysfunctional employee.)
- Is there a good chance of solving the problem?
- How soon can results be obtained?
- What will the benefits be? (If the manager is constantly expending energy on issues that are never resolved, employees will become discouraged and resentful when asked to help.)
- Is there a history of dealing with a particular problem? (Paying attention to what worked and didn't work in the past may save the manager valuable time.)
- How do employees feel about the existing situation?
- If a change is considered, will employees be resistant? (The manager should look beyond the "sour grapes" attitude of some employees to everything suggested and ask him- or herself if the employees that have welcomed new ideas in the past will be resentful of the new idea.)

Whenever a manager wants to be an innovator, the guidelines that Thomas Edison used in gaining acceptance for his inventions should be followed.

First, users of the innovation must see the advantages of the innovation.

Second, users must understand that the consequences of failure will have less potential negative impact than what is currently happening. (These first two points are a must if the new idea is to work.)

Third, the more compatible with the current trend, the greater the acceptance. Little changes are easier to implement than radical changes.

Fourth, if the innovation can be tried one piece at a time, it will be accepted more easily and quickly.

Fifth, supporting activities for the innovation should be kept as simple as possible. For example, simple directions for using a new form should be provided.

Sixth, old vocabulary should be used to describe a new idea. Using terminology already familiar to users makes the mental transition from the old to the new easier.

Seventh, it should be made easy for users to withdraw with minimal pain and cost. When selling the CEO on a new computer system for the office, an account of how the hospital can back out of the purchase if important concerns arise should be provided.

Eighth, the costs in time, money, power, and emotion must be less than the costs of the current situation. If getting the computer system will cost the hospital more money and require more staff, the purchase won't occur.

Ninth, credibility is important. When selling the idea, someone who has the group's trust should sell it. (That someone may not be the manager.)

Tenth, the innovation must be dependable, reliable, and repeatable if it is to gain acceptance.

These guidelines should be used as a challenge to the manager when preparing to sell a new idea. If the manager can satisfy all ten guidelines, he or she will probably succeed. If nine are satisfied, the audience may still accept the idea but there will be more skepticism. If only eight, the audience will be doubtful and will show little interest. If the manager meets less than eight guidelines, the idea should be reworked before presentation.

CHOOSING A MANAGEMENT TOOL

Once the manager has analyzed the problems and has determined which problem will be the best to tackle first, he or she must then choose a management tool to use. There are a wide variety of tools. Two will be discussed in detail and the other only briefly described. They are the flow process chart, work distribution analysis, and motion economy analysis. They may sound dry, but they can be very useful. Flow process charts are best used when the process for completing a job is causing problems, when papers or forms are frequently lost, when employee complaints center around communication with other departments, when there is extensive overtime in the department, when work seems poor in quality and inefficient, or when a task feels awkward and time consuming.

Work distribution analysis is best used to collect data to justify additional employees or the purchase of expensive equipment (e.g., a computer system), to determine if employees are doing too many unrelated tasks, to determine if the actual time spent on tasks reflects the purpose and goals of the department, to ensure that employee skills are being utilized, to determine what skills take the most time, to identify and eliminate unnecessary tasks, and to assist in distributing workload evenly.

Flow Process Chart

To complete a flow process chart (see Exhibit 16-1), the manager, with the help of the employees involved, should list the steps of the identified task in the middle column. The steps should be very specific. (On some of the more detailed flow process charts, the actual distance between objects is measured and recorded.) Once the steps are listed, one of the four categories on the left is chosen to describe the step. If the step involves action, the "Operation" column is marked. If it involves movement, the "Transportation" column is marked. If it involves looking at something with no action occurring, the "Inspection" column is marked. And if there is nothing occurring because the item is on hold, the "Delay" column is marked.

The marked items in the columns are connected by lines, and at the bottom how many marked items there are in each column is noted. Next, each step is analyzed by asking the critical questions listed on the right of the form. In the "Action" column, any suggestions for change that could be made are noted.

Transportation and delay steps are inefficient. The manager should try to eliminate as many of these steps as possible. By asking the critical questions and looking for creative solutions, wasted time and effort can be removed from the process.

The example in Exhibit 16-1 shows a completed chart. Ensure that employees are involved in developing and evaluating the flow process chart. By keeping employees involved, the manager will have a greater chance of successfully implementing change.

Work Distribution Analysis

Work distribution analysis can be used in any size department. To use this tool, each employee records the tasks performed for a week, noting the approximate time spent on each task (to the nearest five minutes). At the end of the week, each employee should have a list containing 10 to 15 tasks in order of priority and noting the total number of hours spent that week on each task. To get the most accurate results, a "typical" week should be chosen, not the week the Joint Commission is coming to visit. The manager should then compile the lists into a department functions list, grouping similar tasks together. The functions should be listed in order of importance and should not exceed ten in number. Every task on each employee's list should fit under a department function. The total number of hours

Exhibit 16-1 Flow Process Chart

Task __Agenda Preparation for the Surgery Department__

Date _____

Critical Questions - Answer each with Y (Yes), N (No), N/A (not applicable)
Is this step (the):

Operation	Transportation	Inspection	Delay	Steps in Completing Task	Best Method	Best Location	Best Time	Necessary	Action
Ⓞ	T	I	D	1. 2 weeks before meeting - Dept. member requests agenda item	Y	Y	Y	Y	Ø
Ⓞ	T	I	D	2. MSSP writes note on item	Y	-	-	Y	Ø
O	Ⓣ	I	D	3. Note is placed in out box on desk (1st 3 steps repeated twice in that wk.)	N	N	N/A	N/A	Establish agenda file
O	T	Ⓘ	D	4. MSSP reviews min. of tissue commit. ident. item for Surg. Dept. (no note made)	N	N/A	Y	Y	Make note for agenda file
Ⓞ	T	I	D	5. 1 week before meeting - Drafts proposed agenda	Y	N/A	Y	Y	Ø
O	T	Ⓘ	D	6. MSSP reviews previous minutes for unfinished business	Y	N/A	Y	Y	Ø
Ⓞ	T	I	D	7. Notes items on agenda under old bus.	Y	Y	Y	Y	Ø
Ⓞ	T	I	D	8. Contacts O.R. Supervisor for new business items	Y	N/A	Y	Y	Ø
Ⓞ	T	I	D	9. Notes them on agenda under new bus.	Y	Y	Y	Y	Ø
O	T	Ⓘ	D	10. Looks for notes on physician requested agenda items	N	N	N/A	Y	Could be avoided with agenda file
O	Ⓣ	I	D	11. Retrieves one item	N	N	Y	Y	Could be avoided with agenda file
Ⓞ	T	I	D	12. Notes it on agenda under new bus.	Y	Y	Y	Y	Ø
O	Ⓣ	I	D	13. Sends rough draft to Dept. Chairman's office for review	N	N	Y	Y	Make ap't. to review in MSSD
O	T	I	Ⓓ	14. Morn. of meeting-Attempts to contact Dept. Chair re unreturned agenda*	N	N	N	N	Can avoid with #13
Ⓞ	T	I	D	15. Copies incomplete draft of agenda for distribution	N	N/A	N	Y	Can avoid with #13
O	T	I	D	16.					
O	T	I	D	17.					
O	T	I	D	18. * (Chair in surgery until meeting)					
O	T	I	D	19.					
O	T	I	D	20.					
8	3	3	1	TOTALS					

Description of Improved Task: Agenda files will be created for each dep't./committee; the dep't./committee chairman will review agendas in the MSSD 1 week prior to meeting.

Source: Adapted from *Medical Record Management*, 7th ed. by Bernice C. Campbell (Ed.), p. 469, with permission of Physician's Record Company, © 1981.

everyone in the department spends on the function should be noted. Exhibit 16-2 shows examples of task and function lists.

After completing these lists, the manager will then complete the department function analysis chart (see Exhibit 16-3). The functions listed on the department function list will be written in the column on the left. Each employee's name will be written in a box across the top of the chart. Using each employee's task list, the number of the task is noted in the appropriate row. The number of hours the employee spent on that task is also indicated.

When adding the hours spent for each employee, the total hours worked each week on the department function analysis chart should equal the number of hours worked on the employee's task list sheet. Then the number of hours spent by everyone on each function is totaled and recorded in the column on the right. For each function, to calculate its percentage of all hours worked, divide the total of all hours worked (add total hours worked per week by each employee across or the total hours spent per function down) by the total number of hours spent on the function in question. See Exhibit 16-3 for a sample completed form.

Department goals and purpose should be reviewed when analyzing the results. Is the department spending the most time on the most important goal? If not, why not? Can consolidation of tasks improve the efficiency of the office? Is the office efficient yet still showing significant overtime? Do the results suggest another employee would reduce overtime? Using the information in this book on justifying a computer system (see Chapter 20), can the hours saved be clearly shown?

Motion Economy Analysis

The last tool is motion economy analysis. Its principles can be used by the manager to organize workspaces or improve the office layout. The purpose of motion economy analysis is to reduce unnecessary movement in completing tasks. It is best used when employees complain of fatigue or have to leave their work stations often or when designing a new office.

The first principle is that motion should be productive and simple. If the Rolodex must be moved every time the stapler is needed, that is not efficient.

Second, motion should be along curved lines. Curved lines are less stressful on the joints and muscles than reaching at an angle.

Third, motion should be rhythmic and smooth, with tools in easy reach. If a person is left-handed, the telephone should be on the right, thus freeing the left hand to write.

Fourth, tools used frequently should be pre-positioned. The keyboard may need to be near the phone so that work will be minimally interrupted.

Fifth, unexercised parts of the body should be used whenever possible. This may be difficult if the majority of the required job is repetitive. It is better to break up repetitive tasks to reduce stress on one area of the body.

Exhibit 16-2 Work Distribution Analysis

Task List

Employee: Cindy Gassiot
Job Title: Medical Staff Coordinator

Tasks:	Hours/wk.
1. credentialing (new applications)—supervise	9
2. reappointments	8
3. meetings—agendas, attend, draft mins.	20
4. support for peer review	4
5. office management—budget plan, etc.	10
6. medical staff social support	2

Task List

Employee: Sharon Lindsey
Job Title: Medical Staff Secretary

Tasks:	Hours/wk.
1. process new applications	10
2. meetings—transcribe minutes	15
3. medical staff social support	5
4. meetings—set up calendar, notification	5
5. physician referral phone	2
6. general clerical support	8

Department Function List

Functions:	Hours/wk.
1. credentialing	22
2. meetings	44
3. management	5
4. physician referral	8
5. medical staff social support	2
6. general clerical support	5

Source: Adapted from *Medical Record Management*, 7th ed. by Bernice C. Campbell (Ed.), p. 486, with permission of Physician's Record Company, © 1981.

Exhibit 16-3 Department Function Analysis Chart

Functions	Employee	Cindy Gassiot	Hours Spent	Sharon Lindsey	Hours Spent		Hours Spent		Hours Spent		Hours Spent	Total Hours Spent per Function	% of All Hours Worked
Credentialing		1	4	1	10							22	24%
		2	8										
Meetings		3	20	2	15							44	47%
		4	4	4	5								
Management		5	10									10	11%
Physician Referral				5	5							5	5%
Medical Staff Social Support		6	2	3	2							4	4%
General Clerical Support				6	8							8	9%
Total hrs. worked/week by each employee		48		45								93	

Total of all hours worked

Source: Adapted from *Medical Record Management*, 7th ed. by Bernice C. Campbell (Ed.), p. 487, with permission of Physician's Record Company, © 1981.

Sixth, tools should be combined whenever possible.

Seventh, the employee should be at ease when working and should keep on the lookout for signs of stress, frustration, or physical discomfort.

The work management tools described above, which are just a few of the tools available, can be used by managers and employees to smooth out the workflow. They should be used only as tools, and careful analysis of the results is always required.

NOTES

1. Donald R. Stabile, "The Du Pont Experiments in Scientific Management: Efficiency and Safety," *Business History Review* 61 (Autumn 1987): 365–86.

2. Addison C. Bennett, "Work Smarter, Not Harder," *Health Care Supervisor* 6 (April 1988): 1–13.

3. Ibid., 3.

4. Ibid., 3–4.

Chapter 17

Planning for the Medical Staff Year

Joyce Gardner, CMSC

One challenge of working in the medical staff services department is that, in most hospitals, the start of a new medical staff year brings with it a whole new world: new officers, new committee chairpersons, new committee members. Although this can be quite disruptive, it is one of the unique characteristics of the job, and the successful medical staff services professional (MSSP) learns to make the best of it. Meeting deadlines is another challenge for the MSSP. There is a deadline to be met almost every day. This chapter will address planning for the new year and needed programs and policies that will facilitate the inevitable transition from year to year as well as planning to meet deadlines.

THE MEDICAL STAFF YEAR

The medical staff organization operates on a yearly cycle, perhaps to coincide with the hospital's fiscal or calendar year, and this must be specified in the medical staff bylaws. Events such as election of officers, election of department chairpersons, committee appointments, and reappointments, and so on, fall within the time frame of the medical staff year.

Election of Officers

The method for electing officers must be specified in the medical staff bylaws. It is the responsibility of the MSSP to oversee the nomination and election process to ensure that the bylaws, policies, and procedures of the medical staff are followed.

If so stated in the bylaws, a nominating committee is appointed prior to the election of officers. The duties of the nominating committee will be to determine the willingness of various candidates to have their names placed in nomination and to ensure that any candidate possesses the proper credentials for the office being considered (as specified in the bylaws). The nominating committee then presents the slate of candidates to the electing body (a particular department or the full medical staff). The slate may be accepted, rejected, or amended by the body. Nominees not proposed by the nominating committee may or may not be added at the meeting, and, again, the applicable rule will be set forth in the bylaws. The slate of nominees must be provided (possibly sent by mail) prior to the meeting at which the actual election occurs.

The MSSP is responsible for preparing ballots. Ballots are contained in a double envelope: One envelope, designated "Ballot," is placed inside an outer envelope on which a staff member's name is written. Since the staff members who are eligible to vote are specified in the bylaws (usually only active staff members), the MSSP must ensure that only those staff members eligible to vote are provided ballots. The outer envelope must be discarded and only the envelope marked "Ballot" will be retained, ensuring voter anonymity.

Following the casting of ballots, either the MSSP and his or her office staff, a committee of the body casting the vote, or a combination of both, may be designated to count the ballots. The ballots should be counted twice to ensure accuracy, and the counting should be witnessed by a person other than the MSSP. The presiding officer is then notified of the results immediately after the counting, and he or she in turn notifies the candidates. Once the election results have been announced to the electing body, the ballots are destroyed. Permission to destroy the counted ballots is granted by a motion at a meeting of the electing body.

Election of officers in a small, nondepartmentalized hospital may be held annually at an assembly of the general staff and may be carried out without discussion or debate. In larger hospitals with many departments and a large general medical staff, election of officers can be a major, sometimes political, event. The MSSP should be totally familiar with the bylaw provisions that specify the method of election of officers, and he or she must monitor the department or staff leaders to see that the procedures are followed exactly.

Once officers have been elected, there may be a lapse between the actual election and the time offices are assumed. The "changing of the guard" can be disruptive and trying. The MSSP is responsible for orienting incoming officers, thus providing continuity of programs and issues held over from one administration to the other.

Orientation Programs

Orientation of incoming medical staff officers may take one of several forms. The session may range from two-hour breakfast or luncheon affairs to half- or full-day educational seminars. The legal climate and escalating control by state, federal, and regulatory agencies have increased the level of responsibility placed upon medical staff leaders, with the result that physicians are more and more reluctant to assume the sometimes difficult leadership positions. Since the bylaws often require a succession of officers, some feel they have only begun to learn their jobs when the term is ended and responsibility falls to those next in line. It is incumbent upon the MSSP to have programs in place that will prevent the incoming group of officers from wasting six or seven months of the term of office "learning the ropes." Areas that must be thoroughly covered in the orientation program are as follows:

1. Precedent-setting legal cases pertaining to medical staff appointments, privileges, and obligations to monitor the work of the medical staff.

2. Requirements of the Joint Commission on Accreditation of Healthcare Organizations as well as state and federal regulatory requirements. New officers should be familiar not only with the global requirements of outside regulatory bodies but with the institution's specific requirements for conducting quality assurance activities and completion of medical records.

3. Responsibilities of officers as specified in the medical staff bylaws, rules, and regulations.

4. Information about the hospital, including detailed financial information. This information might include the hospital's case mix of patients as well as payment sources, occupancy rates, and other pertinent business data.

5. Specific information regarding the credentialing process. The incoming officers should have a clear picture of the hospital's fair hearing plan, including actions that can trigger a hearing situation.

6. A clear description of the hospital's quality assurance (QA) and utilization review (UR) processes. The incoming officers will bear responsibility for carrying out the QA and UR processes, and a detailed explanation of what is done, and why, removes any mystery. At the same time, the orientation session can result in gaining support for the QA and UR functions from any of the officers whose support may have previously been less than optimal.

Once the officers have been elected, oriented, and installed, the MSSP will provide daily guidance and help them to grasp the breadth and depth of their new roles. Once again, the MSSP is placed in a pivotal position between the hospital and the medical staff, providing the linkage necessary to transfer the power and responsibility from one group of officers to another.

Committee Membership

To a lesser extent, the changing of the guard will occur annually at the committee level. Committee membership is less likely to undergo a complete change each year. Rather, some members will be retained whereas others will be replaced. The MSSP must provide continuity to committee members in much the same manner as for staff officers. At the committee level, it is important that no business fall by the wayside in the transition between one chairperson and the next. An orientation session for committees at the beginning of the staff year is appropriate. Topics to be covered at such a session might include the following:

- the purpose of the committee, with a clear explanation of its duties, functions, and authority
- the committee composition (required members, voting members, nonvoting members, exofficio members, chairperson, and vice-chairperson)
- the date, time, and place of the first meeting and whether the committee meets on a regular schedule
- standard agenda items
- attendance requirements (specified in the bylaws); what constitutes an "excused" absence; any specific quorum requirements
- a brief summary of issues or matters left unresolved the previous year

The orientation of committee members will also serve as a refresher for holdovers, so that all members will have a firm grasp of the tasks and issues ahead.

The Master Calendar

Planning for a medical staff year is incomplete without the development of a master calendar. This eliminates conflicts between opposing forces and allows the MSSP to schedule coverage of required functions. If the medical staff services department is organized so that specific personnel have routine and regular assignments, the master calendar reinforces each individual's schedule. If the department assignments are made on a monthly or weekly basis, then the calendar serves as a tool to assist the medical staff services director in staffing required meetings. The master schedule of meetings should be published so that physicians may make a note of the meetings that pertain to them.

An adjunct to the yearly calendar is the monthly calendar of events, which indicates department meetings, committee meetings, general staff meetings, social events such as golf or tennis meets sponsored by the hospital or physician groups, education rounds or conferences, and continuing education programs. The calendar of events may be published in the medical staff newsletter or be provided to the medical staff through some other communication mechanism.

Planning for Reappointments

The medical staff services department will be responsible for planning and scheduling medical staff reappointments This process absorbs a significant number of working hours of department personnel. Mailing the reappointment forms, gathering the information to be entered in the individual physician profiles, and routing the information to appropriate committees and finally to the governing body must be carefully orchestrated so that the medical staff is reappointed prior to the time the current appointments expire. A process for reappointment should be developed after careful review of the medical staff bylaws "procedure for re-appointment" to be absolutely certain that the two are synchronized.

MEETING DEADLINES

Careful planning can eliminate some, but not all, of the day-to-day crises that occur in every medical staff services department. The MSSP's life can become a series of deadlines and emergency situations that must be dealt with posthaste! By scheduling and planning for the known deadlines, crises arise less frequently. For example, the agenda for each meeting should have a deadline, and such a deadline should never come as a surprise to the person responsible for meeting it. Minutes of every meeting should be prepared within a specified time frame. The MSSP must learn early in his or her career to prioritize tasks and duties and to learn effective time management techniques. One of the most important assets for meeting known deadlines is the ability to establish good policies and procedures.

THE POLICY AND PROCEDURE MANUAL AS A PLANNING TOOL

The medical staff services department policy and procedure manual is both an organizing and a planning tool. The manual contains a "road map" for each and every task that is carried out in the department. For example the credentialing procedure, in its entirety, should be spelled out step by step in the manual, with copies of every form used at every step of the process included for reference. The procedure for requesting travel to an educational conference should also be included, as should instructions for recording hours worked by employees, requests for time off, and all departmental activities. The policy and procedure manual not only serves as a guide for the department's activities but provides information to new employees regarding specific tasks and functions.

Good planning and comprehensive policies and procedures will allow any medical staff services department to function more smoothly.

Chapter 18

Managing Medical Staff Meetings

Mimi Cruse, CMSC

As has been previously discussed, the role of the medical staff services profes-sional (MSSP) includes providing assistance to the medical staff organization as it functions in a manner that complies with accrediting body regulations and fulfills the responsibilities assigned to it by the governing body and the administration of the hospital. A very important part of this assistance includes coordination of medical staff committee, department, section, and general meetings. Coordination involves such tasks as providing a calendar for the meetings; sending meeting notices; arranging for rooms, food, and equipment, preparing agendas; recording attendance and minutes; and instituting or directing follow-up as necessary.

The number of meetings in any given time period will depend, of course, on the size of the institution, the size of its medical staff, and how that staff is organized constitutionally. For purposes of this chapter, imagine an institution, Central City Hospital, that has approximately 400 beds, approximately 300 physicians on staff, and numerous clinical departments, including surgery, medicine, family practice, pediatrics, obstetrics/gynecology, and psychiatry. Of the departments mentioned, only surgery and medicine have organized sections. The medical staff committees include the infection control, pharmacy and therapeutics, blood utilization and transfusion review, medical records, critical care, credentials, tissue and surgical practice, medical practice, and medical executive committees as well as temporary ad hoc committees. (As mentioned earlier in the book, many of these committees may be unnecessary.)

MEETING PREPARATION

Scheduling

For efficient and effective scheduling, an annual calendar of medical staff meetings should be prepared and then kept in the medical staff services department.

The MSSP must work closely with the chief of staff and all committee and department chairpersons and section chiefs so that meetings are scheduled at times that will be convenient for the chairpersons and will facilitate the appropriate and timely flow of information between groups. One method suggested for accomplishing this is to think of the meetings as occurring on the face of a clock and then to plug that information into a calendar. For instance, if, as in Figure 18-1, the governing body meeting is at 12 o'clock, the medical executive committee (MEC) at 1, the department of surgery at 2, the credentials committee at 3, the department of medicine at 4, the infection control committee at 5, and so on, there is not a smooth flow of information, since committees report to other committees, sections, and departments; sections report to departments; departments (and most committees) report to the MEC; and the MEC reports to the governing body. Indeed in this scheme of things, there is considerable unnecessary delay.

Figure 18-2 illustrates a far more reasonable schedule that allows for an expeditious flow of information. This schedule then gets transferred to a monthly calendar. It should be noted here that implementing such a meeting schedule may not always be possible for many reasons, not the least of which might be the attitude that "we've always met on the third Thursday and we see no reason to change now." The clock system is simply suggested as one method for achieving good information flow.

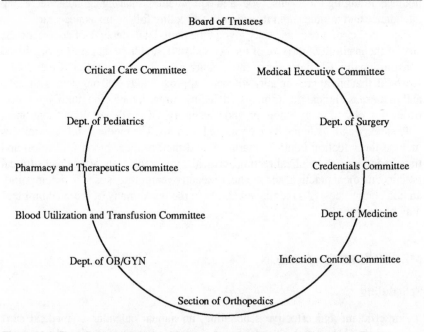

Figure 18-1 Clock System to Schedule Meetings: Poor Organization for Information Flow

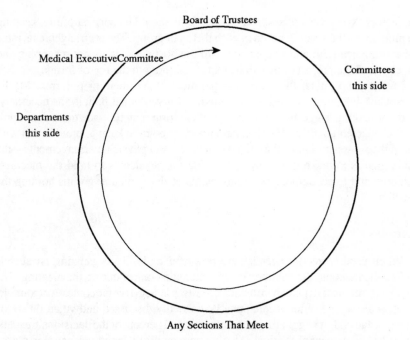

Board of Trustees

Medical ExecutiveCommittee

Committees
this side

Departments
this side

Any Sections That Meet

Figure 18-2 Clock System to Schedule Meetings: Ideal Organization for Information Flow

Notification

After the chief of staff or the persons making appointments and assignments have completed that task, someone in the medical staff services department must notify the appointees. The notices should provide all the necessary information and permit the physicians to mark their own office calendars accordingly for the year. However, because most physicians are quite busy and patients are their first priority, most MSSPs send a reminder notification for any meeting approximately two weeks to ten days ahead of time. Computerization of committee, section, and department lists can simplify this task. Along with the notice, the agenda and any materials requiring review prior to the meeting are included. (Agendas will be discussed in greater detail shortly.)

Physical Preparation

Another responsibility of the MSSP is to make arrangements for meeting rooms; order any dietary items requested by the group, such as lunch or drinks and snacks; and arrange for any special equipment the group may need, such as overhead projectors, X-ray view boxes, and the like. This should be done carefully, keeping in mind all of the specific needs of each different group. These arrangements must be coordinated with other departments in the hospital such as housekeeping and dietary, and the preparations will be expedited through the use of forms.

In many hospitals, the various departments have their own forms. MSSD personnel will simply adjust to the individual institutional policies as necessary, perhaps making suggestions for changes if the forms can be made more communicative, efficient, or cost-effective. An important point to keep in mind is that with all of these preparations—the calendar, notices, and physician arrangements—the main goal is to make it as easy as possible for physicians to hold the meetings required and to accomplish the assignments of the particular groups holding the meetings.

Agendas

When used correctly, agendas are powerful tools. By organizing an agenda before the meeting, the chairperson can maintain control during the meeting. The mere placement of items can influence a positive or negative outcome. For example, an item at the end of an agenda may be hurriedly discussed and voted on so the meeting can end. A negotiating principle is that 80 percent of the decisions are made in the last 20 percent of the time. Also, an item requiring lengthy discussion placed at the beginning of an agenda may mean all items after it will not be discussed.

An agenda lets other committee members prepare for the items to be discussed. If a committee is to be most effective, the decisions made should reflect careful consideration. The physician who will be asked to approve a policy closing the psychiatry section to new members will need to read the policy and think about questions and concerns before coming to the meeting. Providing an agenda promotes efficiency without losing valuable input.

Another asset of a well-planned agenda is improvement in meeting minutes. Minutes that are written around the agenda allow easier retrieval of information. If a form is used for formulating minutes, the agenda item can be pretyped on the form, allowing the rough draft to be written during the meeting.

An agenda should be clear and may state whether a given item is for information, discussion, or action. In addition, the time allowed for discussion or action may also be stated. When the formulation of the agenda occurs during the preliminary planning process, the chairperson can tailor the agenda length to the length of meeting.

To ensure that items from previous meetings requiring additional time are not omitted, previous minutes must be reviewed or a reminder must be placed in an agenda item file. Committee members should be contacted or instructed to submit agenda items, allowing enough time to adequately compile the agenda.

The specific agenda format will vary, but each agenda should include some basic elements, such as approval of previous meeting minutes, committee and officer reports, old or unfinished business, new business, announcements, and adjourn-ment. These basic elements are explained in more detail in *Robert's Rules of Order*. When listing items under the above headings, it is important to ensure that adequate information is included for easy understanding. Use of action verbs to emphasize the expected outcome of each item is helpful.

The timing of the distribution of an agenda will normally depend on the wishes of the chairperson of the group involved. However, having an agenda sent out to those who are to attend a meeting prior to the meeting is usually very beneficial. This is especially true if there are materials sent with the agenda that should be carefully reviewed before discussion occurs.

Please consider the sample agenda for a medical executive committee meeting presented in Exhibit 18-1. The author prefers this type of agenda for MEC meetings because it not only facilitates the writing of minutes but also ensures proper follow-up and the retention of items that have not been resolved. Such items have a tendency to "fall through the cracks," especially (and understandably) when difficult issues are under discussion and the members present are reluctant to take immediate action.

Sources for agenda items are many and varied. Quite often many of the items to appear on an agenda will be dictated by what accrediting agencies such as Joint Commission on Accreditation of Healthcare Organizations (Joint Commission) indicate the group should be considering at its meetings. (See Exhibit 18-2, which indicates those items clinical departments should considered in order to properly accomplish their monthly review of clinical practice.) There will also be unfinished pieces of business from previous meetings and referrals from other groups or persons in the facility who need to have something considered and a recommenda-tion made or an action taken.

An effective way of keeping track of what needs to be put on the agendas of the many committees coordinated by the office is to establish agenda files. One file should be created for every medical staff group that meets. Everyone in the facility and the leaders of the medical staff should be made aware of the existence of these files. Any item that anyone wants considered by a specific group is sent to the med-ical staff services department for placement in the appropriate agenda file. The MSSP also looks over all minutes for referral items and places those in the files. The person compiling an agenda then consults the files prior to preparation, which ensures that no matter who makes up the agenda all items of business needing consideration are there.

THE MEETING

Attendance Sheets

Because most accrediting bodies have standards regarding attendance, it is essential that an accurate record of attendance at all medical staff meetings be kept.

Exhibit 18-1 A Sample Medical Executive Committee Agenda

Central City Hospital Medical Staff
Medical Executive Committee
November 1, 1989

Agenda

____a.m.	1. Call to order, Dr. Jones, Chairperson
( ) approved	2. Review of minutes of previous
( ) amended	meeting held October 4, 1989. (See attachment, pp. 1–4.)
	3. CEO's report—John Smith
	4. Chief of Staff's Report—Dr. Jones
	5. Nursing Report—Mary Ward, RN

Unfinished Business

	6. Bylaws Committee Referral:
( ) follow-up	From Medical Staff Services: Dr. Williams is still conducting research.
	7. Blood Order Form:
( ) follow-up	From Sept. MEC minutes: "Blood order form being developed." From Oct. Blood Utilization Committee minutes: "Dr. Pontius presented draft of form for request of blood. Committee approved first draft and supports use of order form except in cases of emergency. (Draft of form distributed.)

New Business

	8. Medical Records Committee—Dr. George
( ) approved	a. Oncology Ongoing Medical Form recommended by Oncology Section
( ) amended	presented for approval.
( ) disapproved	
( ) deferred	
	9. Pharmacy and Therapeutics—Dr. Lock
( ) received	EPO Protocol from Nephrology Section presented for information. (See attachment, pp. 11–12.)
( ) received	10. Reports of other committees, sections, and departments: Notation is made that minutes of meetings (indicated by date) are on file in the Medical Staff Services Dept., none of which contain any specific recommended actions or items needing consideration by the MEC.

The ideal is to have each person attending sign next to his or her name on a prepared list. The alert MSSP, however, will also note the attendees so that missing names may be filled in and initialed. Maintaining a running tabulation of attendance for each medical staff member, either on computer or manually, allows department chairpersons to easily access summaries to review physician citizenship at the time of reappointment. In addition to the attendance sheet itself, members present, absent, and excused may also be listed someplace in the actual minutes, usually

Exhibit 18-2 Sample Department of Surgery Agenda

Central City Hospital
Department of Surgery
November 22, 1989

Agenda

I. CALL TO ORDER—12:30 p.m.
II. APPROVAL OF MINUTES
III. QUALITY ASSURANCE REPORTS
   A. Follow-up on Case #12345
      Response from Dr. #478
   B. Findings from Surgical Case Review
   C. Findings from Blood Use Review
   D. Findings from Drug Use Review
   E. Findings from Medical Record Review
   F. Findings from Utilization Management
   G. Infection Rate Report
IV. UNFINISHED BUSINESS
   A. Revised Proctoring Protocol for Department (see attachment)
V. NEW BUSINESS
   A. Credentialing
   B. Need for Policy on Second Assistants in Surgery
VI. ADJOURNMENT

---

above the discussion of business. It is also possible to state "Attendance per the Attached Sign-in Sheet" and attach a copy of the sheet to the original minutes.

Conduct of the Meeting

The MSSP does not conduct medical staff meetings; the chairperson does. The MSSP, however, can increase the effectiveness of the meeting by making sure the chairperson understands his or her responsibilities and by helping to prepare the chairperson. For example, it is generally useful to review the agenda and all materials to be considered with the chairperson prior to the meeting. Such a review is not always easy to accomplish, but it is well worth the effort.

Many reference sources are available that define guidelines for chairpersons. One list of such guidelines follows:[1]

1. Start on time and work with an agenda.
2. State the reason for the meeting briefly and clearly.

3. Ensure that members hear all sides of an issue.
4. Direct the meeting but keep a low profile.
5. Keep the meeting moving and insist on order.
6. Speak clearly and to the group, not to individuals.
7. Summarize what has been said on an issue and aim for a decision.
8. Go for closure. Recommend additional outside work if agreement or closure cannot be reached.
9. Ask questions and clarify but do not engage in debate with members.
10. Be sure any opinions stated are identified as such and not as directives.
11. Be sure that accurate minutes are recorded and distributed appropriately.
12. Check at the end of the meeting to ensure that all subjects have been covered.

Two excellent sources for guidelines are *Principles of Medical Staff Services Science*[2] and *The Medical Staff Leader's Complete Practical Guidebook*.[3] Medical staff leaders who must conduct meetings may also find videotapes helpful, such as the one offered by Brighton Books: "The Hospital Medical Staff—Its Changing Form and Function."[4] Needless to say, the better prepared a leader is to conduct a meeting, the easier is the job of the MSSP who is documenting what occurs at the meeting. Therefore, the smart coordinator helps the leader with "homework" to the greatest extent possible.

Parliamentary Procedure

The support person attending medical staff meetings should be familiar with parliamentary procedure or at least have a reference ready at hand during the meetings to help facilitate the conduct of business. Some groups will appoint their own parliamentarian, but a "hard copy" reference on hand will be very helpful if there are disputes.

Probably the most common reference work is still *Robert's Rules of Order*, although some groups may prefer *Sturgis Rules of Order*.[5] In addition, *Principles of Medical Staff Services Science* contains a comprehensive summary of the basics of parliamentary procedure.[6] Further recommended is a very handy booklet that, because of its small size and clever design, permits quick references: E. C. Utter's *Parliamentary Law at a Glance*.[7]

It should be noted that the purpose of parliamentary procedure is to ensure that the majority rules while the minority is guaranteed a voice. In addition, following parliamentary procedure can assist in the orderly consideration of items and issues. Most medical staff meetings are not so formal as to require a strict adherence to proper procedure. In fact, strict adherence might be a hindrance if the procedure becomes the overriding concern, and this must be avoided. Common sense will usually dictate when the rules of order need to be invoked. The most important concerns for the support person are to use common sense, to have a working knowledge of parliamentary procedure, and have on hand an easy-to-use reference.

MINUTES

General Considerations

The most important purpose of preparing medical staff minutes is to document that the medical staff is in compliance with the required functions and standards of accrediting agencies. The second important purpose is to provide a means of communication between the various interacting groups of the medical staff. The person responsible for the minutes needs to keep both of these purposes in mind as the minutes are prepared.

It is essential that the minutes record actions taken. Surveyors for the Joint Commission and other agencies will peruse minutes carefully for evidence of actions taken and resultant documentation of improvement in quality of care. This subject will be examined in greater depth shortly, but first a look at formats.

Formats

There are many formats for minutes, but the three most generally accepted are one-column, two-column, or three-column formats.* A sample of each of these formats is presented in Figure 18-3.

One-Column Format. The most traditional format. Usually a general summary of events, using either complete sentences or the briefer "fragments" style (thoughts and ideas) and one or more paragraphs for each subject. Each subject should be introduced by a title line, either underlined or entirely in upper case letters (or both). The entire width of the page is used from left to right margin.

Two-Column Format. Utilizes two vertical columns, one narrow and one wide. The narrow column may be at either the left or right margin, depending on individual preference. (The right side of the page probably facilitates quick reference.) The wide column contains the "body" of minutes. Next to this, the narrow column contains either subject or action, briefly stated, often entirely in upper case letters. Either complete sentences or the briefer "fragments" style can be utilized with this format.

Three-Column Format. Newer. Utilizes three vertical columns: A wide column in the middle which contains the "body" of the minutes and one narrow column at

---

* Description of one-column, two-column, and three-column formats is reprinted from *Overview*, vol. 14, no. 1, p. 8, with permission of the National Association of Medical Staff Services, © 1987.

A.   One-Column

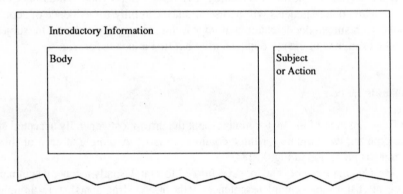

B.   Two-Column

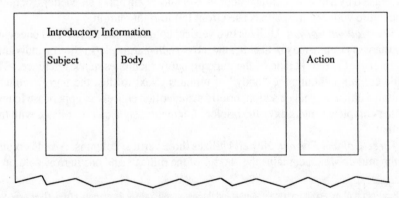

C.   Three-Column

Figure 18-3 Sample Formats for Minutes

each margin, one of which is headed "Subject," the other "Action." Proponents of this format point out that it focuses on what was done—action taken—and contains a provision for "built-in" follow-up. Generally, the body is written in a terse, fragmentary style because of the limitations of space. This format tends to eliminate extraneous material from the minutes.

The three-column format is probably the best format for use in hospital settings today. Its advantages are fairly obvious. However, it is also possible, as the author has found, that some meetings (e.g., medical executive committee meetings, which are longer, have many agenda items, and involve more discussion) lend themselves better to the two-column format. The recorder of the minutes, with consent of the chairperson, should decide on the format based on considerations of efficiency and effectiveness.

Taping

The use of a tape recorder during a meeting is often ill-advised, but occasionally it can be very helpful. Such use, however, will probably require consent of the chairperson and even possibly the entire group. It certainly has been found that a tape can be a valuable tool when issues discussed are complicated or clouded by emotional rhetoric. There is definitely an advantage to being able to sit in the quiet of one's office and listen to the tape in order to sift out the "real meat" of such discussion. Permission given to the support person to tape a meeting entails an obligation to use the tapes only to prepare the minutes. At no time should a tape or any portion of a tape ever be played for anyone other than attendees who dispute the written minutes, and the tapes always should be erased for confidentiality reasons as soon as the chairperson has approved the minutes as prepared.

Phraseology

Great care should be taken to express the *intent* of what is expressed in minutes rather than what is actually said, especially when emotional rhetoric occurs. Most of us, being human and often speaking "off the cuff," fail to express ourselves in the most professional and diplomatic manner. The recorder of minutes can be of assistance simply by altering the phraseology while keeping true to intent. Examples of appropriate alterations follow:

Actual: "I don't see why the bylaws committee expects us to do their work for them! Why don't they get off their royal duffs and do this themselves?"
Reported: Concern was expressed that this issue would more appropriately be resolved by the bylaws committee, and the consensus was that it should be referred to them for action.

Actual: "I think this whole idea stinks! There's no way we should be involved in a project like this cockamamie idea."

Reported: One member expressed concern and suggested that the group not endorse such a project.

Actual: "This is a great idea. I don't see why the committee can't be given the money and the go-ahead."

Reported: A suggestion was made that the committee be funded to investigate the project.

Actual: "That's a heck of a lot of money! Let's not be stupid and spend that kind of money without really looking into it and knowing what we're doing."

Reported: One member suggested that the necessity and feasibility of the project be considered in depth prior to approval of the recommended expenditure.

Identification of Speakers

The recorder of minutes should never attempt to achieve a verbatim transcript; this is totally unnecessary and serves no useful purpose. Motions made, however, are actions taken and should be stated as clearly and accurately as possible. If the recorder, during discussion of a motion, becomes confused as to the statement of the motion, clarification should be requested of the chairperson or the person making the motion (likewise for amendments). This can be accomplished inoffensively by addressing the chairperson in the following way: "Excuse me, Dr. Cureall, but I'm not totally clear on how this motion should be stated in the minutes. Could you or Dr. Doright please restate it?"

Further, there is no reason to identify by name the physicians (or members of the group) who make and second motions unless they explicitly express the desire that this be done. Indeed, some attorneys will advise against it.

As a matter of fact, there exists now a generally accepted theory that the use of names in minutes is to be avoided, especially when reporting items that provoked emotional outbursts. It is quite correct, however, to use names when objective reports are given ("Dr. Jones reported for the medical records committee that . . .") Additionally, if a member requests that his or her name be recorded for whatever reason, then the recorder should do so. This often happens when there are dissenting votes or abstentions. In the case of clinical reviews of actual patient cases, physicians should be identified only by number. Their anonymity in these peer review situations must be protected; otherwise, the validity of the peer review process is compromised.

Content

There are certain items that the minutes of any medical staff group meeting should contain. These items include the following:

- name of institution
- name of group and type of meeting (regular or special)
- date, place, and time of call to order and adjournment
- attendance, including absences and those excused plus guests or visitors
- names of chairperson and recorder
- review and approval of previous minutes (with any corrections noted)

What should then follow is simply a brief description of the items discussed and the actions taken or the follow-up to be done. Minutes should be simply informational and should not put anyone at risk by the inclusion of gossip, hearsay, innuendo, or other potentially embarrassing statements. As Sgt. Friday used to say, "Just the facts, ma'am, just the facts."

Clinical Review Documentation

There are now, and will be for the foreseeable future, accreditation standards that require clinical departments to review the actual clinical practice, note problems discovered during the review, take actions to correct these problems, and track and document the results of the actions taken. Whether this overall activity is called *quality assurance, quality improvement, performance improvement,* or some other name does not matter. What does matter is that the activities must be well documented in the minutes. The MSSP must be aware of current standards and keep the medical staff informed about them. The MSSP must also assist with the performance and documentation of the activities required for compliance with current standards. At the time of this writing, the Joint Commission mandates that the medical staff will perform the following functions:[8]

1. monitoring and evaluation of the quality and appropriateness of care by all individuals with clinical privileges
2. surgical case review
3. drug usage review
4. medical record review
5. blood utilization review
6. pharmacy and therapeutics function
7. utilization review
8. infection control

The performance of these functions is discussed at length in other chapters of this book. What should be noted here is that the performance or review of the performance of these functions must be reflected in minutes. There are no finite or specific rules for recording this information, at least not at the present time. Each MSSP should adopt the method or system that best suits the medical staff and the facility being served.

Confidentiality

There exists today understandable reluctance to include peer review matters in the body of the minutes—even when every attempt is made to protect the anonymity of all concerned—because it is feared they may be discoverable in a court of law. Two possible solutions are suggested:

1. Place the peer review portions of the minutes on a sheet separate from the general business discussions and keep them in a separate section in the minutes book. This section is to be treated as nonreleasable.
2. Keep all material dealing with clinical review and quality assurance matters in a completely separate filing cabinet and stamp them all with a stamp reading, "Privileged and Confidential. Protected by State Statute_____ " (insert the appropriate number).

Each of these solutions does not absolutely guarantee that the materials will never be discovered, but each will help. The hospital legal counsel should, of course, be consulted if a subpoena is received for protected peer review documents.

Follow-Up

The minutes of any medical staff group, no matter how large or small, should indicate when follow-up is required and by whom. The initiation of the follow-up will almost always fall to the person who has prepared the minutes, whether that person is doing the actual follow-up or not. There will be different responsibilities assigned in different institutions depending on the size, organization type, and other factors. For example, in peer review follow-up some MSSPs will be given the duty of preparing review forms and related letters to physicians, whereas other MSSPs may only have to receive and file such items and retrieve them at reappointment time. The fact remains, however, that the minutes, if well-written, will define who is responsible and for what. The MSSP simply must keep in mind that the loop always needs to be closed—the actions taken need to have a documented result, whether favorable or unfavorable—and pending items need to be pursued to that end.

CONCLUSION

The final instruction to readers seeking knowledge about the conduct of meetings and the preparation of minutes is to read as many writings as can be found on the subject. Some of these writings were noted above, but there are many others that can be of help. Mastery of the required skills depends on investigation and concentrated effort. However, the author believes that assisting a medical staff and its leaders in conducting meaningful meetings and then providing proper documentation of those meetings is not necessarily a set of tasks to be endured but can be instead an art to be enjoyed.

NOTES

1. David L. Brannon, "Making Meetings Work" (Paper presented at the annual conference of the National Association of Quality Assurance Professionals, Baltimore, October 1988).

2. Cindy Orsund-Gassiot and Patricia J. Starr, *Priniciples of Medical Staff Services Science*, 2d ed., ed. National Association Medical Staff Services, Education Council (Chicago: National Association Medical Staff Services, 1987).

3. Richard E. Thompson, *The Medical Staff Leader's Complete Practical Guidebook* (Wheaton, Ill.: Senss, 1988).

4. "The Hospital Medical Staff—Its Changing Form and Function," videotape presented by William R. Fifer (Brighton, Colo.: Brighton Books, 1987).

5. Henry M. Robert, *Robert's Rules of Order*, completely revised and edited by Darwin Patnode (New York: Berkley Books, 1989); Alice Sturgis, *Sturgis Standard Code of Parliamentary Procedure*, 2d ed. (New York: McGraw-Hill 1966).

6. See note 2 above.

7. E.C. Utter, *Parliamentary Law at a Glance* (Chicago: Henry Regnery, 1949).

8. Joint Commission on Accreditation of Healthcare Organizations, *1989 Accreditation Manual for Hospitals* (Chicago: Joint Commission on Accreditation of Healthcare Organizations, 1988), 117–22.

Chapter 19

Preparing Medical Staff Services for an Accreditation Survey

Cindy Orsund-Gassiot, CMSC

As discussed in Chapter 2, there are several agencies that accredit health care institutions. As the majority of hospitals in the country are accredited by the Joint Commission on Accreditation of Healthcare Organizations (Joint Commission), this chapter will address preparing for a survey by that agency. All accreditation surveys are similar, however, and these suggestions will serve as a guide for surveys by other accrediting bodies as well.

The health care facility initiates the accreditation survey by applying to the Joint Commission for an on-site survey. A detailed questionnaire related to the standards is mailed to the hospital for completion prior to the survey and is returned to the Joint Commission for analysis.

It is helpful for the health care facility to conduct a self-survey using the accreditation scoring guidelines published by the Joint Commission. Areas that are deficient or weak can be identified and improved using this tool. The self-survey must be done at least a year in advance of the Joint Commission survey, however, in order to establish a minimum 12-month track record of compliance with the standards.

The on-site survey is scheduled in advance, and the hospital is notified of the dates and names of the survey team members. The team usually consists of a physician, a registered nurse, and an administrator, although other health care professionals sometimes accompany the survey team. In some states, a cooperative survey is conducted by representatives of the state hospital licensing agency and the Joint Commission. In at least one state (California) representatives of the state medical association and state licensing agency also conduct various parts of the survey, and each group accepts the others' findings. In 39 states, however, the state hospital licensing agency accepts the findings of the Joint Commission, with a sample validated by independent survey.

During an accreditation survey, the medical staff organization receives primary attention. The physician member (or members) of the survey team devotes his or her time exclusively to (1) observing and reviewing matters related to the functions of the medical staff organization and (2) interviewing the medical staff leadership. The medical staff services professional also must be available to the physician member of the survey team in order to provide requested documentation and answer questions concerning the particular medical staff being surveyed. It is not unusual for the medical staff services professional to spend the entire three days (the survey period in larger hospitals) with the physician surveyor, even accompanying the surveyor on the inspection tour of the hospital departments that are basically medical in nature.

DOCUMENTS NEEDED FOR THE SURVEY

When the hospital receives written notice of an impending accreditation survey, a list is included of documents the surveyors will want to review. Those related to the survey of the medical staff include the medical staff bylaws, rules and regulations, and related policies; credentials files (records of appointments and reappointments); and minutes of medical staff committee and department meetings, including results of quality assurance activities.

The surveyor will provide at the time of the survey a list of the credentials files he or she wishes to review. The list usually includes files for one practitioner from each specialty represented on the medical staff membership and for several allied health professionals. Sometimes the surveyor requests the credentials files for each department chairperson and each medical director of clinical support services. Prior to the survey, the medical staff services professional should plan for the credentials files to be presented, ensuring that they are in good order and contain copies of current licensure and narcotics registration and any other documentation required by the medical staff bylaws. If the results of quality assurance activities regarding specific practitioners are maintained in files separate from the credentials file, these files should also be readied.

In addition to looking for documentation of current licensure, the surveyor checks the files for adequacy of privilege delineation and appropriate source verification of education, training, and experience. Reappointment documentation is checked to determine whether there is a profile of physician performance information that supports the clinical privileges exercised by the staff member and whether health status has been appraised by the department chief.

Minutes of medical staff committee and department meetings from the past three years must be made ready for review and should be presented in an organized, professional manner. Most hospitals store meeting minutes in three-ring binders. In the front of each binder, a record of attendance of the group is maintained and minute sets are divided by month. Although a full accreditation survey occurs once every three years, the surveyor usually focuses on the documentation of more recent activities. Minutes for the three-year period being surveyed must be readily available if requested, but the surveyor will probably review records from only the past year or two due to time constraints.

The surveyor will review meeting minutes to determine whether the medical staff is monitoring and evaluating the quality of care delivered by its members. The surveyor will look specifically for (1) documentation of conclusions, recommendations, and actions taken as a result of these findings and (2) follow-up directed toward determining whether the actions taken were effective. The minutes of all groups will be reviewed to see whether all required functions are being performed effectively. Administrative matters addressed by most medical staffs are of little interest to the physician surveyor. Instead, the focus is on documentation that indicates the degree of concern for the quality and safety of patient care in the health care facility.

OTHER ARRANGEMENTS PRIOR TO THE SURVEY

Because of the large volume of documentation that will be reviewed by the physician surveyor, a meeting room should be scheduled for the review of medical staff–related activities that will accommodate all of the minute books, credentials files, and other documents. A comfortable setting should be arranged, as the surveyor will spend the majority of survey time looking through documents.

In most cases, the entire medical staff leadership should be available for the survey. At a minimum, the chief of staff should spend some time with the physician surveyor. It is also advisable, if time permits, for the department chairpersons to meet with the surveyor. If the physicians are unable to be interviewed individually by the surveyor, they should attend a meeting scheduled ahead of time for this purpose. The meeting can be a luncheon set up especially for this purpose or it can be the summation conference that is usually held at the end of the final day of the survey.

AVOIDING LAST-MINUTE PANIC

Panic and pandemonium in the hospital always seem to precede an accreditation survey. In the experience of the author, some hospital employees stay up the entire night before a survey doing things at the last minute that should have been done weeks or months before. Although some tidying up of records and files is important prior to a survey, this should not be left undone until the night before. If the documentation necessary for an accreditation survey has not been appropriately maintained all along, it is doubtful that it can produced at the last minute.

THE SURVEY

The hospital is surveyed for substantial compliance with the accreditation standards. As noted above, evidence of medical staff compliance with the standards will be found (or not found) in the documentation presented. The physical environment of the hospital is also inspected for safety by the other members of the survey team. If the surveyor finds that a particular area is not in substantial compliance or needs improvement, he or she may well offer sample documents from other surveyed hospitals or advice and recommendations for improvement. It behooves the medical staff services professional to graciously accept any proffered advice or sample documentation from other sources.

At the end of the survey, an exit conference will be held. The attendees will include the surveyors and the hospital's chief executive officer, the governing board chairperson, the senior elected official of the medical staff, and the nursing administrator. During this conference, the hospital will learn about problems identified by the surveyors. A written report of survey findings and the accreditation decision will be mailed to the hospital at a later date.

THE ACCREDITATION DECISION

A hospital may be granted full three-year accreditation or accreditation with recommendations. The latter type occurs when there are deficiencies that will require written progress reports or another on-site survey to determine if the deficiencies have been corrected. Type I recommendations are those that bear directly on the accreditation decision, and they should be given a high priority by the institution. Type II recommendations should receive serious attention by the institution in its plans for improvement. A hospital found not to be in substantial compliance with the standards but found to be capable of expeditious resolution of identified deficiencies will receive conditional accreditation. Conditional accreditation procedures allow a hospital 30 days to submit a written plan of corrective action, which, if approved by the Joint Commission, will allow the institution six months to address specific deficiencies. At that time, another on-site survey is held. A nonaccreditation decision indicates the hospital was not in compliance with the standards. In this case, the hospital may appeal through a procedure outlined by the accrediting body.

COMMON ACCREDITATION PROBLEMS

According to data from the Joint Commission, the following areas related to the functions of the medical staff organization were most frequently cited as deficient and resulted in recommendations (Table 19-1).

Table 19-1 Deficient Areas of Medical Staff Organizations

Area Surveyed	Percentage of Hospitals Cited
Medical staff monitoring and evaluation	59
Surgical case review	51
Radiology monitoring and evaluation	5
Pathology monitoring and evaluation	42
Clinical privileges	40
Appointment/reappointment	35

Medical staffs most often fail to analyze the data collected for monitoring patient care or to take action on the findings (see Chapter 9). Standards for surgical case review are frequently not met due to failure to review indications for all surgery performed or to review invasive procedures in which no surgical specimen is removed, such as endoscopy procedures. Many hospitals continue to be cited for failure to adequately delineate the clinical privileges granted to staff members or to use findings from quality assurance activities in the reappointment process[1] (see Chapter 8).

NOTE

1. American Hospital Association, "How to Avert Common JCAHO Contingencies," *Medical Staff Leader* 18 (August 1989): 1,8.

Chapter 20

How To Propose and Justify a Computerized Medical Staff Office System

Sue King, CMSC, Vicki L. Searcy, CMSC, and Meg L. Terry, MS

GETTING STARTED

Many medical staff offices, faced with the need for increased data collection and management responsibilities, have initiated changes to upgrade from their file cabinet and word processing programs to an integrated data management system. A computerized system can reduce the workload associated with changing medical staff information by providing a centralized data entry and management tool. It can also ensure consistency of information and provide a vehicle for communicating this information to those who need it.

Any system justification needs to begin with a feasibility study or analysis. What problems will be solved with a computerized system? How much faster can tasks be accomplished? How can the quality of work be enhanced?

Three key reference points to stress and identify throughout the written cost benefit analysis are:

1. Quality—it can help produce a higher standard of work by . . .
2. Efficiency—it can help do this job faster by . . .
3. Effectiveness—it can make the office more effective by . . .

The approach to system justification should occur in three phases:

- Phase I
  —Assess the current situation.
  —Identify objectives.
  —Gain leadership commitment.
  —Encourage participation.

- —Establish a task force.
- —Develop a plan.
- Phase II
- —Review potential solutions.
- —Present the solution to the decision makers.
- Phase III
- —Implement and evaluate the solution.

PHASE I: ASSESSMENT

Begin by developing a complete set of objectives which incorporates all the functions of the medical staff office. This provides a foundation to justify the need for a system. Objectives should be measurable and specific. Begin this process by listing the medical staff office functions and services that are currently provided or that would be desirable to implement (see Exhibit 20-1). Then review the number of staff or full time equivalents (FTEs) allocated to the office, including job descriptions. Assign a percentage of each staff member's time next to each function. Review the short and long range goals for the office. It's likely that these goals can easily be transferred into objectives for a system. The work management tool for task analysis discussed in this text can also be used to collect this information.

Next, list existing problems and frustrations to eliminate or reduce by implementing a system. Naturally, all problems cannot be eliminated with any computerized system, but most information needs can be met. For example, if keeping track of expiring malpractice insurance coverage is a problem, a computerized "tickler" system can streamline this important task.

During the objective-setting process solicit input from those closely involved with the operation. This can be done with either a formal or informal survey or an interview. This provides two benefits—(1) it enlarges the view of the situation, and (2) it can provide a sense of ownership and commitment to the solution by others. It may also identify weaknesses in the planning process.

Rank the objectives or assign levels of importance to them. More than likely every objective on the list will not be met, but it will help in differentiating musts and wants and will keep the planner from getting side-tracked into looking for answers to relatively insignificant problems. It will also help in keeping the "big picture" in mind (see Exhibit 20-2). A sample of medical staff office objectives might include:

1. *To identify a system that will maintain all pertinent medical staff demographic information in one centralized system.* Make a list of what information is necessary to include in the physician data base. Keep in mind that a

Exhibit 20-1 Sample Medical Staff Office Functions Worksheet

	Current % of Staff Time	Anticipated % with Computer

Expiration Date Tracking
(average savings with computer of 25%; up to 50%; plus in some cases the ability to keep close track for the first time)

• licenses	___	___
• DEA	___	___
• malpractice coverage	___	___
• dues	___	___
• temporary privileges	___	___

Processing new applications
(average savings with computer of 30%; as high as 50%)*

• verification letters	___	___
• tracking	___	___
• approval	___	___

Privilege Maintenance
(savings on average 30%, reporting ability greatly enhanced)

• list creation and approval	___	___
• file maintenance	___	___
• reports	___	___

Responding to data requests
(staff time savings with computer up to 70%; plus the ability, in some cases, to provide the data for the first time)

• to other facilities	___	___
• surveys to:		
–Joint Commission	___	___
–PRO	___	___
• inter-departmental requests	___	___
• medical staff needs	___	___

Reports
(staff savings to 100%; ability and speed greatly enhanced)

• internal	___	___
• external	___	___
• rosters	___	___
• directories	___	___

Reappointment Process
(average time savings with computer of 30%; as high as 50%)

• identification of physicians	___	___
• notification	___	___
• data collection	___	___
• profile generation	___	___
• approval process	___	___

Ancillary Services
(savings vary depending on current duties. HealthLine Systems has software systems available to aid in these areas)

• physician referral	___	___
• QA integration	___	___

Bylaws and Documents
(not handled by software)

• revision	___	___

Meeting Management
(average savings with computer of 30%; as high as 60%)

• notices	___	___
• sign-in sheets	___	___
• calendar	___	___
• attendance tracking	___	___
• minutes	___	___
• CME tracking	___	___

Physician Relations
(not handled by software)

• relations	___	___

Other

___	___	___

* Savings with computer are given as guidelines; they are taken from client interviews and are for the category as a whole. Individual staff savings on line-items can be much higher; or in cases where the item is not currently accomplished often, lower.

Source: Reprinted from *How to Propose and Justify a Computerized Medical Staff Office System* by S. King, V. Searcy, and M. Terry, p. 9, with permission of HealthLine Systems, Inc., © 1989.

Exhibit 20-2 Objectives Worksheet

	Currently Handled Adequately (Y/N)	New System Must	New System Want* 1–5
Complete physician file			
• name	___	___	___
• addresses	___	___	___
• training	___	___	___
• licenses	___	___	___
• privileges	___	___	___
• CME	___	___	___
• education	___	___	___
• board certification	___	___	___
• malpractice insurance	___	___	___
• appointment dates	___	___	___
• staff category, departments	___	___	___
• committee assignments	___	___	___
Letter generation included			
• physician letters	___	___	___
• verification letters	___	___	___
• mailing labels	___	___	___
• rosters	___	___	___
• meeting calendar	___	___	___
• sign-in sheets	___	___	___
Features			
• standard reports	___	___	___
• custom reports	___	___	___
• statistical analysis	___	___	___
• physician profiles	___	___	___

Hardware Requirements

• single-user PC	___	___	___
• LAN PC	___	___	___
• Integration to mainframe	___	___	___
• Industry-standard file structures	___	___	___

User defined

• _____	___	___	___
• _____	___	___	___

Vendor Requirements

• easily understood documentation	___	___	___
• on-site training	___	___	___
• user groups/ newsletter	___	___	___
• updates	___	___	___
• toll-free phone support	___	___	___
• modem support	___	___	___
• source code escrow	___	___	___
• annual user's conference	___	___	___

Integration with Quality Assurance

• vendor produced system	___	___	___
• electronic interface between programs	___	___	___

*The authors recommend ranking your "wants" on a 1–5 scale with "1" being highly desirable. Your selection should meet all of your "musts" and several of your highly ranked "wants."

Source: Reprinted from *How to Propose and Justify a Computerized Medical Staff Office System* by S. King, V. Searcy, and M. Terry, p. 10, with permission of HealthLine Systems, Inc., © 1989.

data base that does not contain all information will lead to frustration and is not a true automation for the office. The solution should provide for easy retrieval without the need to review individual files.

2. *To produce reports and meet the management needs of the department today and in the future.* Define the reports the system is expected to generate. Consider printing styles, number of columns per page, rosters, sign-in sheets, numeric listings, age reports, etc.

3. *To streamline the physician appointment and reappointment process.* Identify the steps to complete the credentialing process (identification of staff, profile and letter generation, etc.).

4. *To identify a method to interface the system with existing hospital data bases for sharing of information.* Identify what interfaces the office requires (quality assurance, medical records, admitting statistics, etc.).

Look to solve both immediate and long-range needs and consider current and projected staff size and the system capacity needed to meet this growth.

The decision to automate the medical staff office should be based upon the ability of a computer system to improve operational efficiency. Calculate the average time staff spends per month completing major tasks. For example, medical staff office surveys indicate that an average of 10 to 17 hours are spent to process one new staff member application. A computerized system with automatic verification letter generation can reduce this process by 4 to 7 hours. Project the time savings by determining the monthly average of new applications currently processed, then complete the worksheet, Exhibit 20-3. Use these same formulas for each task on the list.

The "bottom line" cost benefit of installing any system is difficult to determine.

It is also difficult to quantify increased work production. A computerized system can improve the ability to produce accurate reports and can streamline the appointment and reappointment process; even the production of a staff roster can be accomplished in a few minutes. With additional resources like "after hours batch reporting" a computer can work after hours without overtime costs. And undoubtedly, the medical staff office operation will be upgraded as the ability to manage data increases. The quality and quantity of work will improve.

A few of the more tangible benefits of computerizing include:

1. immediate and easy access to information
2. increased productivity without additional staff
3. no additional costs for special projects and mailings
4. ability to create reports as needs arise—without additional programming costs and delays

Exhibit 20-3 Costs Worksheet

	Current	Projected w/ system			
			Custom Programming		
			• cost	___	___
First Year:			**Supplies**		
Staffing Costs			• _____	___	___
• FTEs	___	___	Total First Year:	___	___
• costs	___	___			
(Do not forget to figure in staff time savings from Exhibit 2-1)			**Additional 5 year costs:**		
Computer Equipment			**Computer Equipment**		
• hardware	___	___	• upgrades	___	___
• printer	___	___	• maintenance	___	___
• training	___	___			
• 1 year maintenance	___	___	**Software**		
Software			• upgrades	___	___
			• maintenance	___	___
• cost	___	___	• continuing education	___	___
• training	___	___			
• maintenance	___	___	Total Additional:	___	___

Source: Reprinted from *How to Propose and Justify a Computerized Medical Staff Office System* by S. King, V. Searcy, and M. Terry, p. 11, with permission of HealthLine Systems, Inc., © 1989.

5. integration of many hospital areas and services into one centralized data base
6. easy access to fact-based information in order to make informed medical staff decisions for strategic planning
7. automated application processing
8. streamlined reappointment
9. department, staff, and committee meeting attendance automation
10. compliance with Joint Commission requirements
11. assurance that licenses are current
12. summarization of QA and malpractice incidents
13. individual privilege lists tracked
14. production of meaningful administrative reports

PHASE II: REVIEW POTENTIAL SOLUTIONS

After having assessed the situation and needs, the next step is to identify what solutions are most appropriate. Begin by reviewing and selecting the software system that will best meet the medical staff office's needs. After identifying the software solution, select the type of equipment configuration (computer hardware) to operate the software.

Choosing Software

The first step in Phase II is to identify the software features needed. Two alternatives are possible. Purchase a commercially available package or develop a program either internally or by using a local consultant.

A Commercial or Internal System?

Advantages to selecting a commercially available program include:

1. The package has been designed exclusively for the medical staff office.
2. Development time is eliminated.
3. The system has been tested and "debugged."
4. Most packages include training and documentation for staff.
5. On-going support and program enhancements are available to keep the system up to date.
6. A network of other users are available for questions and reference.

Advantages of an internally developed program are:

1. A tailored system is developed to meet specific needs.
2. On-site help and training is provided by the data processing department, which has been intimately involved in the program development.
3. Changes to the software may be accomplished immediately rather than through an enhancement schedule offered by the vendor.

The internal data processing department will be a terrific resource during this evaluation process. The ideal situation is to have their expertise, agreement, and support in either case.

In developing an inhouse program, their involvement is a must. Software design is a painstaking process where all parties involved may not speak the same language. Gain the commitment of the data processing office before proceeding.

Software Features: What to Look for

The statement "the information you are storing is worth more than the computer itself" is true. The software purchased or developed should be an easy-to-use, menu driven system that encompasses all areas of the medical staff office. Begin by comparing the list of objectives with the vendor's product description. Eliminate those vendors whose product does not meet or exceed the objectives.

The software selected should use an industry standard language and file structure (the way the data base is handled within the software program). Having these elements "industry standard" enhances the software's ability to interface ("talk to") other hospital systems.

Consider the overall system design and ease of use. If the software is complicated to operate it may not be able to be used to its full advantage. The best method by which to judge a program is to evaluate it during a software demonstration. During this review, have the list made in Phase I available in order to comprehensively rank all areas that are of importance—not just those the vendor wants seen. Specifically look at:

1. Equipment requirements. (Does it require a particular printer or extra components to operate the software?)
2. Does the software come in both single and multi-user (or local area network or LAN) versions? What is the difference in price?
3. What is included in the training? (Is training an additional charge?)
4. How much computer experience is needed to operate the program?
5. Does it allow the user to perform the functions outlined in terms of day-to-day operations and management?

After reviewing the options and reducing the list, continue the process by examining the vendor's qualifications. Remember not to just buy software, but look for a company to provide training and support. Ask the vendor:

1. To provide a no-cost demonstration.
2. To supply a client list. Call current users, inquire about ease of use, training, and support.
3. To describe the maintenance program. What is included? Maintenance is a cost-effective protection of the investment.
4. What is the vendor's enhancement schedule and costs of future releases?
5. What is included in the training program?
6. What pre-implementation support is provided? Does the vendor offer conversion of existing information and is there a charge for this service?
7. What support after installation is offered (toll-free hot-line, modem connection, etc.)?

8. How many total staff and support staff are available for assistance?
9. What is the average problem response time?
10. Is software source code provided, or an escrow account for source code? Having source code or an escrow account ensures that program changes or modifications to the software may be made if the vendor should go out of business or fail to support the program.

After viewing each software finalist, make the decision. It is valuable to have materials management or legal staff review the vendor's license agreement (the document that governs the sale of the software) prior to its execution.

Choosing Hardware

Once software is selected, identify the various hardware solutions that will operate the program. Hardware selection is crucial. An underpowered computer will always be a source of frustration. Keep in mind that computer re-sale rarely provides an opportunity to re-coup expenses. The fastest quality machine the budget will allow should be purchased, particularly with a large medical staff.

A personal computer (PC) based solution for *most* medical staff offices is recommended. PCs are cost-effective, take up little space, and are relatively easy to operate and manage. Local area network technology is such that linking PCs can be accomplished without substantially increasing the price. A major advantage of a PC is the variety of off-the-shelf software programs available that require minimal computer experience to operate.

About PCs

Microprocessors. Even though there are many different vendors, operating systems, and configurations there are really three different types of *IBM compatible PC computers*. They differ mainly in the type of microprocessor they have. Think of the central processing unit (CPU) or microprocessor as the engine that makes the PC run. Engine selection is extremely important; it determines how fast your system will perform. For the sake of clarity we have described the microprocessor in simplified terms:

1. *4 cylinder CHEVETTE—8088 microprocessor:* The first generation of PC, the 8088 machines are often called "XTs" since IBM used this microprocessor for its PC and PC-XT computers. The 8088 was the first generation of PC chip and is found in many of the older PCs. While this is a dependable machine, the processing time may be too slow for most medical staff offices.
2. *6 cylinder CAMARO—80286 microprocessor:* The second generation of PC, this type of microprocessor is found in IBM AT (286) type machines and

is the workhorse of the PC industry. This type of "engine" is recommended for most medical staff offices, single-user or LAN configurations.

3. 8 cylinder CADILLAC—80386 microprocessor: The most recent engine developed. The 386 considerably increases speed of performance and is recommended for those large hospitals that intend to use a large LAN.

Co-Processors. Beware of software that requires math co-processors. This is an indication of a slow software package. Oftentimes software requiring math co-processors uses non-standard structures and needs the "extra help" of a co-processor just to "keep up."

Disk Storage Space. Hard disk space, often referred to as MB, or megabytes, is the amount of information the computer can store. A computer that does not have a hard disk for storage will be inadequate for any medical staff office management system use. The size of the hard disk the office will need is dependent upon the size of the medical staff and the number of different software programs intended for operation.

RAM. Random access memory is how much information the computer can process at one time. Most commercially available software programs require 640K of RAM for operation.

Printers. Consider the speed of printing (number of pages per minute), the quality of type, and the noise (if noise is important in the work location). Be certain that the software selected is compatible with the printer.

Single-User System of Multi-User LAN (Local Area Network). A single-user PC system is appropriate if the medical staff office has only one staff member or tasks and responsibilities are divided in such a way that sharing a computer presents no problem. Be certain that the equipment purchased for the single-user station will operate on a network to be implemented later if this is part of the plan.

PHASE III: IMPLEMENT AND EVALUATE THE SOLUTION

Once the needs and potential solutions have been identified, the plan is completed by filling in the cost information based upon the hardware and software solutions selected (see Exhibit 20-3). Projecting these costs over a five-year period should be considered. Maintenance costs and upgrades to hardware that may be selected must be kept in mind. A final word though about costs—*the last consideration in the decision process should be cost*. No matter how inexpensive, if the solution doesn't meet the needs, it is not money wisely spent.

The plan is then presented to the decision makers in the facility. Refining the plan as the process proceeds may be expected. A phased approach that can grow as the medical staff office expands its responsibilities should be considered.

Once approval has been gained, the implementation phase begins. Depending upon many factors (purchasing steps, budget cycles, etc.), the average implementation time is four to eight weeks. During this time, purchase orders can be sent to vendors, pre-installation assessments completed, existing data converted, and the selected hardware and software installed and learned. As with any new skill, a learning curve exists—60 to 90 days should be allowed to master the basics and enter and update the records. Using temporary help to input the data should be considered.

Chapter 21

Promoting the Medical Staff Organization

Vicki L. Searcy, CMSC and Sue King, CMSC

MARKETING THE HOSPITAL TO PHYSICIANS

The hospital's number one customer is the physician. Physicians make the majority of decisions as to which hospital they will place their patients. Thus, marketing the hospital and its services to the medical staff may be key to the survival of the hospital.

Why do physicians choose one hospital over another? This issue has been heavily researched over the past few years as the competition for physicians and patients has escalated. The reasons for physician preference include the following:

- physician mix (specialists available)
- quality services (including nursing care)
- proximity to office
- efficient admitting and discharge capabilities
- open communication between physicians and administrators
- good "image" of hospital and medical staff
- modernness and cleanliness of physical plant[1]

Each hospital should take a good look at itself from a physician's viewpoint to help determine what its marketing strengths are. Consideration of the following questions may be helpful:

- Is there convenient parking for the medical staff (e.g., close to the emergency room entrance)?
- How easy is it for physicians to "sign in" once they are in the facility so that they can be reached by office personnel and other physicians? (Do they have to notify the operator or merely punch a button conveniently located at the doctors' entrance?)

299

- Are there adequate physician lounges, including changing areas (for both men and women) and a place for physicians to sleep when they are on call or must stay overnight to care for critically ill patients?
- Is there a library with current journals and other publications and research services?
- What are the arrangements for physicians to eat in the facility (perhaps a special physicians' dining room)?
- How does a physician know where his or her patients are located in the facility when he or she arrives? (Is there a computerized printout?)
- What is the turn-around time for radiology reports, laboratory reports, etc.?
- How easy is it for a physician to complete medical records? (Does a hospital employee pull any of the physician's charts that need dictation or a signature?)
- Is the nursing department adequately staffed with qualified registered nurses and other professionals to care for the physicians' patients?
- How good is the quality of respiratory care services, physical therapy, dietary, etc.?
- Is there adequate staff for patient teaching? (This is an important concern for physicians who treat diabetic patients or others with diseases requiring specific education.)
- Is administration responsive to the medical staff's needs? (For example, an obstetrician is hard pressed these days to get an expectant mother to go to a hospital where there are no birthing rooms or where the environment is aesthetically displeasing.)
- Are the administration, governing body, and medical staff working together on issues such as physician recruitment, handling of outpatients, etc.?
- How easy is it to schedule surgery cases?
- Is the chief executive officer accessible?

The above list of questions is intended to get the thinking process started. The fundamental question is this: What are strengths of the facility that can be promoted so that physicians will perceive it as the preferred place in which to admit their patients?

The relationship between a physician and the physician's office staff is often an overlooked area. An excellent way to effectively work with the medical staff is via their office personnel (including clerical and clinical employees). A physician's office staff frequently does not understand how the hospital operates; how to access resources, services, etc.; or even what services are available. Regular group meetings can be scheduled with these important individuals in a busy physician's practice to problem solve (e.g., discuss how surgery scheduling can be handled more efficiently for both the hospital and physician), introduce them to key individuals within the hospital's hierarchy, discuss new services the hospital plans to provide, and discuss important hospital strategies (e.g., explain why the hospital has a utilization management program and how it works).

In addition to the type of information discussed above, hospitals may wish to provide physician office personnel with seminars on medical terminology, business office functions, and other topics relevant to office management. All of these types of activities will help create a team spirit instead of the "us versus them" atmosphere prevalent in many hospitals.

Building a "winning" medical staff organization also will help in promoting the hospital. What is a winning medical staff organization? According to the authors, the following statements are likely to describe it:

- Its leaders are properly equipped and trained to actually lead it forward.
- Through its organizational structure, it can appropriately handle its functions and responsibilities (e.g., performing peer reviews, dealing with "problem" practitioners, overseeing the quality of care provided in the institution, etc.).
- It communicates to the administration and the governing body through defined channels.
- It has a streamlined organizational structure so that time spent in committee and department meetings is productive and meaningful.
- Through its leaders, it enforces its own bylaws, rules, and regulations.

Winning medical staff organizations do not just happen. It takes support, money, time, effort, and commitment to develop a medical staff organization that is more than just a group of loosely organized physicians who reluctantly attend medical staff meetings. Medical staff leadership orientation programs are one of the most important keys to a successful medical staff organization. Physicians are not taught in medical school about the responsibilities of the medical staff organization or how to be effective leaders. Why expect them to be successful at leadership if they have had no training?

There are many different types of leadership training sessions, ranging from two- or three-hour afterdinner meetings to weekend retreats. Some topics that might be addressed at such sessions are as follows:

- medical staff organization functions, authority, and responsibilities
- overview of the credentialing system
- importance of the medical staff bylaws, rules and regulations (and why they must be enforced)
- the medical staff and peer review
- the relationships between the governing body and the medical staff

- the role of the medical executive committee
- key leadership roles in the credentialing and clinical monitoring processes
- handling disciplinary problems
- dealing with the impaired physician
- confidentiality of medical staff activities, files, and documents

Medical staff newsletters should be used to promote good communication with members of the medical staff. Newsletters can be used to introduce new practitioners to the staff; communicate the actions of the executive committee; introduce new hospital services, equipment acquisitions, or key hospital employees; and alert and educate medical staff members regarding new requirements or laws that affect the hospital and physician practices.

New-physician orientation programs should involve more than just giving new medical staff members a parking card, a medical staff roster, and a copy of the medical staff bylaws. The orientation can be a means to begin building a good relationship between the new physician and the hospital employees the physician will be interacting with on a routine basis. For example, if there is a new urologist on staff, a lunch attended by the urologist, his or her office nurse, the hospital surgery supervisor, and the head nurse of the surgery floor may be a very important part of the orientation process. Although the urologist will of course be introduced to the chairperson of the department of surgery and be given information to ensure he or she understands the requirements associated with provisional staff status and knows how to access medical record dictation lines, and so on, the luncheon mentioned above may be far more meaningful from the urologist's viewpoint.

Social activities for the medical staff should not be overlooked. They should be held as often as funds permit and should be entertaining and fun. The development of good relationships between the administration, the medical staff, and governing body can often be enhanced by allowing members of these groups the opportunity to socialize with each other in a nonmedical environment.

PHYSICIAN PRACTICE MARKETING

In an effort to strengthen relationships with their physicians, hospitals are focusing much of their efforts on assisting private practice physicians in enhancing and expanding their practices. Hospital executives want physicians on staff whose practices are financially stable. The assumption, of course, is that successful, loyal physicians will, in turn, utilize the hospital when their patients need hospital or outpatient services provided by the hospital. Hospitals are instituting programs such as practice marketing, practice management, specialized business services, and financial aid to assist physicians.

Some hospital practice enhancement programs offer monthly business management seminars on all aspects of running a group practice. In providing these seminars, hospitals sometimes use their own employees. Hospital employees from departments such as marketing, public relations, human resources, and the print shop meet individually with physicians and their office personnel to offer expertise and support. Other facilities provide free consultations with firms specializing in marketing and advertising the physician practices or in physician-office management techniques.

Practice marketing encompasses various types of activities concerned with expanding the natural focus of a physician practice. The focus for an obstetrician/gynecologist would, of course, be on marketing to women. The focus for an ophthalmology practice might be on marketing cataract surgery and intraocular lens implant services to the elderly.

To market a physician practice, the practice itself should first be assessed to identify opportunities to improve revenues. The assessment should include a complete evaluation of the financial, personnel management, marketing strategies, and managed care components of the practice.

The next step is to perform a market analysis to determine if the practice is positioned to capture the maximum market share.

The objective of such practice management strategies is to gather information that will enable physicians to learn the market's specific attitudes and needs, real or perceived. The information can then assist physicians in making decisions that will affect growth, management, and positioning. Important data include the following:

- market share
- competitive position
- business opportunities
- office efficiency
- patient satisfaction
- financial profile

The purpose of obtaining the above data is to design a practice development plan.

There are almost as many types of physician practice management services as there are physician specialties. The most common services are these:

1. *Office staff training.* This is usually provided by the hospital through the same in-service educational programs offered to the hospital's own employees.

2. *Personnel recruitment.* The hospital's human resources department usually provides this service. A human resources department commonly has applications on file for various positions within the hospital. Applicants for jobs

in the business office, medical transcription, and nursing are most often referred to physician offices by the department.

3. *Group purchasing.* Hospitals and physician practice groups, such as independent practice associations (IPAs), have discovered the great savings that can be realized through group purchases. Most hospitals are eager to assist their private staff physicians in this manner. However, there are state and federal laws that curtail group purchases (depending on the structure of the hospital and the relationship between the hospital and the physician).

4. *Information systems.* During recent years, hospitals have begun to create bonds with physicians via on-line information systems. Some hospitals have provided computers free of charge to their loyal practicing physicians. The computers are linked to the hospital information network. Physicians and their office personnel can then have direct access to patient information, such as admissions information, lab results, X-ray reports, medical records, and insurance and billing information. Most of these systems have built-in confidentiality features to limit access to data on patients admitted by a given physician or patients for whom the physician is providing consultation.

Specialized business services are another important component of physician practice management. Using their own personnel or outside consultants, hospitals provide business services such as personnel management, financial management, equipment purchasing advice, malpractice insurance and hospital-funded life and health insurance (with premium discounts).

Some hospitals offer complete contract management services to their staff physicians. Comprehensive services ranging from personnel management to financial management and advanced marketing and planning techniques are provided.

It is widely known that some hospitals provide financial assistance in the form of guaranteed loans. Others make available the services of accountants, tax attorneys, and financial planners.

Hospitals providing physician practice management programs have learned one very important lesson during the past decade: Physicians want to be part of a strong, viable institution. More importantly, they want to maintain their individuality—they do not want to be controlled or held captive.

MARKETING THE MEDICAL STAFF ORGANIZATION TO THE COMMUNITY

Marketing the quality of the medical staff organization to third-party payers is a somewhat new concept. Because of the recent release of information to news sources (e.g., mortality statistics and, more recently, the names of hospitals with conditional accreditation), emphasizing the quality of the medical staff to third-party payers and to the community has become a necessity. It is time for hospitals to take a proactive stance rather than wait for consumers to ask, "How do I know that I am going to receive quality care at your institution?"

There are a variety of ways the medical staff and the services provided by the hospital can be marketed to the outside world, including the following:

- *Health forums.* A topic of interest to consumers in the community can be addressed by a physician or group of physicians. This provides an excellent opportunity to showcase specific physician members of the medical staff together with specific services provided by the hospital. For example, a community with a large senior citizen population may be very interested in attending an informational forum on ophthalmology. A hospital that has recently purchased lasers to be used for ophthalmology procedures can showcase the new equipment and the streamlined outpatient registration procedures they have put in place. The ophthalmologists on the staff can present information and answer questions regarding common eye procedures. Another health forum might be held on diabetes, with participation by physicians who treat this disease and nurses who are prepared to educate patients regarding diabetic care.

- *Newspaper ads.* Hospitals are putting newspaper advertisement to good use. Individual physicians can be incorporated into these ads. For example, the hospital may run an ad featuring its obstetric services and also showcase the physicians who care for mothers and babies.

- *Radio spots.* Radio spots may also be used to showcase hospital services and the medical staff. In at least one community, there is a regular weekly program called "Ask the Doc." This program is advertised widely, and the physician of the week gives a brief presentation regarding his or her specialty and the types of patients seen. Phone-in questions from the listening audience are then addressed.

- *Screening programs.* Offering screening programs is yet another way hospitals and the medical staff can work together to market services and practitioners. Screening programs for breast cancer, cholesterol, hypertension, diabetes, and so on, are now familiar and provide an opportunity for hospital staff and physicians to participate together in meeting new potential consumers for hospital and physician services.

- *Speakers bureaus.* These have become popular in some areas. Organizing a speakers bureau may be as simple as identifying physician members of the medical staff who are willing and able to speak to the public on selected topics. In the typical community, there are many organizations that might want to utilize such a bureau. School systems and other community groups can be informed that speakers are available. Speaking engagements can then be used to showcase the medical staff and services available at the facility.

There are many opportunities to market the medical staff to the community. By continually sending messages concerning available services and practitioners, the hospital will gain the public's confidence.

PHYSICIAN REFERRAL SERVICES AND NETWORKS

Referral Services

For many years, the health care industry focused marketing efforts on consumer choices. However, recent research found that new and improved patient services and the development of marketing programs to communicate those services to consumers proved to be of questionable benefit to the hospital.[2] In the late 1980s, a new awareness developed among hospital executives that referrals of patients come most often from private practice physicians.[3] The result was a shift from direct consumer appeal to recapturing the loyalty and allegiance of such physicians.

According to an article in *Hospitals*, "In all hospitals [surveyed], practice building programs and physician referral services are considered to be among the most productive and important physician marketing activities."[4] Hospitals have indeed found physician referral services to be extremely effective.

Hospitals and medical societies have had physician referral services for many years. The American Hospital Association reported[5] that hospitals have always kept informal lists of available physicians for referrals. Local medical societies created referral panels 30 years ago to help members attract patients. However, callers were simply given the names of a few doctors who fit the caller's general medical requirements—most often primary care physicians. In hospitals, the switchboard operator usually transferred the telephone requests to the medical staff services office. As hospital executives became more aware of the importance of treating physicians as customers, the traditional physician referral service took on a new look.

Computerized physician referral systems have placed physician referral services "center stage" in the marketing efforts of many hospitals. Such services include physician data bases that store retrievable, modifiable files for each participating physician. It is imperative that these data bases be constantly updated.

All types of information can be included in a computerized system. Decisions regarding release of information are best left to an advisory committee made up of staff physicians and hospital administrators. The consumer's right to know is an important issue, and the approach to what information should be released is usually dictated by what is public information in each state.

Health care attorneys have suggested several ways to minimize the risks associated with a physician referral service:[6]

- A thorough and systematic initial appointment and reappointment process should be in place at each facility.
- All physicians included on the referral list should be subject to peer review and quality assurance systems.
- The physician referral list should be reviewed by the advisory committee at least quarterly to be certain only physicians of "high quality" are on the list.
- Requiring physicians to refer patients to the hospital or specialty staff should be avoided.
- Tying compensation, pricing or any other form of remuneration to referrals should be avoided.
- Termination of the hospital-physician relationship because admissions or referrals do not meet expectations should be avoided.
- Tying loans or other obligations to referrals should be avoided.

Employees manning physician referral services must be carefully trained and supported. Triage nurses should be available (perhaps in the emergency department) to assist in screening calls. Trained physician referral specialists know how to ask questions leading to appropriate referrals and avoid making clinical judgments or giving advice to callers.

A computerized referral service has the ability to search and sort through the physician data base to select criteria, such as physician specialty, physician subspecialty, office location, and health care insurance accepted. This helps eliminate confusion over the choice of a physician.

Consumers have become much more sophisticated in their search for the "right" physician, and they expect and demand more information about physicians. Additionally, many insurance companies are mandating second opinions, and some patients spend hours trying to locate a qualified physician to give a second opinion. Physician referral services provide easily accessible and reliable information.

The benefits to a hospital from a comprehensive computerized referral service include the following:

- The service can help develop an image of the hospital as service-minded and community-oriented.
- The service can assist the hospital in developing and sustaining marketing programs that will increase its market share by providing vital data on physicians and consumers.
- The service can help to enlarge the service market and can assist the hospital in penetrating new geographic areas.
- The service can provide new customer names and demographics for cross-marketing hospital services.

Referral Networks

A comprehensive physician referral service can easily be expanded into a referral network.

A referral network or telecommunications department has several components. The primary component is that of the physician referral service. However, the referral network also provides information on hospital services and on educational programs offered by the hospital. For example, when a young pregnant woman calls for an obstetrician, she will be given the names of physicians or be provided with an appointment. The referral specialist should also inform the caller about the hospital's prenatal services, including prenatal classes. Nutritional and fitness programs might also be suggested (or information on all of the appropriate services might be mailed to the caller).

The components of a flexible physician referral network include the following:

- physician referral service
  —appropriate new patients for private physicians
  —emergency and urgent care center referrals
  —integration of patient follow-up from the emergency department and urgent care centers
  —physician-to-physician consultation line
- Educational programs
  —information about professional continuing medical education (for physicians, nursing, technical staff)
  —lay educational programs
  —speakers bureau for outreach educational offerings
  —data base for future promotions and programs offered by the hospital
  —cross-referrals to hospital services and physicians
- Hospital services
  —internal hospitalwide coordination of services
  —elimination of "blind" telephone call transfers for patients who need additional information on a service
  —increase in data base for marketing purposes

Follow-Up and Tracking

In order to maximize the benefits of a physician referral service or network to the hospital and physicians, it is important to solicit feedback from the consumers as well as from the physicians to whom the consumers have been referred.

A well-formulated questionnaire mailed to callers on a timely basis provides useful information for assessing the effectiveness of the service. It is difficult for hospitals to determine whether the physician referral service has impacted on hospital census without an effective tracking system. Hospitals that have such a tracking program depend on both consumer questionnaires and physician responses. By utilizing the information gained and merging it with their hospital information systems, they are able to determine the actual return on the investment.

It is now well accepted that a physician referral system is an effective marketing tool and helps to attract both physicians and patients to the hospital.

NOTES

1. Richard B. Nordstrom, Yvonne Horton, and Myron E. Hatcher, "How to Create a Marketing Strategy Based on Hospital Characteristics That Attract Physicians," *Journal of Healthcare Marketing* 7 (March 1987): 29–35.
2. Ronald Sullivan, "Referral Services Grow as Physicians Reach for New Customers," *New York Times*, Dec. 17. 1987.
3. Ibid.
4. Therese Droste, "Physician Marketing Budgets to Grow in '88," *Hospitals* 62 (January 20, 1988): 32.
5. Sullivan, "Referral Services Grow."
6. David Burda, "Referral Services Can Link Hospitals with Lawsuits," *Hospitals* 61 (May 20, 1987): 36; Elise Dunitz Brennan, "Legal Focus" (From a presentation at a user conference of HealthLine Systems, Inc., Las Vegas, October 1989).

Index

Q

R